VOICES FROM THE BLUE

JENNIFER REES
AND
ROBERT J. STRANGE

ROBINSON

ROBINSON

First published in Great Britain in 2019 by Robinson
This paperback edition published in 2020 by Robinson

1 3 5 7 9 10 8 6 4 2

ISBN: 978-1-47214-310-5

Typeset in Electra LT by Hewer Text UK Ltd, Edinburgh
Printed and bound in Great Britain by Clays Ltd, Elcograf S.p.A.

Papers used by Robinson are from well-managed
forests and other responsible sources.

Robinson
An imprint of
Little, Brown Book Group
Carmelite House
50 Victoria Embankment
London EC4Y 0DZ

An Hachette UK Company
www.hachette.co.uk

www.littlebrown.co.uk

This book is dedicated to all former and serving
women officers of the Metropolitan Police

CONTENTS

INTRODUCTION

Exactly one hundred years ago a group of just twenty-five courageous women stormed the previously unassailable, male bastion of the Metropolitan Police Service to become the first women officers to patrol the streets of London. In an age of prejudice, gender discrimination and casual sexual harassment, women police were at first resented by both the public and many of their male colleagues. They had to battle misogynistic expectations that they were there to 'Make the tea, luv', and fight for the right to do anything other than care for women and children.

Yet, with an ever-growing level of professionalism, female officers won the acceptance and respect they deserved. Even so, it would be years before they were granted the same powers of arrest as the men, more than fifty years before they gained full equality and equal pay, and almost a century before London's first female Commissioner, Cressida Dick, took charge of the entire organisation.

I served for more than thirty years in the Metropolitan Police, first as a police officer and then as a forensic specialist: my co-author, Bob Strange, is a former Fleet Street crime reporter. Until we began interviewing former and serving female officers for this book, neither of us had expected to find ourselves in New Scotland Yard, chatting to Cressida Dick. We spoke about her career and shared stories with her of the humour, courage and moving emotional triumphs and tragedies now handled everyday by the thousands of female police officers under her command. We found that the Commissioner's own stories were in many ways typical of the tales we have heard from the hundreds of other female officers whom we have met: their 'voices from the blue' revealing both the challenges and the sheer fun and fascination of being a female police officer.

A similar pure enjoyment of being a police officer shone out of Cressida as we spoke. She had been slightly late for our meeting, apologising because she had been out of her office on her own, walking the streets of Westminster, keeping in touch with the public and refreshing her own 'feel' for policing life in London. She explained that the fun of working in the police service still motivated her, and that she still has to regularly pinch herself to remember that she is now the Commissioner, the most senior police officer not only in London but in the whole of the United Kingdom.

Cressida Dick's position at the top of the Met Police command structure is a fitting reminder of the entire point of this book: women's own accounts of a hundred-year struggle that has seen them advance from jobs as police matrons and baby-minders through to equality with their male colleagues. This is their story of that century-long journey, overcoming difficulties that seem almost unbelievable to today's #MeToo generation: a journey which has finally proved that female officers are every bit the measure of their male counterparts.

Jennifer Rees
Robert J. Strange

1

IT'S A FAIR COP, LUV

Amanda (M Div) 1990s

A speeding car smashes into a lamppost right in front of us. We slam on the brakes as three armed men run towards us. A huge guy, well over six feet tall, with a bull neck, cannons into the front of our area car. I give chase but, next thing I know, I'm on my own: a 5'6", lightly built policewoman chasing three armed robbers through a deserted council estate in the dead of night. I don't even have a truncheon – not that it would be much help: if you're lucky you can just about break a car window with the ones we female officers are given. They're so small, and designed to fit into a skirt pocket without ruining the line. I mean, for goodness' sake!

Because he is a bit slower, I zero in on the big guy; not a great choice, but the adrenalin is pumping. I see one suspect in the distance, and another ducks down into a hedge. That leaves me and the big guy, with me catching up till my fingers brush the back of his sweatshirt. Then he turns on me . . . and I freeze. I know they've held up a wine bar, but it's not till the gun is in my face that I actually register ... these guys have GUNS! This is also the point where I realise how big my suspect is. I'm dwarfed. I can't believe it when, instead of shooting me, he throws the gun over my head and swings at my face, breaking my glasses and grabbing me round the neck. Somehow I manage a judo move to reverse the headlock, and his neck is now locked under my arm.

The guy in the bushes is taking aim at me but, because his gun has a hair trigger, he shoots himself in the foot instead and is a tad distracted. My suspect is big enough to just lift me up and toss me into the distance as easily as he tossed the gun aside, so with just one option – holding on for dear life and knowing I have to keep him off balance – I carry on squeezing his neck and start spinning him around as fast as I can so he can't lift me off the ground. At the same time I keep an eye on the gun, getting ready to make a dash for it.

It feels like forever, but finally my driver comes charging round the corner. The look on his face when he sees me spinning this massive guy around makes me all too aware of the trouble I've got myself into. I have never been so relieved to see anyone. He cuffs my still-spinning suspect and I stagger off and finally secure the gun: it's one of those small derringers, the sort you see in the purses of women in Westerns. The relief ... it's a toy! I hadn't nearly been killed.

Days later I find out it was a real gun and it was loaded. We had been toe-to-toe; any shot could have been fatal.

'Amanda', now retired but wheelchair-bound from injuries received protecting a woman from a violent husband, is just one of the many women police officers I met while writing this book. Before then my knowledge about arrests made by women police

officers was confined to my own limited years of service as a policewoman in the Metropolitan Police. I had no idea of the wealth of diverse tales of courage, of fun, of tragedy and of laughter I would hear from so many serving and former women police officers who have patrolled the streets of London over the past hundred years.

The more women police I talked to, the more I realised that changes in their working lives mirror how attitudes to women have evolved through the decades. A century ago the first female officers were thought incapable of dealing with anything other than 'fallen women', young children and administrative duties. Nothing illustrates society's changes better than the way that policewomen increasingly carry out what many believe to be the primary duty of the police – arresting those who break the law.

Of course, among the men and women of the Metropolitan Police there are 'thief takers' . . . and then there's me!

When I became a WPC in the late 1960s I received the same training as the men, but there was less pressure on women to get arrests. When we patrolled the streets it was a general wander to show the uniform, to be a police presence, to get to school crossing duty, to go to addresses where a problem relating to women and children had been highlighted, or to make 'alien enquiries' about people's immigration status.

All police officers truly want to be seen to be arresting criminals. So when I took one new WPC out to 'show her the ropes', I thought I would try to get her an arrest. Drunks abounded on our ground in East

London, and I soon picked out a short, dark-haired, middle-aged man staggering towards us. I knew by heart the short definition of an 'arrestable drunk' – the description we would lay before the magistrate in court: 'He was unsteady on his feet, his speech was slurred, and he smelled of alcohol. He was drunk, Your Honour.' With this chap weaving all over the pavement I had him in my sights as a perfect arrest.

We approached him. 'Are you all right, Sir? I asked.

He smiled. 'Oh yes,' he said. There was no trace of his speech being slurred by alcohol. 'I'm fine . . . just my bad leg playing me up again . . . thanks for asking.'

We left him to go on his unsteady, yet utterly sober, way. Luckily for the safety of all Londoners, many other women police officers have proved better than me at making arrests.

The idea that women officers might one day actually be called upon to arrest drunks, let alone tackle hardened criminals, was barely even contemplated when the first 'Women Patrols' were recruited into the Police Service in 1919. Indeed, an early Met Police Commissioner, Sir William Horwood, railed against suggestions that women should be sworn in as 'warranted officers', a step which would have granted them the same powers of arrest as their male counterparts.

'If women patrols were "sworn in" they would have to carry out certain duties which, as must be obvious to everyone, they are not physically fitted to perform and

I should hesitate to accept the responsibility of any of these women being called upon by the general public to carry out a police duty which it is not within their power to perform.'

Brigadier-General Sir William Thomas Francis
Horwood GBE KCB DSO, Commissioner of
Police for the Metropolis 1920s
Metropolitan Police Archives

The Commissioner's comments reflected society's view at that time. Women were still thought of as 'the fairer sex', with neither the physical strength, nor the determination, to tackle violent criminals. Those who believed the fair sex too gentle to make arrests perhaps failed to take into account the determination women would bring to the job. There was no recognition of the fact that physical strength is far from being the only way of influencing events. Sometimes women may defuse situations in a way that a man might not, and even laughter can be a powerful weapon to aid in an arrest.

Jenny (formerly WPC 381 H Division)

Shirley (Z Div) 1950s

There was a problem with street-betting on Lavender Hill's ground. After a week in which PCs tried but failed to make arrests I was asked if I would have a go. I dressed up in old clothing, carrying my shopping bag and clutching my betting slip (a piece of paper) in my hand. I was assured by the PC that he would be on hand to come to my assistance. I walked down the road and saw the tout with the agent. As I got to the tout, he stepped back for me to approach the agent, I said who I was . . . and arrested him. There was quite a scuffle, with me hanging on to the 'prisoner', and the tout trying to part me from the agent. Suddenly the agent said, 'All right, Miss. I'll come quietly.' It was then that the PC decided to appear. We travelled by bus back to the nick. At court on the Monday morning, the public gallery was full of men. The PC told me they had all come to see me. That way I could not be used again as I would be recognised.

Daisy (E Div) 1950s

On Boat Race day, a drunk was causing trouble somewhere up Caledonian Road. When I got there he was being abusive and loud and swearing. I got a neighbour to phone in and ask for the van to come, but the reply was: 'We haven't got one available, you will have to walk him in.' I could see trouble, but he came with me like a lamb – much to the surprise of the front office who thought they were going to have a good laugh. Actually, I always found that drunken women were far more aggressive than drunken men.

Margaret (H Div) 1960s

Being a woman can work in your favour sometimes. When I was at Commercial Street nick, a man came running out of a local basement café crying for help because this big man had terrified him. I led the way down into the café where there was this huge man . . . enormous: he'd got the one-arm bandit machine and was rocking it backwards and forwards like it was a toy.

He wasn't drunk, just angry. I thought, 'Christ, what am I going to do?' Then a vanload of PCs tumbled down the stairs. When they saw the size of him they all stopped dead in their tracks, bumping into each other 'boom . . . boom . . . boom', like characters out of a silent Keystones Cops movie. It was hilarious.

He turned his head to me, winked, and held his arm out. I said, 'I'm arresting you for malicious damage', or something like that, and he walked off with me as calm as a pussy cat. When I put my hands round his arm, my fingers didn't meet, he was that big. He loved it, he really loved it. The men were gobsmacked when we got back to the nick. He was charged, but as soon as I walked out of the charge room he went berserk.

Aggie (H Div) 1960s

We didn't need to patrol in pairs in those days, and we didn't all have radios. I was patrolling the pedestrian underpass beneath Whitechapel when I came across a chap squatting by the wall, emptying his bowels into a well-defined cowpat. Being a novice, knowing this must be an offence but unsure as to whether it was an arrestable one, I retraced my steps, found a police box and called in. The Station Sergeant, knowing I was new, advised me to arrest the man *and* bring in the evidence. Fortunately, a fellow officer passing by told me I was having my leg pulled. We just moved the man off with a caution and contacted the council to come and clear up the mess.

Terri (H Div) 1960s

Another policewoman and I chased a young male absconder who jumped onto an old tyre on a building site and catapulted up on top of a high wall. With that, my colleague also jumped onto the tyre . . . which unfortunately sank under her weight. Instead of springing up onto the wall, she missed the top and slid down like a cartoon character. The young lad laughed so much he fell off the wall . . . onto our side. He gave himself up, saying, 'I've not had such a good laugh for ages.'

Diana (H Div) 1960s

My first arrest on Division was of a large drunk found lying in a garage forecourt. Well, I thought I should arrest him, so recited his rights. I then didn't know how to get him to the station: no radio, and certainly no mobiles in those days. Fortunately, a fire engine came by and the firemen hoisted him onto the tender before they 'ding-a-linged' us back to Leman Street nick.

With just a whistle, no radios, and no truncheons or handcuffs, we often had to use tact and good humour as our working tools. I got a commendation for arresting a young lad in Cable Street who seemed to me to be too small for the big motorbike he was pushing: I suspected he had nicked it and had run out of petrol. He was limping and told me he had tried to kick-start the bike, but a 'kick-back' had injured his ankle. To avoid any violent confrontation I suggested we go to the station for medical help. Bless him . . . off we went together. As soon as we got to the police station yard I told him he was being arrested and took him to be charged. The CID appeared and took over, but I didn't mind because the arrest was mine.

Janis (D Div) 1970s

When I was patrolling my beat in the 1970s there was still respect for females, even among men who were otherwise capable of extreme violence. That meant that I would get little hassle on the streets even when reporting or arresting someone. I was posted one day on a van when a call came out about a man armed with a knife. As the passenger in our van, I got out fast and was the first to reach him. He was a scary guy armed with a knife, but I think his respect for me as a woman actually outweighed his 'thuggery'. He stopped his threats, I arrested him and we took him to the police station. Had I been a male officer I think he would have reacted differently. Good news really as I only had a handbag, not even a truncheon, to defend myself.

As in any job I don't believe you can characterise police officers merely by gender. There are plenty of female police more than capable of handling themselves in a fight. At training school we were shown self-defence and restraint methods such as using a 'hammer lock-and-bar' or a 'wrist lock' to control violent suspects. Both holds are painful and both quickly immobilise most people. The problem, however, is that no training can truly equip you for real-life violence on the streets. In school we were attacked by fellow officers playing at being offenders. They were more compliant than any real criminal would be; offering up arms to be twisted up backs, or hands to have thumbs pulled down to their wrists. I know women from the 1950s were given judo lessons, but in my training days the restraint holds were all we had.

I've always been tall for a woman, and strong enough to hold my own in those mock fights. But on the streets the fighting was for real. In my probation-ary period I was patrolling with a Detective Constable who detained a man he'd been looking for. The DC, a big, beefy Scotsman, had no trouble controlling his prisoner, but the suspect's girlfriend was not happy and tried to join in. I grabbed her and

*we grappled. Unlike in training school, the wriggling
girl had no intention of assisting me; instead it took
all my strength to just keep hold.*

*Afterwards the DC wanted me to arrest her for
obstructing police, but I refused. She had been
worried about her boyfriend and hadn't actually hurt
anyone . . . or so I thought. Back at the nick, I found
my arms were covered in bruises: so much for self-
defence classes. I learned a lesson that day: when
you're up against it, instinct takes over because the
training was nowhere near intensive enough to be of
real-life value.*

*I did do my job that day, along with other women
who over the last century have consistently proved
themselves every bit the equal of men. That was not
enough, however, for some male officers who twisted
facts when it suited them to try and maintain their
fiction that the 'fair sex' needed men to look after
them.*

*Even criminals felt hard done by when arrested by
a woman. A former colleague who served in the
Flying Squad, the real-life 'Sweeney', recounted a
story of detaining a prolific burglar who begged her
colleagues not to tell anyone he had been arrested by
'a bloody tart'.*

Jenny

Deryl (P Div) 1970s

My very first Duty Officer was a powerful woman. A typical
encounter was her putting a 'shout up' for suspects, and when
we got there she'd have some guy bent over the bonnet of a car,
face down, with an elbow pinning his neck, his arm up his back,

while she rolled a fag with her other hand. There was no way she was going to put up with any sort of sexism. Unfortunately, I later worked with a male officer who was almost the opposite in attitude to her. There was a male probationer who, like me, couldn't drive, but he was always posted as the passenger in a patrol car, while I was left to walk the beat alone by day and night. The new Inspector would delight in comparing our work records: not surprisingly the probationer reached more crimes, more speedily, in a car than I could on foot and so the comparison made him look good . . . and me look bad.

Sexist attitudes like those sometimes extended to falsifying facts to downplay the role of women officers. Once when I did get to go out in the car we took a call on Chislehurst's ground [the area worked by a given police station]. We were talking to a couple of chaps having split them up, when mine took off. I caught him as he tripped up a kerb and discovered he had a shillelagh hidden under his coat. I arrested him and took him to Chislehurst where I related the facts to the male Station Officer.

To my astonishment he showed my male driver as the arresting officer. Even worse, he was blatant in his explanation of what he was doing: 'We've never had a woman in my charge book . . . I am not changing that now.' His ploy didn't work on that occasion, though. As the officers involved, we both wrote our notes showing me as the arresting officer and telling the truth that the driver was not even with me at the time. The case ended up in No 1 Court at the Old Bailey because the guy I arrested turned out to have been responsible for a very serious GBH with the weapon a little earlier in the evening.

At the time I joined the Met I felt safe as a woman in uniform – although I doubt I would say the same if I was serving today. All I had to protect myself was a handbag, although later in my service I could sometimes get hold of a radio. It was the size of a brick – and about as much use when it came to communicating with the station. I suppose it did at least add weight when swinging my handbag.

Most women contributors to this book told me they did not have truncheons until 1986, around twelve years after female officers had been supposedly integrated in every way with the male reliefs [the name given to our individual police teams on duty]. That integration increased the risks for women required to work solo patrols, and made them as vulnerable to attack as the men. There was some slow recognition of that danger, yet women still did not have the same protective equipment as the men.

Size matters. Men carried a full-size truncheon, whereas women were given far smaller 'girlie' truncheons they could fit in their handbags. It was a remnant of the idea that women were incapable of wielding larger pieces of equipment. That is a concept hard to justify when women officers were not only meeting violence on the streets but also were being used as decoys on covert operations to catch offenders known to be targeting vulnerable women.

Jenny

Annie (E Div) 1970s

There were not many female officers back in the late 1970s so I was regularly selected for decoy work. It amounted to walking with your handbag, in plain clothes at a crime hotspot, trying to look like a young, vulnerable girl. You were closely monitored by two or three male colleagues in the hope that the local robber would select you as his next victim and be arrested in the act.

I was used as a decoy to capture a bloke targeting and attacking young girls as they entered lifts in the West End. He would leap in as the doors were closing and indecently assault them by grabbing their breasts. I have always been a 'buxom lass', which probably went some way towards ensuring my selection.

I was deployed with my minders. Briefing instructions were to wear a tightly fitting jumper and skirt, and to look provocative. However, this was very different from being out on the street, visible and with other people milling around. Once you got into that lift, you were alone. Your covert back-up did their best, but they couldn't always get vision on the lift doors. I can still remember standing in that first lift, shaking with fear, and hiding a truncheon in my handbag. My hand never left that stick. It was to be drawn the second this miscreant stormed the lift.

After a few days of my feet aching in high-heeled shoes, and with no likely approaches, I started to relax. So, I'm in the lift, doors starting to close, when I hear the sound of running footsteps. My heart rate goes through the roof. In jumps a young man. I unleash a primeval screech and draw my truncheon. He drops to the floor, screaming, 'Take my wallet, take my wallet . . . don't hurt me!' Oh my God – he thinks I'm a robber. He is wailing like a wounded animal and, adding to the carnage, my two beefcake colleagues are trying to rip the lift doors open. Anyway, we pick him up, give him a hug and take him for a large glass of ale at the nearest pub to calm his nerves. He took it very well, and after the third pint was actually laughing.

Needless to say, 'Operation Breast Grabber' was wound down.

Cressida (C Div) 1980s

The one thing about the West End, there's always been a high number of officers per square metre, so if you shouted you got help very quickly. The first arrest I ever made was like that. I was walking down Old Compton Street when I saw a bloke go into a red telephone box, get out a screwdriver and try to get the money out. This guy was a great big bloke and I thought, 'Oh yikes, this could be quite tricky. He's got a screwdriver and I haven't. All I have is this little truncheon in the depths of my handbag.'

So I thought, 'What am I going to do?' We didn't have a truncheon pocket at that point, just a normal skirt. We didn't have any of the safety training or physical skills they have now (which is marvellous to watch in terms of how professional they are). I ran up and said, 'Oi.' He turned round and looked absolutely horrified. The door of the telephone box was half-open and I said, 'I'm arresting you.' And he said, 'No you're bloody not.' And I said, 'Yes I am.'

And I thought, 'There's only one thing for it', and I slammed the door shut and leant back as hard as I could against it, because I could see he would have been able to overpower me in a second. Two members of the public came and helped keep the door shut until my friends came charging round the corner.

Despite increasing dangers we women were stuck with the smaller truncheon for decades, until finally policewomen were allowed to wear trousers with a purpose-made truncheon pocket. A lot of police equipment was only gradually standardised across the gender divide as women took a more active role in the fight against crime. Today, men and women have

near-identical equipment including stab vests, rein-
forced hats, extendable batons, CS gas canisters and
Tasers, which rolled out in service across London from
2011 onwards.

Jenny

Jane (H Div) 1990s

Our relief had an unprecedented number of WPCs on it. My friend and I went to deal with a 'domestic'. We separated the couple and I took the man into the lounge. He was really angry and had been drinking. He started shouting that he wanted to deal with a policeman, not a woman. So I called up for another unit to come and help. Along came another two WPCs. By now he was really steaming and demanding to speak to a policeman. Of course, we got on the radio and told the operations room he was not happy; could they dispatch another car? Which they did . . . and yes – you've guessed it – another two WPCs turned up! He literally held his hands out and said, 'I give in.' Brilliant.

Mary (L Div) 1990s

I was Section Sergeant at Walworth at a time when racial tensions were high. I'd been to several incidents where locals were barracking police officers and I considered it would have taken very little to turn the situation into large-scale public disorder. There was an armed robbery at a local shop, involving a tall black man with a handgun who took all the banknotes from the till. I stopped a man who loosely answered the description. He was affable and said he'd been at a friend's flat watching videos. My Inspector told me to let him go, but I didn't. I asked another male officer to search him; nothing was found. The CCTV was inconclusive. My Inspector again told

me to let him go. I asked the man to take me to his friend's flat,
and he replied he'd forgotten which flat it was. I arrested him,
to the evident distress of my Inspector. At the station all the
cash was found in his underpants and the handgun was found
by a police dog, having been posted through the letterbox of a
nearby house. The man admitted his involvement and I got a
big bunch of flowers from the CID.

Sam (P Div) 1990s

I went round to this flat to arrest a woman who'd been stealing
from a pensioner. So I go round to nick her, and she's in bed
in this not-very-nice flat. There were dogs everywhere and as
she's getting out of bed she treads in a pile of dog poo. She
doesn't clean her foot, just puts it into her white stiletto shoe.
We get ready to go and she says, 'I can't go without tidying up.'
I thought. 'You've got to be kidding.' She says, 'At least let me
make the bed.' So she shakes it, and all this shit flies off the bed
where the dogs have been sleeping; disgusting. I've been to
some places where I don't know how I've managed to go in.

Annie (CID) 1990s

I stopped a car driven by a middle-aged man who set off my
antenna. Eventually we found a stash of jewellery and cash,
which we later discovered was from a number of burglaries he
had committed that night, in a high-value residential area. I
was seconded onto the subsequent investigation. He admitted
over 2650 similar offences and nearly one million pounds'
worth of lost items. He would do five to ten houses in a single
street by checking the voters' register at the local library and
calling directory enquiries for the telephone number of each
home. If no one answered the phone he would burgle the
house.

I am afraid of heights which led to some embarrassment with other arrests. One night I chased a burglar who got up onto a flat roof. I went after him, arrested him up there . . . but couldn't get down. The Fire Brigade had to be called. A similar incident happened at Chelsea football ground where I had to come down the terrace stairs backwards with my prisoner, because it was so steep it made me feel ill. The crowd thought it was hilarious.

Caroline (Traffic) 2000s

Hammersmith Robbery Squad were having problems with youths stealing laptops, mobile phones and posh watches from lone females in soft-top cars stuck in traffic on the A40. Groups of youths from the local council estate would attack them mob-handed. I was used as a decoy and sat in my soft-top car, pretending to read a newspaper. I was wearing a real Rolex which had been lent to us, and had a fake mobile phone and laptop out on display. Sure enough a group of about twenty youths turned up and started discussing what they would do to get these items.

The officers in our observation van could hear that they intended to slash my face with a knife and, if I resisted, to stab me. I couldn't hear those details, but my gut feeling was that I was in a dangerous position. I remember only being able to hear my heartbeat . . . all other sounds disappeared ('audible exclusion' or something it's called, when you go into high-stress situations). Anyway, the sergeant decided it was too dangerous and warned me, 'Get the fuck out of there' as they were coming for me. They scattered as I drove off, and may have damaged their bikes but tough shit . . . no one ever reported it.

With the exception of a couple of damaged bicycles,
that incident had a safe ending. Sadly that is not
always the case. I admire the sheer guts and raw cour-
age of policewomen and particularly the bravery of
Amanda, the woman officer who chased three armed
robbers and whose story began this chapter.

Deservedly she received a commendation for what
she did that day; showing courage which helped put
three dangerous men behind bars for long prison
sentences. Her family were delighted to hear of her
award, but understandably worried about her.

'If you're not careful you'll end up in a wheelchair,'
said her grandmother. That chilling warning was to
come horribly true. I think Amanda's final story, told
below, is a clear illustration of the dangers facing any
police office making an arrest; a fitting closure for
this chapter.

Jenny

Amanda (M Div) 1990s

At around midnight we get a shout to a domestic incident in the
New Kent Road. We pull up, blue lights flashing and are met by
the caller – a lady in her mid-twenties, wearing only knickers and
a T-shirt. In her flat we find a tall, skinny bloke sitting in an
armchair. We ascertain that he has been drinking and has recently
been discharged under the Care in the Community Scheme. As
she doesn't want to press any charges I give him a warning and tell
him if we get called back then he'll get nicked. He's behaving
himself while we are there, and promises to go to bed.

A short time later we're called back, and again she is outside
in knickers and T-shirt, but this time carrying a small orna-
mental brass iron that the male has hit her with. In the flat he

is sitting exactly as before. This is just a couple of days after we had been issued with a baton and trained how to use it, so I have mine in a low profile 'draw' position behind my left leg, as does the probationer constable who is with me. I inform the man that I am arresting him for assault and ask him to come quietly. He says that isn't happening. When I approach to apply cuffs he pulls his jumper sleeve over his hand to prevent the cuffs from fitting, grabs my arm and tries to drag me towards him. I leap backwards, twisting my arm away. I reiterate that he is under arrest, and that if he makes another move without direct instruction I will strike with my baton.

He stands, and I tell him to place his hands behind his back and turn around. As he turns he rips a wooden shelf off the wall and throws it . . . just missing me. I shout into my radio for 'urgent assistance' then dart forward and strike him twice on his right leg, just to the side of his kneecap, as hard as I can. During training we had been told this would be enough to cause serious damage to anyone's leg . . . but he just looks at me, tilts his head and waggles his finger at me in a 'tut-tut' fashion. What the training did not cover was dealing with a schizophrenic who'd been taking drugs during the time between our two call-outs to him. I had damaged his knee, but he just didn't notice because he was high.

I know we're in trouble when he charges. I strike him with the baton, as does my probationer, but it doesn't even slow him down. During our desperate fight to suppress him, I hear hammering on the communal door and yelling coming over the radio, 'Open the door', but we're too busy fighting. Our back-up can't get through the heavy security door, and no one in the block is prepared to buzz the police in.

The male has me pinned against the kitchen cabinet with his arms wrapped around me and is doing his best to pull my head off. I twist and turn till I manage to whip myself backwards and away from the cabinet. Even at the time I realise this is not the way you are supposed to treat your spine and back muscles. My probationer keeps hitting him with his baton, but my attacker hasn't even noticed his presence. I break free and get a gap between us, but he picks up a broom handle. He's about to attack again when the back-up guys burst through the door.

The male spins round and swings at one of the officers, breaking his knuckle. Now he has his back to me, so I jump on him, wrap my legs around his torso and my arms around his neck. With my weight behind him, and my colleagues fighting to the front of him, he topples backwards, pinning me to the floor with his full bodyweight. He starts bucking wildly, swinging the broom at the incoming officers, preventing them from helping me. I manage to free an arm and begin applying pressure on his neck. Finally he starts to slow down, but not before throwing a bowl of what smells like cat's pee all over me. Arms pull me from under the bloke, but it takes six strapping male police officers to restrain and cuff him.

By this point he is quite battered, even though he doesn't realise it, and it's decided to take him to A&E under heavy escort. I am also taken to get checked over, along with the PC with a broken knuckle. While at Guys Hospital the bloke manages to get an arm loose and injure a nurse. Subsequently in prison he assaulted a guard who had to retire due to his injuries.

That night my back hurt and I was tired. We finished up, and the following day I still had some paperwork to do from the arrest. I was sitting at the newly installed computers when a mate came to congratulate me on 'a good shout'. He pushed down on both of my shoulders in a supportive gesture; instantly things started popping, and overwhelming pain tore down through my back and body. I was taken straight home and saw my GP the next day.

I made multiple attempts to get back to work, but the pain was excruciating and my legs weakened to the point that it felt they would buckle beneath me. At that time you could stay on sick leave for an extended period following an assault and not have to worry about pay. I didn't want to just hang on like that. If I couldn't be a copper any more I wanted to move on. My family was in Yorkshire and I wanted to go home. The Medical Officer agreed, and I was retired on an injury pension.

Over the next couple of years my back deteriorated and complications resulted in spinal fixation surgery, which increased weakness in my legs and left me only able to walk short distances, with sticks, around the house. The rest of the time I have to use a wheelchair. It doesn't bother me, though. I have my two kids, a lovely husband and my Support dog, Jupiter. I've climbed Snowdon in a wheelchair; become a Serious Incident Investigator for the Ambulance Service, and been selected for the Paralympic Para-potential programme for archery. I'm not sure where that last one will take me because I'd never shot an arrow before ... but it's a great honour to have got this far.

2

THIS IS THE JOB FOR ME

The headmaster of my secondary modern school believed a girl's career should be restricted to marriage, being a housewife and having babies. He did concede that in the meantime we might work in a shop or an office. Goodness knows what he would have thought of me joining the Police Force.

My own career with the London Force began on 8 April 1969, fifty years after the first women joined the Metropolitan Police. Barely nineteen, I was a naïve bundle of hope, fired with the desire to do good and to help the general public. I was also, if I'm honest, craving security. My mother died when I was seventeen. She had been the lynchpin that held my family together, and without her we fell apart. I left home shortly after her death.

The first step of my recruitment into the Met was a visit by a sergeant from the local police station. He came to vet my home conditions even though I was living with a friend's family at the time. Stage two was a day of interviews and medicals at the recruitment centre in Borough High Street in Southwark, South London. The day was both daunting and embarrassing. It was daunting because interview followed interview, making me feel like a bug under a microscope with Woman Chief Superintendent Shirley Becke, head of the Women's Branch, and a panel of men overseeing the day. The embarrassing part was standing, half-naked, in front of a panel of two women and one man, all sitting comfortably behind a desk in the interview room. I just hoped the man was indeed a doctor.

The mortifying police medical is a memory which seems to be etched on the minds of all female recruits, up to and including the current Met Commissioner, Cressida Dick (although she assures me that it no longer follows the same format in the modern recruitment process). In the days when she and I were recruited, we were told to strip down to our knickers, bend over and touch our toes, turn around with our back to the panel . . . and do the same again. There was no explanation as to what medical facts this might conceivably have offered.

The rest of the medical was more understandable. Eye tests, a weigh-in and the all-important measurement of my height. The minimum height for a WPC then was 5'4" – just as it had been for the first Women Patrols in 1919. I stood 5'9" in my stockinged feet so I knew there was no problem there. However, they put my official height as 5'8¾". Robbed of that all-important quarter inch I demanded a re-match with the measuring stick. To my disgust they recorded the lesser figure once again. It's something that still rankles to this day.

Lastly we had general knowledge, English and maths tests. I was, and still am, a complete dipstick when it comes to maths and expected to fail. To my surprise I passed, and a week later was given my joining instructions.

Different women did, of course, have different reasons for wanting to join the police; reasons which have evolved through the decades. My research found that some former women officers had a limited choice of professions. Part of their motivation was that join-ing the Police Service was better than working in an office, or behind the counter in Woolworths. Yet even with the passing of time, one of the abiding reasons given has been a desire to 'make a difference', and to serve those who live and work in London.

Looking through older records of the Met Police, many of which I found at the National Archives in Kew, it's clear that the first women recruits were expected to be of 'a certain class' in society.

Jenny

Lilian 1918

I am a single woman of 35 years of age with no children and I am a British subject. Both of my parents were born in Britain. I was educated in private schools and have previously worked as an unpaid volunteer Women Patrol, and as a Children's Governess with a family in Hampstead. I have some experi-ence of social work from volunteer work with All Saints Church at Dalston in the East End of London.

Application for employment of Lilian Wyles, 1918
Metropolitan Police Archives

Maureen (V Div) 1940s

My reasons for joining the Police Force might sound a little ridiculous, but were important to me at the time. My mother was an invalid so it was perhaps natural that I became a State Registered Nurse at a hospital during the war. This is the bit that sounds ridiculous: I'm on the bus one day and I see a policewoman walking by. She's wearing black stockings. Stockings were still on ration coupons at the time, which meant they were in short supply.

'Ah,' I thought. 'I've got black stockings: I could do that job.' So I got the forms and went for an interview, where they were very nice and agreed I could live at home, once I had passed the training, because my mother was not all that well. By 1947 I was twenty-three-years old, and had joined the Metropolitan Police.

Audrey (Q Div) 1950s

I was a secretary in a solicitor's office, fascinated by the law and wanting a more worthwhile job than typing and shorthand. I considered becoming a probation officer, or joining the police. I chose the Police Service because I did not have a School Certificate and, in those days, I would have had to do a course at the London School of Economics to train as a probation officer. That seems hard to believe now. There were three recruitment days for the police. Out of the original hundred applicants of both sexes, only about ten of us were accepted. I was proud to be one of the few.

Mary (D Div) 1950s

I was brought up on a farm in Dumfries and Galloway and wanted to see what the rest of the world was like. So I upped and volunteered for four years with the WRAF in Singapore. I applied for the police when I was there. It was an unusual choice of career I suppose, but I wanted to work in London, and was lucky to get in because I was twenty-two and they had only recently begun taking recruits as young as that.

I remember that the medicals for both jobs were similar: we had to strip down to our knickers in front of the doctor, bend over to touch toes and then they peeked down our pants to check for any 'infection'. I remember they asked what experience I thought I had gained from being out in Changi. I was able to tell them about life there because, of course, there was an emergency out there then. They were fighting the communists in the jungle. I think they were looking for girls with some experience. Miss Bather was the Chief Superintendent in charge of women in the Met and she was an ex-WRAF, so I thought I stood a good chance. I was right. I got in.

Shirley (Z Div) 1950s
I saw two WPCs on the beat in Croydon when I was twelve years old, and thought 'that's the job I would like to do'. When I was sixteen I went to my local police station and asked a male sergeant at the front desk what I could do before applying for the Job, I was told not to waste his time. I left the Station, thinking if I got into the Job, I would never treat anyone like that. I later found out he could have lifted a phone and asked the WPC on reserve to speak to me. Undeterred, I did apply and went for a one-day interview. My medical was in front of a doctor and the women officers. It amounted to them watching you stand on brown paper in your pants and taking a look at your hands; that was it!

Pamela (H Div) 1960s
I joined in 1960 when I was twenty-one years old. I had left school at fifteen in Aberystwyth and always fancied being a

hospital almoner but didn't have the qualifications. So I diversified towards the Metropolitan Women Police, partly influenced by the knowledge that suitable accommodation would be made available for me in London. I was interviewed by a panel of a woman and two men, and part of the medical was wearing only pants and bra. We had to bend down and touch toes, exposing the back of legs and rear area to the panel. I think it was meant to expose varicose veins, but all I was conscious of was a ladder in my nylon pants. Very embarrassing!

Monica (C Div) 1960s

In my interview they asked about any family connections to the police. I told them my grandfather joined Thames Police in 1864, the start of an almost continuous line of family members since then, including the Royal Irish Constabulary and the Australian Police. Two senior women officers and an elderly doctor were on my board. For the medical we were stripped to our knickers and wore a huge dressing gown. As we entered the room, the dressing gown was whipped from our shoulders by the woman Inspector and we were told to stand on a set of footprints, about ten feet from the other people sitting behind a large desk. The aged doctor got up and listened to heart, front and back with his stethoscope and tapped us with his fingers. He looked in my mouth and checked ears. I have never understood why those other people were present during a medical . . . but I have my own theory!

Carol (C Div) 1960s

My father was a police sergeant in the Norfolk Constabulary and I applied to the Met because he bet me I was not bright enough to get in and that, even if I did, I'd not last six months. Winning would recoup me a total of £10. As I was only earning £4.50 a week at the time, it seemed worth giving it a go. There were written tests of some sort and then the medical which, as a green, nicely brought-up young lady, I found horrendous. My lovely mum had given me some pretty, scanty, lace knickers to wear and, to my undying shame, I was made to bend down in front of this board with my rear end mooning at them. They were all women apart from the doctor, I think, but I was mortified. Their main concern, however, seemed to be whether or not I suffered from chilblains. I had lived in police property all my life and central heating had not been heard of in Norfolk, so of course I did have chilblains; everyone did in those days.

Pet (Q Div) 1970s

As far as I know I was the second black female to join the Met. I was born in Jamaica, came to England when I was twelve, got married at seventeen and had three children by the time I joined the police at the age of twenty-four.

It was a fluke how I joined really. My husband and I had just moved to Harlesden and I was going for an interview for a totally different job but couldn't find the place. I asked this man who told me to ask at the police station round the corner. There was an ad for a typist on the board outside, so I went in and said, 'I'm here for the job.' The cheek of it! But I got the job. For me it was a good insight into the work of the police. What I did, I used to look through the books in admin. I was nosy and read through all the books and letters which made me interested in police work. I was a married woman with three children and I think the job took a risk with me. It was really strange how as a typist I became a police officer. I tell people it's the best job I've ever done, it opens your eyes to so many different things.

Lorraine (S Div) 1970s

When I went for my medical to become a Special Police Constable, I wore glasses. My eyesight was really bad. I was told to take my glasses off. When I went to the guy for the medical check he said, 'Can you read that board over there?'

Me and my humour. I said, 'Oh yes I can, thank you.'

He replied, 'OK,' and signed me off. That's how I got in. I thought, 'If you knew how bad my eyesight was, mate, you'd never have let me in.'

Jo (T Div) 1970s

I can remember the application form was especially designed for female adults; it was pink! The exams were easy because I was still in education and my mind was sharp. This was single-sex recruitment and, while we were waiting to be tested, girls were called out and we never saw them again. They asked me would I be scared and I answered, 'Yes, but I would climb a mountain just to have the experience, scared or not.'

Susan (P Div) 1970s

My parents had a rather volatile relationship and it was quite common for a neighbour to call the police, as there would be screaming and shouting. The local cops would come out with a lovely woman police constable. I remember she would chat to me and my sister, and then, as if by magic, things would quieten down.

At my interview at Paddington Green I had taken a lot of care with my 'up' hairdo and I wore a small amount of make-up. One of the men on the board asked if I would mind wearing a uniform as he felt I was obviously a follower of fashion. I answered that it would be a relief to wear a uniform and not have to pick what to wear. Then I got a letter to start at Hendon on 4 November 1974. I was still living at home with my mum, who was proud of me. I travelled with a great big case full of clothes, toiletries, a shoe-cleaning kit, several pairs of black tights, and a writing set of Basildon Bond pad, envelopes, stamps and pens. I was so excited.

Sally (W Div) 1970s
My dad said I could join the police cadets but not the police. He was a Chief Superintendent in the Met at the time and was a bit dubious about women in the Job because they didn't respect women that much in those days. On the way back from interviewing for the cadets I was walking through the tube station where a busker was singing, 'Let me take you by the hand and lead you through the streets of London.' I couldn't believe it; I thought, 'Well, someone's telling me something.'

Gina (G Div) 1970s
I was just 5' 3" tall, which at the time was under the height limit for joining the Met. I was also only about seven stone, and had done ballet, so was quite 'diddy'. I remember being asked how I thought I could cope. Surprisingly, I was still allowed in because I had A-level GCE qualifications, which was unusual at the time. I did not grow after that.

Cheryl (Q Div) 1970s–1980s
I am afraid my reason for joining is not a long-held dream of being a police officer. It was just a case of, 'OK, I'll give it a try,' as the other option then was a job as a shop assistant at John Lewis, Brent Cross. I had a wonderful career, made the most amazing friends and do not regret a single moment. Hand on heart I can count on one hand the number of times I didn't feel like going to work over my thirty-four-year career; and all

from my dad suggesting trying the cadets as I had no other prospects.

Mary (R Div) 1980s
For my interview and medical I had to strip down to my pants then stand on footprints on a mat in front of a man (whom I trust was a doctor). He asked me to show him my hands and I walked towards him. Startled, he shouted at me to stop and go back on the footprints . . . I think my over-generous breasts had alarmed him.

Jane (Z Div) 1980s
I dipped my interview board the first time. I wasn't as prepared or as fit as I should have been. Also you had to do this test around your knowledge of London. They said mine was appalling and I failed. Second time around I was much better prepared. We had to do six times round the track, do sit-ups, and pull-ups which were difficult for a female. You had this bar and had to lift your body weight. I don't think many of us excelled at that. My warrant number is just four figures; women still had their own warrant numbers then. We're the old girls now and it's amazing how proud you are at having four figures. I begrudge the double zero that we have to put on the front for computers.

Caroline (T Div) 1980s
You know the sort of person who can't walk past something that shouldn't be happening? The sort who always wants to help? That's me. I wanted to be a policewoman since I was twelve years old. At my interview three white, old males sat behind a desk, with the light coming in from the window behind so I couldn't actually see them. I remember one asking, 'How do you cope with your monthly periods? Are you able to

perform normal tasks? Do you have to lie down or do you just get on with it?'

Cressida (C Div) 1980s

As a teenager I became quite interested in becoming a police officer. I thought it looked interesting, I thought it looked like I could help people; sounds a bit cheesy, I know. I lived in Oxford and was lucky because Thames Valley Police had an access programme at the time. I spent a week at their training centre when I was fifteen and was able to look at how policing was. That was great, and then I went off to university and studied, but I still had policing in the back of my mind. I applied for Thames Valley in my last year, like you do, and they turned me down. That was a bit of a setback, and I went off and did accountancy in the City. So I came to London and shared a house with my brother and started as a trainee accountant. That really helped because I worked out exactly what I *didn't* want to do. You'd go home at the end of the day and wonder, what did we achieve? It was all the same thing. Not very exciting, although I liked a lot of things about it. I wasn't particularly brilliant. But I think they were very surprised when I walked in and said, after nine months, I was leaving. And I was leaving because I'd put in an application for the Met. I hadn't actually heard that I'd got it. So I spent the summer working in a fish-and-chip shop and doing different things.

I was only just, if at all, 5'4". You had to be 5'6" for the City and 5'4" for the Met in 1983. I literally hung from the banisters and did anything I could think of to ensure I wouldn't be thought too short. This very nice nurse at the medical took one look at me and I could see what she was thinking. She said, 'Don't worry,' and I got in. Everyone since has said that I'm not really 5'4".

I remember putting on this very short, white gown and having to go in front of this panel of people where you had to turn around and bend over and touch your toes for no apparent reason; we never knew why. I wasn't traumatised by it – I just remember thinking it was an odd thing, and talking to people about it afterwards, I seem to have been the least bothered. On the beach I'll strip off, none of that worries me, it never has – but I can remember thinking what a funny thing to be doing. That does not happen any more. I do know that.

Jacqui (G Div) 2000s

Having worked at Holloway Prison, I thought I'd try the police. I was the only female 'person of colour' on my interview board and I recall a male officer giving me a scenario about cannabis. He insisted that I *must* know people who smoked it. I felt he was alluding to my race. That day I got the highest scores in the tests . . . yet 'failed' my interview! But the following week I was given an opportunity with another examiner, and passed.

Megan (K Div) 2010s

My degree hasn't helped me at all. I went for the graduate entry scheme but took myself off it because I thought, 'How can I lead people if I haven't experienced what they experienced? How am I going to get respect?' I love this job, but the way it is now we don't have people who genuinely want to stay in the Job and who are really good at it. They join out of university because they don't know what they want to do. And now, you have to be a graduate to join, and all those who are in the Job will have to take a degree.

3

WELCOME TO THE MET . . .

With my whole life packed into numerous bags, I was deposited at Peto House, a Victorian building off Oxford Street in Central London. This was to be home for the next thirteen weeks while I was bussed each day to the Police Training School, Hendon. It was an adventure and I loved it, despite being drilled and verbally abused by the parade Inspector who shouted, 'I wouldn't let my daughter walk down the street looking like that.' My crime was to have a few strands of hair hanging over the back of my uniform collar. Such treatment was meant to strengthen our character in preparation for facing a sometimes none-too-friendly public.

My abiding memory of Hendon's canteen food is of being served shoe leather disguised as pork chops. By contrast, we girls enjoyed freshly cooked meals each evening at Peto House, with the luxury of toast available any time of the day or night. Butter and jam were always at the ready. I was in heaven.

We may have been better fed than the boys but they did have one advantage over us; they had the more practical uniforms. Ours were designed by The Queen's dressmaker, Norman Hartnell. I liked the jacket, the cape and the pillbox hat, but the skirts were awful; straight boxes without any pleats which might have helped us to actually move and perhaps, one day, chase after villains. It was smart but utterly impractical. Even so, along with the great majority of women who have joined in the past hundred years, I wore the uniform with pride.

Jenny

Maureen (V Div) 1940s

Our training billet was in Wandsworth stables, although I don't remember if the horses were there with us. I do remember we had no men and that Miss Saville was in charge of us all. We hadn't got any young instructors, but we got on well with the men there. As a trained nurse, I used to argue with the first-aider when it came to putting on a splint. I said, 'It's not the way to put it on.' And he'd say, 'Yes it is.' I think the instructors were afraid that if they upset us we might go; they wanted women, you see. We started off with three of us girls in a class, but one of them only stayed two days. She was with the Land Army and said she 'wasn't putting up with this' and left. We did have to learn an awful lot. We had this book of words, the 'Instruction Book'. I used to know the first sentence of it, because everyone knew it off by heart . . . but not now.

Audrey (Q Div) 1950s

I and three other women on my course were housed in Peto House in Marylebone. This was not my first time away from home as I had been at boarding school from the age of nine, and I became good friends with the other women. The instructors were strict but fair, but I found the training hard. We had to learn the 'Instruction Book' parrot-fashion and learn judo. Particularly frustrating for me was trying to get a mirror shine on my toecaps with spit and polish. I spent many an evening doing this! It was a good basis for the outside world, but nothing can prepare you for the real thing. I think donning the uniform gave me a lot of confidence and pride.

Shirley (Z Div) 1950s

There were three women, including me, in our class, along with nineteen men. I remember the photographer who took the class photo stood me on two 'IBs' ('Instruction Books') because I was short and unbalanced the photo. It was my first time away from home and scary because I so wanted to pass the exams and remain in the Job. One or two instructors did seem to think Women Police were a waste of space but, on the whole, they treated us well. Women Police had extra training in the Children and Young Persons Act, 1933, because our main work was dealing with vulnerable young people. If necessary we would take them to court as in need of care and protection and present the case to the magistrates.

Pat (C Div) 1960s

During training we were issued with shirts, separate collars, stockings, a gabardine mac, hat, gloves and bag. We wore our own plain skirts and lace-up shoes. Our tailored uniform was ready for when we were posted. I was nineteen years old and loved the camaraderie on the course . . . although camaraderie with the men once got me into trouble. I was seen chatting to a male recruit in the lunch queue at Peel House. I was sent to the front of the queue ... and the man was sent to the back. Once posted, I shared a room at Pembridge Hall women's section house in Notting Hill. No visitors allowed in rooms, although we could 'book' a small sitting room to entertain, and we had a kitchen too. In some other section houses women had a separate floor, often the top. Men weren't allowed there, and you could be sacked if caught on the men's floor.

Margaret (H Div) 1960s

One morning we were waiting patiently for the driver of the coach taking us to train at Hendon. The engine was running and, having foolishly asked everyone on board if I should drive it, they all dared me. I put the coach into gear and drove it about two inches. Everyone cheered. I pulled up with a hiss of air brakes and went back to my seat feeling very clever ... until the Section House Sergeant asked me to step outside.

He looked stern. 'Have you asked the owner's permission to drive this vehicle, and are you insured?' He informed me he had every right to chuck me out of the Police Force for taking and driving away without the permission of the owner, and driving without insurance. I thought I was on the point of being dishonourably discharged. I can only say a heartfelt thank you to this sergeant, because he didn't report me and I went on to pass out of Hendon and get a posting to Commercial Street.

Sandra (T Div) 1960s

We all had our own little room. Evening meals were served punctually at 6 p.m. and if you didn't come down then, you didn't eat. If we wanted to go out or do late-night shopping we could ask permission that morning. The extension would be till 8 p.m. and our meal would be kept warm for us, as long as we were back . . . on the dot. I have to admit it felt regimented at first, but after the first week we became a very close-knit group who used to gather in the big kitchen at Peto House, have snacks before bed and chat about all kinds of things.

I am only 5'4", and was so slim then that the stores didn't have a uniform small enough to alter. Pete, one of the PCs, was 6'4" and his uniform was huge. One day while waiting for the instructor, they decided I should be dressed in Pete's great-coat and helmet. It totally swamped me and I disappeared under it. Naturally that's when the instructor decided to appear. Even he roared with laughter. We all enjoyed the teasing; nobody felt picked on.

Monica (C Div) 1960s

The training was comprehensive and covered most of the Acts [of Parliament] that we would deal with on a day-to-day basis. The rote learning of what they called the 'A' reports struck fear into us constantly. Many hours were spent pacing up and down trying to learn them by heart, and all these years later I can still recall a lot of them.

Drill in the yard was great fun. The Drill Sergeant, 'Herbie' Castle, an ex-boxer with a flattened nose, barked out his orders. One morning I was set up to go and ask him what he was shouting out. He spent the next ten minutes demonstrating to me in slow motion. When the Superintendent came down for daily inspection he leaned in two inches from my face: 'There's only room for one joker here, Miss . . . and it's not you.'

Self-defence classes consisted of the women being shown a wrist hold (very painful – and I did use it several times) and a sideways chopping action just under the nose (also very pain-ful.) Both were useful if a prisoner was resisting arrest.

Carol (C Div) 1960s

This was my first time away from home, and I struggled with simple little things. I did not know, for example, that you could get your dry cleaning done in two hours. So I was often pulled up for being scruffy, which I had never been before. Living in London was a whole new learning process, albeit my mother was a Londoner and I had visited it often. I do remember that women were often written off as 'only being there to find a husband'. Two really good pieces of advice I was given then were that friendships are transient ... but camaraderie is important, and that I should pay a full National Insurance stamp, even though women could still pay a reduced stamp at that time.

Deryl (P Div) 1970s

Home had been an old farmhouse with no heating other than an open fire downstairs, but my bedroom window had never been closed. The first few nights in the Hendon tower block I got up every hour to open/close the window.

I got sworn at, which I was not used to. I had to ask a classmate what the words 'fucking' and 'cunt' meant after one of the instructors put his nose an inch from mine and screamed, 'You are a useless fucking cunt ... what are you?' I dutifully repeated, 'I'm a useless fucking cunt, Sergeant'. I did guess the words were not complimentary. I was eighteen years old, but neither my Methodist youth club nor girls' grammar school had equipped me with such knowledge. Nothing ever upset me on the streets ... so I suppose it worked.

Gina (G Div) 1970s

I came from the incredibly sheltered background of a private girls' boarding school in Wales where we weren't allowed to talk to boys and where manners were paramount. I remember arriving at Hendon, putting my case down, and hearing a sergeant shouting at me, 'Get that fucking case off the grass!' I'd never heard the word before. It was a huge shock to me, someone shouting at me like that for something so trivial. I don't think he could believe I was actually that naïve – and I think they were shouting at everyone.

I was used as a trigger for the whole psychology thing for the blokes. The sergeant asked me one day, 'Why have you joined?' I started to go through the whole, 'I want to help people . . .', but he kicked my desk. 'You cow,' he said. 'You're either a dyke . . . or you've joined to find a husband.' So I said, 'What do mean, I'm a dyke?' I didn't know what that meant and, 'If I was looking for a husband I wouldn't have joined the Police Force for a husband.' Several of the blokes were trying to protect me, and one who'd been in the army was all ready for lamping him. Then this sergeant turned around with a big smile on his face and wrote on the blackboard 'Aggression' – the whole thing was about recognising people's reactions. I was used many times for that sort of thing because it seemed I was this sweet naïve young thing; that couldn't have been further from the truth.

Janis (C Div) 1970s

I lived at Hendon during training and hardly ate in the week as the canteen was infested with cockroaches. I lived just thirty minutes away by car and was grateful to be able to go home at the weekends and have decent meals. Living on one floor, in a block dominated by male officers on other floors, had its challenges, and we were often seen as easy targets. We did feel vulnerable at times and some of the females were put in compromising situations, such as having men come to their rooms. There were occasional sexual innuendos, usually ignorance rather than intentional, which in this day and age would not go down well. But I was a twenty-two-year-old when I joined in 1973 and, having experience of life 'outside', I was able to deal with varying degrees of sexual remarks.

Margaret (N Div) 1970s

It was great living five minutes from Oxford Street. Because we wore uniform for work and were fed and watered, all of our money was disposable . . . so we disposed with great alacrity! We used to go off and spend our wages (paid in cash in a little brown envelope on a Friday evening, I think) on clothes and shoes. I can still remember some of the dresses I bought, and the shoes; platforms were just coming in – low ones for me, though. I did the Women Police Senior Training course and was taught how to interview rape victims, search female prisoners, and deal with care and protection. It was great, in-depth training and, to my mind, far superior to anything the men had.

Pet (Q Div) 1970s

I never expected in a million years the work to be so hard. I got 4 out of 10 for my first test. My instructor said, 'You're not going to be the teacher's pet if you continue to get marks like this.' I was ashamed, so that weekend I went home and told my husband, 'I'm not going to do anything, I have got to study.' There's no way I was going to be the dunce in the class. Anyway, Monday, 8 out of 10; I never looked back. The Chief Superintendent came in and said he wanted to praise someone . . . and it was me.

Jo (T Div) 1970s

When learning the 'old-style' police caution we were fined a few pence if we got it wrong. We were tested ad hoc by the instructor who would all of a sudden ask a student to recite it. The money went in the kitty for the end-of-training party. I was asked to be 'Mother Bunny' at training school, a role I can only describe as being a listening ear to other females who felt over-whelmed or needed advice. What could an eighteen-year-old give counsel on? I was fairly green myself.

We all had to take the oath of allegiance and I remember feeling very proud, and wondering how my career would pan out. I was posted to Heathrow Airport where the upside was that I was not alone. All females at TS Division were posted to Heathrow at that time. The ethos was that they would need females to man a casualty bureau should a major event happen at Heathrow. These days that would be classed as discrimina-tion – back then it was just expected.

Susan (P Div) 1970s

A woman sergeant explained the rules: 'No men on our floor, and no noise.' CID officers were in our block, and we were to be very careful around these 'sex-crazed' men. My name tag read 'Susan' and, when in the lift with CID men on their courses, they'd stare at the tag . . . and ask what the other breast was called. I didn't realise how much time we would spend pressing our uniforms. The woman police sergeant explained how to press the crease down the sleeves of the jacket and told us how to 'bull' our shoes with the famous 'spit and polish'. I spent many happy hours in the lounge area, chatting, ironing and cleaning shoes.

The parade ground practice was split between fun and terror with the famous Sergeant Sid Butcher teaching us to march and how to 'dress' to get proper gaps in the parade line. In inspections he enjoyed going on at the girls for not being smart enough, or for having hair on their collars and suchlike. Sometimes tube trains went by and I could see people laughing.

A woman Inspector called us into the canteen one night to tell us what it would be like after we were posted to Divisions. She warned us to be careful of the men taking advantage of us. She didn't want anyone going sick with 'period pains'; the proper name was dysmenorrhea! Later I had to laugh when I saw how every Reserve Room in the Met had the word 'diarrhoea' written on the wall because they couldn't spell it when people phoned in sick.

Sue (B Div) 1980s

The accommodation was pretty grim, and over the years it just got worse. Men were not allowed on the women's floor of course; though there seemed to be a fair bit of scurrying up and down the stairwell. Early on I was told that women only lasted five years on average, and so we wouldn't get much specialist training. Years later I worked with the same sergeant who was mortified when I reminded him of what he had said. As per usual in the police, if you proved yourself, then they were generally OK.

One sexist guy in our class got kicked out later in the course; the rest were lovely. We were all in it together and helped each other out. One guy spent ages trying to teach me to dive for the life-saving exam – I failed. Others would bull my shoes or patiently show me how to do it. I met my husband at training school. He sat behind me and his opening line was quite novel: 'So, are you one of those stone-faced lesbians . . . or do you like men?' Despite this dodgy intro we became great friends and when we met again after training school he cooked dinner, and the rest is history.

Women didn't do boxing, we didn't do public order. We wore lovely navy knickers and little PE skirts. Plenty of wise-cracks all round – mostly taken in good humour – and if things got out of hand the other male students would step in. We were in the bar one night and some lads were singing a bawdy song about a sailor who couldn't satisfy his wife. I just said: 'He obviously hasn't found her clitoris then.' They were shocked, and one of our tutors nearly fell off his chair laughing.

Debbie (A Div) 1980s
I remember derogatory comments from the drill instructor, who introduced himself as, 'My name is Butcher . . . B-A-S-T-A-R-D . . . Butcher.' Some Instructors would call men with beards 'fungus face', and any officer with glasses was 'four eyes'. I recall one instructor calling a black WPC 'Coco', and female officers were referred to as 'split arses'. In one PT session we were playing tunnel-ball and the instructor said to the female officers, 'Forget what your mother told you . . . open your legs wide'. I hated the early starts but it taught me discipline. I was only nineteen and used to lying in half the day and staying out all hours.

Jane (H Div) 1980s
We went to Hounslow for riot training and, as we were enter-ing the changing rooms, I was laughing. One of the instructors said, 'We've got a right one here,' indicating me. We had to line up at the end. The instructors had bits of lost property and the owners had to step forward to collect them and do forfeit star-jumps. The last item was a suspender belt. I remember standing to attention thinking, 'Oh no, someone's in for a

tough time'. As no one came forward he said, 'It's OK, it has a name in it.' Everyone started laughing, including me . . . until he read out my name. I was mortified and went a delightful shade of puce. I couldn't think of any way of telling people it wasn't mine without showing them! (I didn't though). After they dismissed us the cheeky instructor came to find me and ask me out. I reckon he did it every time.

Janet (Y Div) 1980s

One of the instructors made a comment about me putting on some weight since my joining photo had been taken. With a smirk on his face he said something like, 'So you like the food here then?' My weight has been an up/down issue for me since childhood, so that did not make me feel very happy or confident. I was a twenty-three-year-old trainee being spoken to by one of my class sergeants. They were more or less God at the time, so what was I to say?

I enjoyed most of my time in training, although I ended up with an anxiety issue because of my fear of heights and the threat of being made to jump from the top board of the swimming pool. I was kept behind once and continually made to jump in from the side. Seemingly the instructor thought I'd get better the more I did it, but actually I got more and more distressed. I was sobbing uncontrollably towards the end and it was not nice. I think many instructors were teaching because it was an easy posting, and they should have had more professional training.

I enjoyed feeling part of something that was like a family; a job for life, a place where you felt you belonged and were 'looked after', had housing, got prescription, dental and eye-test charges back, and things like plain clothes allowance. All these things have now gone, and the organisation seems to be coming from a very different ethos. You only have to look at the current state of the site where the training school was: the new Peel House at Hendon can't hold a candle to the vast and impressive site that once was Hendon Training School and all that that encompassed. I could say much about that analogy in the context of the way the Job has gone over the last fifteen or so years . . . eroded, replaced and shrunk beyond measure.

Jacqui (G Div) 2000s

I was a thirty-six-year-old single parent when I joined. Both my parents are from the Caribbean and my family was really proud of me when I joined. Nobody likes the police when they're being arrested but I've had no problem with the people in Hackney. I'm from there, and people will give you the 'kissing of the teeth', but I've said, 'I'm talking to you politely . . . so don't be silly.' That's just how I am, there's no need for the rudeness. I've arrested many a black person, but only once has somebody said, 'You're arresting me because I'm black.' My reply was, 'If you say so.'

Caroline (T Div) 2000s

I was sent to Heathrow so had the three weeks' Standard Firearms course at Lippitts Hill. There was just me and one other girl on the course of twenty men. I remember the instructors putting a load of body armour in a heap on the floor of the classroom. We all had to make up our own body armour, but there was nothing for the female form. My body armour was too big, and too long, for me. When drawing my Glock pistol from my left hip, I had to bend over to the right in order to lift the armour. I could then get my hand on the pistol and pull it out.

Caroline (Royalty Protection) 2000s–2010s

The firearms' training was second to none. Whenever anything went wrong, or we were dealing with an incident, the training really did kick in. The protocol was: 'You're not going out there to shoot people . . . it's an additional tool.' As time went on we had more things on our utility belt to assist us. We had Tasers, CS gas, we had the ASPs (extendable batons) all as options . . . as indeed was the firearm; you didn't just go straight for your firearm.

In training we gauged circumstances according to the scenarios. If you've got a man running towards you with a machete, as I had once in a scenario for my Royalty Protection bit, you just shoot him. Action always beats reaction; he's running towards my Principal (the person I must protect) with a machete, I shoot him. Sometimes one of the scenarios was that someone has already attacked with a knife or a gun and he's walking away from you . . . but still on the loose: what do you do? I shot him in the back. My colleagues said you can't shoot someone in the back and I said, 'Yes you can: he's still a loose cannon.' The instructors always like to encourage conversation among the other students so they let it go on for a while. Underneath I was beginning to wonder if I'd done the right thing, but I went with my gut feeling that this man was still out and about, there were members of the public everywhere, he was going towards a school (that was part of the scenario) he had a gun in his hand, and he'd already killed someone. No, I was going to take him, and I did, and I was praised for that.

Obviously you always have to shout a warning first. 'Armed police – show me your hands. Armed police – show me your hands.' Some students get locked into that, it's like a repeat cycle – 'Armed police – show me your hands' – and they're not actually listening to what the suspect is saying. You have to put in that challenge so every member of the public will know, and when they make a statement they will say, 'Oh yes they were saying, "Armed police . . . put down your gun".'

But you've got to start listening to the suspect as well, because it might be that you give the warning and they do put their gun down straightaway. Then it's a matter of lowering the tension, lowering the voice, 'OK, turn around, put your hands on your head and interlace your fingers, and walk to me, slowly, backwards, look to your left, look away from me.' It might be the case that he still comes straight towards you and you start backing away; but you can't keep backing away because this man is a danger, not only to you but also to others. You want to come to a peaceful, safe conclusion for everyone, including the suspect; everyone has a right to life.

In the Special Escort Group we were trained to shoot from cars, ambushes, shoot from motorcycles, use motorcycles as cover . . . all very Annie Oakley. Then with Close-Protection you'd be driving around with a Principal and they'd throw in a smoke grenade, and the instructor would shout, 'Right, front car immobilise, rear car immobilise.' So you'd be blocked out and you had to get out and get your Principal out, evacuate him or her. They throw in smoke bombs, explosions and mobs. It's all very gung-ho, but with a very serious message underneath.

For one of the assessments for Close-Protection work you go into the gym at Gravesend. There's all these big, rufty-tufty instructors in these bodysuits and they always pick the big buggers to start attacking you. Your Principal is on the other side of the gym, and you have to work round the two sides of the room to get to them. So you start fighting, using all the approved moves and yelling, 'Get back, get down.' It's knacker-ing, and you go from that really physical activity to fine motor skills. You go to the first corner and there'll be an instructor telling you there's a Glock which has got a stoppage; you can see the shell has come out, and he says, 'Right clear it.' And he's shouting in your ear, 'Fucking come on, fucking come on, come on.' I remember I just blocked him out completely, cleared the stoppage, bash . . . and then I'm fighting my way through to the next corner shouting, 'Get back . . . get down.'

I get to my Principal and then I have to take him from that far corner to the other far corner. I can honestly say it felt like the floor of the gym went uphill, it felt like I was fighting uphill. It was knackering, absolutely knackering because the adrenalin is pumping and these lads are coming at you and fighting you, and pushing you back. Then you look round and you've lost hold of your Principal and you're shouting, 'Come on!' And all the while your adrenalin is pumping. One bloke came out and threw up. Looking back, I enjoyed it.

One of the instructors said, 'We could see you flagging, like everyone does, but we knew you were going to pass because you were knackered but suddenly you screamed at your Principal, "You fucking come here" and you pushed him, and we knew you'd got those reserves from your toes up and we knew in a real incident you could do it.'

There were twelve on that course . . . and only four of us passed.

Kim (H Div) 2010s

I wish I had joined at a time when traditional residential training took place.

The initial twelve-week training was OK, but I didn't enjoy the coached patrol. One officer was extremely old school and enjoyed making the students feel small. Maybe this was to 'toughen us up', but I did not appreciate it – especially as I was older than the average recruit at the time. He was not the most politically correct person either, which made me uncomfortable. He was the only person who gave me an experience that I felt was similar to how women would have felt thirty years ago. He's since retired.

Anon (Senior Officer) 2010s

The training now is almost non-existent: you have to assume they can't read or write. You might as well stop a bus and take twenty people off it to be police officers. They have the certificate in policing which frankly teaches them nothing. You give them a uniform and tell them to get on with it. There's none of this twenty weeks of working hard.

4

THE PRUDE ON THE PROWL

'We have no place for the prude on the prowl. All our
women are most carefully chosen. They must be of
good education; tact, kindliness, and a sympathetic
personality are among the desirable attributes. Great
stress is laid upon the fact that they are trained for
general work, but their special duties are concerned
with the prevention of crime among women and children. Women police, by the way, are not doing all-
night duty, although their hours may be very late.'

Mrs Sophia Stanley,
Superintendent Women Patrols 1919
Metropolitan Police Archives

At training school I learned that many of the laws in
force then dated back to the days of Robert Peel, the
founder of the Metropolitan Police. It was fascinating
to be taught some of the history of the service, and of
women's gradual inclusion in the ranks. How odd

that some women started as suffragettes on the wrong side of the law, only to become poacher-turned-game-keeper as pioneer members of the first Women Patrols!

Metropolitan Police archives record that on 17 February 1919 the first twenty-five women patrols left Peel House Training establishment for duty, under the leadership of Woman Superintendent Mrs Sophia Stanley. The hundred-year history of women police in London is a story of slow integration and slow acceptance that women can perform the same roles as men. Those first hesitant steps in a male-dominated force were controversial. Women battled against institutional and deeply ingrained sexism. In those early days such attitudes were the norm in a society where suffragettes had fought a long and bitter struggle. The journey towards equality between male and female officers began with a single notice in Police Orders, the official Scotland Yard publication sent to every police station in the Metropolitan Force.

Jenny

The force of Women Patrols of the Metropolitan police will for the present consist of 100 Patrols and 10 Patrol Sergeants, under a Superintendent. Applications for enrolment are now being dealt with. The success of this experiment, for which there is a widespread public demand, must depend very largely upon a spirit of co-operation between the regular Force and the Women Patrols. The Commissioner looks, therefore, to all ranks to use their best endeavours with this object. Pay is 30s. [£1.50] a week and a war bonus of 12s. [60p] for patrols and 42s [£2.10] plus the war bonus for sergeants.

Police Orders, 1919
Metropolitan Police Archives

'This woman's contract expired on 21/7/21 and although she expressed a wish to serve for a further period, in view of the unsatisfactory reports I had of her work, I did not allow her to sign the renewed contract. At first she worked better, but latterly she has fallen back into her idle habits and I think she is incurably lazy. She is a grumbler, dirty, and a mischief-maker in the Section House. Recommend her services to be terminated.'

Report on 'Ellen', a serving member of the
Women's Patrol – Mrs Sophia Stanley,
Superintendent Women Patrols 1921
Metropolitan Police Archives

'Required to resign. Found sitting in a Ladies lavatory in company with another patrol, whilst on duty, having been previously cautioned for a similar offence.'

Report on 'Madge', a serving member of the
Women's Patrol – *Police Orders*, December 1921
Metropolitan Police Archives

'Women Patrols are to be given access to (Police) Informations and other publications. Their attention will also be to the description of local women and children reported missing or found. The principal duties of Women Patrols consist of dealing with women and

children ill, injured, destitute, homeless and those who
have been the victims of sexual offences, or are believed
to be in danger of drifting towards an immoral life.
They may also work in connection with cases in which
females are concerned such as: white slave traffic, disor-
derly houses, night clubs frequented by both sexes,
Vagrancy Act, fortune telling, watching female prison-
ers detained, or females who have attempted suicide . . .
and prostitutes. Women Patrols are not invested with
the full powers of arrest but Superintendents are to
report when and where, in their opinion, Women
Patrols could with advantage be employed.'

Signed C. F. N. Macready,
Metropolitan Police Commissioner 1920s
Metropolitan Police Archives

In the regulations in 1931, the first duty allotted to
policewomen is Patrol Duty . . . for uniformed police-
women to patrol parks and public places in the inter-
ests of public order and decency and for the protection
of young girls and children. The small force of 50
policewomen for the Metropolitan Area of 700 square
miles is mainly employed on this duty.

Edith Tancred National Council of Women 1930s
Metropolitan Women Police Association Archives,
February 1932

'I think we must protest – as always – on the grounds
that the number in London is quite inadequate for the
duties allotted to them; and if the regulations are not
a complete farce, it is laid down that "numbers shall
be sufficient" to perform allotted duties – we know the

> *London policewomen have allotted duties contained
> in police orders, and it is palpably ridiculous to assert
> that 50 women can carry out these allotted duties.'*
> Letter to Miss Green from Edith Tancred
> 1932 – The Open University and
> Metropolitan Police Authority 2009
> Metropolitan Police Archives

Audrey (Q Div) 1950s

Women police officers were a rarity in the 1950s, especially out in the sticks where I was in Edgware. Our jobs were general patrolling, keeping an eye out for absconders or young girls on the street, and following up on complaints regarding women and children. There seemed to be little crime. 'Soliciting', 'drunk and disorderly' and shoplifting were what I came in contact with. I mostly patrolled with a push-bike and reported to the station using the police box phones, which were handy as we could write up our pocket books in them. A police whistle was all we had to get attention, so it was important to ring in to the station on time.

We were required to deal with traffic offences and be on point duty. Duties involved a lot of house visiting to inspect the au pairs' 'Aliens Certificates' and I did quite a bit of escorting women prisoners to court, or in the court cells. I sometimes was required to man the switchboard at Edgware police station so the civilian staff could go for refreshments, and on a few occasions, I helped the Inspector make up the wage packets for the PCs. Bank transfers for pay had not been introduced yet.

Daisy (E Div) 1950s

Back when I joined, I felt that the whole point of being a woman officer was that we *did* do things differently and that there were things only women could do. That's what made us special, and I also believe that a lot of that 'specialism' was lost when everyone became equal. I know it's the law now, but I can't remember ever thinking that I was being discriminated against back then. Throughout my ten years I was a 'specialist', I felt special and almost always was treated as such. For many years I was the only female in the office, so I suppose I just got used to it. Maybe I was just super-lucky.

After training I was posted to King's Cross Road police station. My number was WPC 212 E. At King's Cross we had the mounted police with their beautiful horses and next door was Clerkenwell Magistrates' Court, a very grand building, although last time I was in that area it was, to my amazement, a backpackers' hostel.

I was introduced to WPC Prendergast with whom I was to work. She had been in the police all through the war and was a very experienced officer. There were four women at King's Cross but night duty was done at Bow Street with only one woman on duty. I had to patrol alone from 11 p.m. till 1 a.m. then go back to Bow Street and write up traffic reports by hand in huge ledger-type books ready to be processed. The men welcomed the women police and used us for any women-connected enquiries. We worked well with the CID and I was never, and I repeat *never*, subjected to anything other than respect and appreciation and kindness by the men.

Jan (H Div) 1960s

I was engaged and married during my service. Back in those days it would have been unusual for a WPC with a small baby to return to working shifts and unsocial hours and so, after the birth of our first child, I had to resign. My late husband was a career police officer and he would not have been prepared, or able, to take a major role in child care. We were reduced to one income, increasing mortgage interest rates and, oh boy, were we hard up. I have to say that when I was working we were not equal: there were jobs which were much more suitable for females than men, and we were employed accordingly. No one really complained or expected it to be otherwise. I think the Equality Act came into force shortly after I left.

We spent lots of time patrolling beats, usually in twos, and on one week in every twelve we did night duty covering the whole Division. If another station needed a WPC they would just come and get us. We 'arrested', or more accurately 'rescued', lots of young runaway teenage girls who had hitched lifts in lorries bound for the Wapping docks. Hopefully we saved a few young women from getting caught up in the lowlife of Cable Street with its unsavoury lifestyle and where it was never boring to patrol.

Our female sergeants and Inspector were responsible for us; we never paraded with the men. We were often asked to man the switchboard (one of those dolls' eye things) and as a typist I was occasionally called on to do some typing for our Chief Inspector, which was a bit of a bonus in the cold, wet weather. We also worked closely with the Social Services and particularly dealt with women and children; which of course we were especially trained for.

Kathy (C Div) 1960s

On patrol we were specifically looking for approved-school absconders and missing children yet I remember stopping a man in Oxford Street underground station. I took him in to a telephone box and called the Criminal Records Office to do a check. The man on the other end asked if I was alone, and I said that I was. Within minutes, coming down every tunnel, were policemen running. I looked around to see what I had missed – I hadn't missed anything – they all ran towards me and grabbed the man. I was left with the phone in my hand and the man on the other end asking if I was all right. I said, 'Yes', and asked what it was all about. He told me that there were outstanding warrants on the man, including one for GBH on a policeman! Gulp . . . I thanked him and walked back to the nick.

I met Norman Hartnell, the designer of the new women police uniform. He stopped me, introduced himself and asked me what I thought of it. I very politely, without causing any offence, told him that I felt like a French railway porter and didn't like having to hoist my skirt when I had to run. I was asked to model that uniform on a couple of occasions.

Kathy (K Div) 1970s

On one occasion at Dagenham the Cup Final was on and the telephonist asked me if I could relieve him so he could go and watch it, and I agreed. Then the Station Officer came in and asked if I would mind doing 'Station Officer' which, of course, I agreed to do. A few minutes later the Duty Officer came in and asked if I would relieve him too. I just wanted the phone to ring and for the person on the other end to say, 'Can I speak to the Reserve please?' – speaking – 'In that case can I speak to the Station Officer?' – speaking – 'Umm the Duty Officer? . . .' But it never happened.

Margaret (Mounted Branch) 1970s

I was engaged to my future husband when I applied to join the Mounted Branch and they made it clear that they weren't too happy about that. One of their questions was how would I cope with cleaning a horse's stifle? I told them I'd probably use a warm sponge. I wasn't a particularly expert horsewoman, and

didn't own my own horse like some of the other fifteen applicants, so I knew I would have to do something to be noticed. I
waited until everyone else was back on the coach and made
sure I was still in the stables asking questions when they came
looking for me. It got me the job and I became one of the first
women officers ever to join the Metropolitan Police's formerly
'male-only preserve', the Mounted Branch.

Wendy (Mounted Branch) 1970s

I transferred to the Met from Avon and Somerset in 1974
because although I had been a rider for most of my life I was
told, 'We have no intention of taking women into the Branch
at this stage.' So I telephoned Mounted Branch in the Met and
spoke to the Superintendent. He said I would have to apply to
transfer to the Met and do a normal tour of duty and then
apply to join the Mounted Branch, so that's what I did. I transferred in 1976 and joined the Mounted Branch in 1977. I
trained at Imber Court and loved it. I came third in the class
and was posted to Great Scotland Yard.

They don't give you your own horse to start with so I started
with a 'strapper', which is whatever horse was spare on the day.
I did Changing the Guard and patrolling. On one particular
patrol I was riding round Soho somewhere and got lost. I didn't
know London very well, and we didn't have radios at the time,
so after passing the same street for the third time, I had to stop
and ask a taxi driver, 'Can you tell me the way back to Great
Scotland Yard?'

There were three of us women at the time and about twenty
men. I got on fine with them for my six months there before
they sent me to an outer division. No women had ever been
posted out of A Division before, so I'd be the pioneer. The day
I arrived, there were snide, back-stabbing comments. They'd

be rude to my face, rude behind my back, and they would sabotage my kit. They slackened off some of the buckles though, fortunately, I always used to check because I suspected something like that would happen. One day I was grooming a particularly nervous horse when a wet sponge came flying across the stables, hitting the horse in the ear. He reared up and nearly came down on top of me.

The atmosphere was not good. Two PCs were supportive, two were indifferent and the other two were totally anti . . . and made it known. I was given the oldest horses and over the period of my posting lost all three. Then one of the PCs got hit on the head with a brick at QPR and they ruled that all officers must wear protective headwear. All the men were given protective hats straight away and we said, 'Where's ours?' They said they had none for women and that we could not do any public order duties.

So from going to Wembley and Tottenham and QPR and ceremonials I suddenly found myself stuck at the stables. It was soul-destroying and I became the skivvy, the general dogs-body. The men of course were getting even more resentful saying, 'She's bloody swanning back at the stables, and we've got to get up at 3 a.m. and go off to football matches or what-ever: fucking lazy cow.' And so the resentment got worse. It wasn't my fault but I couldn't do anything right.

I put up with this for three years until one morning the Commander said, 'Are you all right?' I just burst into tears and told him what it was like; that I was being given all the sick, lame and lazy horses in the Met and I couldn't go on public order or do the job I joined up for. He was very good and said, 'How would Potters Bar suit you in two weeks' time?' I almost bit his hand off and basically left the Mounted Branch.

5

BE A GOOD GIRL . . .
MAKE THE TEA

Mary (D Div) 1950s
I joined on 4 May 1953, just prior to the Coronation of Queen
Elizabeth II. Male recruits were given to an experienced
officer and allowed out on the streets. But because Monica,
Mary and I were so inexperienced we were marched up to
Old Scotland Yard by Sergeant Buxton. The public who'd
been there overnight cheered everybody, including the road
sweepers – and us. When we got there, we found we were just
making refreshments for all the *men* coming in. We were
doing all the teas! Finally, we were allowed out and did get to
see the procession . . . then it was back inside to make more
tea.

> *During my service with the Met in the 1970s I was*
> *never told, as was Mary in her story above, to 'make*
> *the tea', or man the switchboard. Perhaps I was*

fortunate, because it's clear that many women did suffer gender discrimination during their time in the Job.

I do think, however, that when I was a policewoman we more readily accepted what were considered the common courtesies of the day: a man opening a door for a woman, or walking on the kerb side to protect her from stampeding horses. There weren't too many rampaging horses in my day, but I appreciated men seeking to be polite. Women today may object to such 'gentlemanly' civilities, deeming them to be, in themselves, discriminatory. Rightly, we now demand and deserve parity, but courtesy from either sex towards their colleagues never goes amiss.

That said, the women who trailblazed their way through the service in earlier years did have to fight to make their way in a distinctly male-dominated world. Their efforts in the early days were not helped by the ingrained views that women could play only 'limited roles' in the world of work.

Jenny

'I would ask that the men of this grand body have the decency to respect their new women colleagues, to treat them as they would the women of their own household, and to give them a chance in the limited role in which they may be of use.

'I have always thought that this demand [for women to be sworn-in as constables] arose through an entirely false appreciation of the situation. Any subject of His Majesty has the right of arrest in most cases. The only *advantage a Constable has is that he can arrest on reasonable suspicion that a felony has been committed, whereas the ordinary individual in the street can only arrest when a felony has been committed and he has witnessed it. In carrying out the duties which are now allotted to them these Women Patrols are not required to perform the full duties of a Police Constable.'*

Brigadier-General Sir William Thomas Francis Horwood GBE KCB DSO, Commissioner of Police for the Metropolis 1922 Metropolitan Police Archives

'The demand has been renewed that the women shall be sworn in as constables and I see no serious objection to this, in fact, I think it is preferable to place these women on exactly the same footing as men.'

William Bridgeman, 1st Viscount Bridgeman, Home Secretary 1922 Metropolitan Police Archives

'The Women police are being sworn in as Constables. They will have exactly the same standing and powers as male officers of the Force. It will be understood however that they are not expected to undertake any duty which they may be physically unfitted to carry out. The term "Woman Constable" will in future be used instead of 'Woman patrol.'

Home Office (draft) public announcement, January 1923 Metropolitan Police Archives

Monica (C Div) 1960s

By today's standards we were subject to discriminatory behaviour, but it was not viewed as it is now. We women were small in number at that time as the Met had just finished recruiting most PCs from National Service. We were working in a male-dominated environment and having to prove that you could do the job well, while also handling some of the downside. Before I joined I was told that the measure of 'you' was how you dealt with it. The right look, the right comment and good humour, allied with a quick riposte, solved most situations. Once you demonstrated that you were competent and not prone to 'girlie' tactics, all was well.

June (J Div) 1960s

I was told by a Station Sergeant that I wouldn't last a month. The general opinion of most men – of whatever rank – was that WPCs were only looking for husbands.

Deryl (L Div) 1970s

It was only the women who were posted to cover as telephonists, always a busy job. One day I was single 'womanning' the switchboard in office hours, lights were flashing everywhere, buzzers buzzing and wires crisscrossing all over the 'dolls' eye' board. Extension number two was flashing. I had been told the lowest numbers were top priority, so answered it with, 'Switchboard.'

Divisional Chief Superintendent: 'The phone in the adjacent office is ringing. It should be obvious to any idiot that it is not going to be answered. Stop it.'

Me: 'Can you tell me the extension number please sir?'

Him: 'No, I fucking can't, I'm not fucking God.'

Me: 'And I'm not a fucking telephonist.'

I started pulling out lots of the wires. Minutes later I was relieved from switchboard duty and had to see the Chief Superintendent for my bawling out. My response was that with minimal training, and with only me on duty, I was doing my best, I could do no more. He didn't mention me swearing at him, but I was then sent to see my sub-divisional Chief Superintendent. I gave him my side of the story, telling him it was unfair I had to cover the switchboard every time it was short, just because I was the only female available. His only comment was, 'Try not to upset the Chief Superintendent.' The next morning on early-turn parade a male officer was posted as the telephonist. He turned to me and demanded to know why I wasn't doing it. I shrugged my shoulders.

There were so many unfair abstractions off patrol work for women, and your record of work was then compared with male officers who had more time on the streets. On one occasion I was posted on the 'RT' car [the main car with radio transmission capabilities] for a week of night duty. What followed were the arrests of three burglars from two different burglaries, four arrests for taking and driving away motor vehicles, several arrests for carrying an offensive weapon and one for causing grievous bodily harm, another for actual bodily harm, a making off without payment . . . and a murder. Suddenly the sun was shining out of my proverbial.

We women still had to take a turn as matron at Juvenile Court, and at night would travel all over Bromley Borough if there were women needing to be searched or if a juvenile was detained. Sometimes we had to escort them up to the Matron Station at Camberwell. I think the police wanted to keep the number of women down to around 5 per cent of the Force: there were certainly not enough to go around.

Ann (M Div) 1970s

I found most police officers were fair and treated the women equitably. I was probably lucky; I know some girls had a different experience. However, I had a woman police sergeant who didn't believe married women should be in the Job. She made sure I got all the worst jobs, found fault with everything I did, and generally made my life miserable. Because of her I resigned from the police.

Mary (S Div) 1980s

I was posted to the Area car as operator and had to take a package to HQ. I was seen in the car by a senior officer who promptly phoned every station on the District to find out which Area car had a female operator. My Inspector was told to remove me immediately. The only other person available was a male probationer, and the Area car driver refused to take him out because he was too inexperienced. The Inspector tried to insist that he took him but the driver said, 'Sorry, I've had to take the car off the road with a mechanical defect.' He then took time off.

On many occasions there was sexist treatment and comments to female officers, though we gave as good as we got. The majority of it was just banter and we had a lot of laughs. I felt I was as good as, if not better than, many of the men I worked with, and I have several ex-male colleagues who still say, 'You were the best WPC I ever worked with.'

Annette (Y Div) 1980s

As a probationer you prove your worth by the number of arrests you make, but I was given no opportunities. If I did arrest someone I would be told to hand the case over to a male colleague who earned the credit. It made my work record look poor – another ploy by the men running the station to get rid of me completely. The bullying didn't stop there; on one occasion one guy was in a filthy mood and completely lost his temper. He grabbed hold of me, dragged me struggling from the Front Office out into the street, tied me to the railings outside the station and left me there. I was only rescued by a passing member of the public who cut me free.

Cheryl (E Div) 1980s

I cannot tell you how many times I turned up at calls to be informed that they had called for a policeman, not for a woman. A rather obnoxious lady told me that she had a plumbing problem, and that a woman was no good to her. She actually needed her radiators bleeding, which I did for her. She still showed no gratitude – probably because I pointed out she should have called a plumber, not the police. On another occasion I was called to a launderette where there were six inches of boiling water all over the floor. I waded in to find a stopcock, and a member of the public, seeing me in there, complained that I was doing my washing on duty.

Sue (B Div) 1980s

As an Inspector I did a mandatory Firearms Awareness course, but women weren't allowed to carry firearms at all on Borough. Women didn't even have truncheons when I joined. The thinking apparently was that it might be taken off us and then used against us. Later we got small truncheons, which we initially kept in our handbags, and then in pockets that were fitted into uniform skirts.

Women were not allowed to be 'public order' trained and therefore missed out on lots of overtime. We weren't allowed to go to the miners' strike because there was no suitable accommodation. When the Tottenham riots happened all the men were deployed in Tottenham while the handful of women left at the station carried on routine policing.

I wanted to join the Crime Squad, and then the CID, but I was told there was no point in applying because they already had a female on the Crime Squad. I knew some female armed Close-Protection Officers at Special Branch. They stored their guns in special handbags; so I applied for Special Branch instead.

Janet (Y Div) 1980s
It was considered normal banter to refer to female officers as 'plonks' or a 'Dozy Doris'. The stock reply if you bit back was, 'If you can't take a joke, you shouldn't have joined the Job.' A common comment was that as a female in the Job you had to be either 'a bike . . . or a dyke'. There were often unfair postings where female officers were stuck working in the station office, or on the front counter, for months on end. As such you weren't out and about, getting the experience you needed in dealing with crime. I was once posted to the station office for over six months in a row. This no doubt had an effect on my gaining experience and on my confidence. It made it more difficult to move on and get promoted.

Early in my service many such attitudes were the norm, and the inaction of supervisors unwittingly discouraged women from considering promotion. Woman leaving or taking career breaks to have children also meant that they often missed the boat when it came to promotion. The attitude seemed to be that if you stayed working you were serious about the Job; if you did anything else you couldn't have been serious, and were more easily overlooked.

Deryl (P Div) 1980s

On my promotion to sergeant, one male PC who I vaguely knew gave a speech in the canteen about a woman's place being in the home, barefoot and pregnant, etc. I totally blanked him. When he asked me about his thoughts I told him: 'As long as you do what I say, when I say and how I say . . . I don't give a shit what you think.'

Debbie (Y Div) 1990s

As a young Woman Detective Constable it was always assumed that I would deal with all the child abuse and rape offences. This often meant that I wasn't given the same opportunity to deal with burglaries or robberies, or be posted to the Crime Squad. Yet it also meant that I earned lots of overtime and got to work with some very experienced Detective Inspectors. I did learn a lot . . . swings and roundabouts.

I did notice a reluctance to post female officers to Murder Squads, which then were made up of junior officers from a number of Divisions. They wanted to keep you on the Division so you would be available to deal with sexual offences. Some male officers would also take credit for your work. If I found something on a search, interviewed a witness or suspect and ascertained an important piece of information, some male officers would tell the story at a debrief and claim credit.

Whenever we turned up at a crime scene where we weren't known, the public and every officer on the scene, whatever their rank, would automatically talk to the older male officer, even when I was the one in charge. I just let them carry on until we were leaving and they asked for the DC's name; the aide would then tell them who I was, much to their embarrassment.

Despite all that, the only incident of discrimination from the public came late in my service when I was a Detective Sergeant at Tottenham. I had to show witness albums to a Hassidic Jew from Stamford Hill who had been the victim of a street robbery. He would not shake my hand because he said his culture did not allow him to touch a female. He made it clear he did not think I was suitable to do the job. I respected his religious beliefs and kept my counsel – but it made me wonder why some cultures are allowed to belittle someone purely on the grounds of sex. It would appear that some 'protected characteristics' under the Equality Act are more equal than others.

Mary (M Div) 1990s

I was the only female Supervisor at the station and so had to share the locker room with male police sergeants and an Inspector. I asked for a lock to be fitted and sure enough they fitted one . . . on the outside . . . so they could lock me in!

Annie (RCS) 1990s

I did meet a handful of male colleagues who were particularly hateful because I was a female. While on the Regional Crime Squad one DS took delight in giving me the worst postings on an op. I eventually spoke to a more senior officer and threatened to leave, stating I'd complain to the senior management team. He quickly got a grip of it. There were also others who thought you were only there to make tea and look after female prisoners . . . they were soon put right.

Karen (C Div) 1990s

A female officer had to be ten times better than a male colleague in order to achieve the same standing and status.

The environment was sexist and misogynistic. A woman sergeant I worked with was extremely highly regarded and talented, but constantly overlooked for promotion.

Kate (K Div) 2000s

When I worked in Walthamstow I had difficulties with some Asian men who would ignore me and talk to the younger male officers instead. On one occasion I took a brand-new probationer out with me but the Asian male victim refused to speak to me and would only speak to the male I was with.

The only other time I felt discriminated against was when I was chosen for a new role with the Parks Police. I felt it would be appropriate to let them know I was eight weeks' pregnant. The Inspector said I would still be able to perform the role, but the second line manager pulled me from the position and replaced me with a male officer.

Even so, I have had more difficulties with women than with men in this job. Some women seem to no longer support each other but instead fight against each other. One such line manager called me names in front of other officers in a very childish manner. I feel that women are still under-represented throughout the Met, and this is why I feel strongly we should be supporting each other.

Louise (ARV Operational Support) 2010

A real antique, an old-school firearms instructor, made comments about 'plonks' in a very derogatory way in front of me; it didn't go down well. He was talking about a mock scenario in an assessment for firearms training and was talking about a female officer who apparently screamed down the radio, 'The man's got a gun . . . the man's got a gun.'

'Ah you know them plonks,' he said. 'Always screaming, doing what they do best – screaming and panicking.' There was just me and a couple of men and he thought it was funny. I took him aside and spoke quite directly, giving him the benefit of my thoughts and feelings on the matter.

No bullshit: his answer was, 'Oh – give us a kiss, darling!' He thought that was OK . . . but it wasn't OK at all.

6

ARE YOU A BIKE ... OR A DYKE?

The #MeToo movement of 2018 highlighted the casual sexual abuse and harassment that has existed for many years in all sorts of jobs. The Police Service, of course, reflects the society from which its members are drawn. As such, it has not been immune in the past from similar abusive attitudes from male officers towards their female colleagues.

In my early days in the Job I did hear about the legendary custom of 'station-stamping,' where men would slap a date-stamp upon a new WPC's breasts or buttocks. It was an era when women were expected to put up with sexual comments and approaches that would not be tolerated today. I think the force field I could generate with one look made men think twice about trying that on me. The men I worked with teased me, swore like troopers in front of me, made sexist jokes ... but always treated me with professional courtesy and kindness.

Clearly, from what they've told me, some other policewomen were not so fortunate.

Jenny

Margaret (H Div) 1960s

It was after 5 p.m. on a late turn and everyone in the offices had gone. Some PCs tried to stick me on top of the filing cabinet, pull down my pants and station-stamp my bottom. I was furious and fought like a tigress so they couldn't actually do it. It was still sexual assault, and they thought nothing of it; they felt they could do it to everyone. There were no other women on duty with me, but because I fought so hard, they then, in a way, respected me. It's a terrible way to get respect.

These men were buggers. One morning I came in hot and sweaty after cycling from my flat to work. A senior officer, a weasely-looking man, said, 'You look hot . . . you can use the shower in my room . . . if I can watch.' Shocking.

Jan (W Div) 1960s

I realise that things have changed enormously, with a huge shift in what is deemed acceptable or unacceptable. But I believed then that if a male colleague made a suggestive remark, or was coming on to me, I was more than able to deflect such a thing without resorting to reporting him or making a great fuss about it. Of course there was banter – and worse – but a female officer who was unable to deal with that was hardly likely to be able to do her job efficiently anyway.

Wendy (G Div) 1970s

I loved my time at Hackney. It could be hard work, but there was also a lot of fun and high jinks with the men. Station-stamping was just one of those things that happened. I took it in the way it was meant, as just a bit of fun. One New Year's Eve I was station-stamped with the old year's date on one cheek of my bottom, and then, with the chimes of midnight still ringing out, I duly 'turned the other cheek', which was then station-stamped with the New Year date. I had a bottom that spanned two years.

Pet (Q Div) 1970s

The Chief Superintendent was trying to give me guidance. 'Remember this,' he said, 'a standing prick has got no shame.' I tell you what – it was good advice. He meant that a man with an erection has no shame, and he was telling the only WPC on a relief to be careful. He was just preparing me for working with men. That was my introduction to what men could be like and how to handle them. But it was true. It happened . . . but you could deal with that. I was very lucky, the men I worked with, I wouldn't say they wouldn't try anything . . . men were men . . . but they had a little respect. Being a married woman did make a difference. They could chat you up but I was in control of the distance, and that worked. I had no problem with that, although I was more naïve than I thought, even at that age.

Margaret (N Div) 1970s

The governor at one station tried to undo my shirt while I was standing at attention. I managed to move out of the way and avoided any such vulnerability in the future. Years later I found out that the PCs at my first nick would push the duty-book to the back of the desk when they saw me coming on duty. Being a fashionable young girl I was inevitably wearing a miniskirt. Signing-on duty meant I had to lean right over.

Generally speaking, you endeavoured to be 'one of the lads'. If you showed an interest in any one person it was guaranteed to start rumours. To be honest, we did use our femininity as well to get favours from the men. Getting a lift in the Panda car (they were new then, so it was quite exciting) or not getting reported if we were a bit late, things like that.

Judy (L Div) 1970s

When I first went to Division I was initiated into station-stamping. I was held down by three policemen while about forty watched as my breasts were station-stamped. It's something I never got over or forgot. Another colleague, fresh out of training, had the same thing done to her bottom but never got over it. She resigned the following day, too distressed to remain in the Force.

Gina (G Div) 1970s

I always had my own boundaries. As far as I was concerned I went to work to do a professional job and to be taken seriously. Therefore I didn't lark around, I didn't flirt, and I didn't mess around with blokes. Some of the girls didn't have the same approach and – I hate to say they were 'asking for it', because that's completely taboo – but I maintain all the way through I never had any problems and the girls who *did* have problems either didn't mind it . . . or they asked for it.

Oh, they *threatened* me with station-stamping, but I said, 'Under no circumstances. It won't happen.' A female colleague said to me, 'You'll be the first one who hasn't been station-stamped.' I said, 'It will not happen.' Nobody, but nobody, ever tried, whereas one of my poor colleagues was getting it all the time, but then she actually liked it. She was tipped upside-down with her head in the dustbin. I would have been mortified, but she was laughing – and if you're happy with that, that's fine. But nobody does it to me!

Lyn (C Div) 1970s

We had a PC, big chap, who'd come in and he had a way of slipping his hand up the back of your blouse and unclipping your bra, but you'd think, 'Oh that's him', and run into the teleprinter room to sort it. I remember thinking, 'How does he do that with one hand?' I thought he was clever. We weren't offended by it. The same man hired a van and helped me move from the section house. There was no malice. They'd wind you up. Then there was the thing about the station-stamp; it was nothing, it was banter.

Cheryl (Q Div) 1980s

I was subjected to the station-stamp tradition. But it was tried on a bitterly cold winter's day and I think they gave up after the two layers of PE knickers. In the current climate, of course it was wrong.

Cressida (C Div) 1980s

It was an evening do for this guy who was getting married. I didn't know him very well, but I was having a drink and everything was fine when suddenly these guys grabbed hold of me. It wasn't aggressive, but there was no way I was going to be able to move. They said, 'Stand by Cress,' and picked me up, one each side, and took me across the dance floor to the groom-to-be. He'd had quite a lot to drink, had no clothes on at all and was covered in butter or something disgusting. They just wrapped me round him and said, 'Right, you've got to dance.' He was really, really out of it, drunk.

His fiancée was at the do, which struck me as very unwise. I thought, 'What am I supposed to do? This is ridiculous.' I didn't feel assaulted, affronted or anything. I thought, 'This is ridiculous, what are they doing?' I disentangled myself quite quickly and went off to the ladies' to wash my hands. His poor fiancée had locked herself in the ladies' loo in floods of tears; the whole thing was a nightmare. I remember thinking, 'I hope she doesn't think I'm a part of this.' But looking back we were all adults, we weren't children. What were people thinking? It wasn't even funny. As I say I didn't feel remotely abused by it, it was just stupid.

It was of the age. If you'd gone into the Royal Marines' mess, or you'd gone into even the firm of accountants on their night out, it would have been something similar.

Debbie (G Div) 1980s

Officers would 'try it on' on duty; driving the car to a quiet street and chatting me up or, on some occasions, trying to touch me. This was tiresome and often fraught with danger, because when you said 'No' some men would see it as a personal insult and take offence. That could make your working life difficult, particularly if they had rank: unbelievable by today's standards. There was the usual station-stamp for WPCs. Fortunately I was very fit and could run, and most of those chasing were not, so I didn't get caught.

As a young detective you would regularly be asked if you had 'the kit' on . . . meaning stockings and suspenders. We also all remember the lab where, if you hadn't completed your lab form properly, you could avoid 'fines' by showing a glimpse of stocking-top. CID office lunches were always 'fun'. Being the only woman with sometimes up to eighty men who had been drinking meant you had to keep your wits about you. Most female detectives dealt well with it, and in my case I think they were more scared of me than I was of them: and I also encountered a number of female officers of all sexual persuasions who could be as predatory as some of the men.

One occasion of sexual harassment that really made me cross was when a fellow officer bit my backside when I was leaning across a desk. I nearly took his head off with a swinging right arm. He didn't do it again!

Mary (Training School) 1980s

I was in one of the three housing blocks where the top floors were reserved for women. I faced an all-male block, and some of the male recruits would shout across or flash torches at us . . . or worse. Once I looked out to where a PC was apparently naked in his room. I could see him from the naval up and could see that his arm was moving rapidly back and forth. 'Dirty bastard,' I thought . . . then he held up a beautifully bulled boot. 'The Knicker Police' were very active at Hendon, and generally the women were the ones being investigated. It seemed the emphasis was on us not to encourage the men into misbehaving. I can't recall a male officer having to account for his sexual activity or behaviour.

Mary (R Div) 1980s

On day one I turned up on Division expecting to be made welcome and developed into a good officer. But not a bit of it: the first question was, 'Are you a dyke . . . or a bike?'

I was informed my nickname was 'Udders' . . . no guesses as to why, and I felt like a glove puppet because I had so many hands up my skirt. When making the tea, I kept a spoon in boiling water to use when they came in to show me their penises. One PC, who I'd rightly been avoiding, cornered me in the tea room and tried to have sex with me. He didn't succeed as I fought back, but he pinned me down. When I told him I'd scream he said, 'You scream girl, you'll lose your job for being a trouble maker, I'll just get another move.'

Deryl (P Div) 1980s

An attempt to station-stamp me was abandoned after I fought them off, but I was indecently assaulted in the reserve room. I was leaning over the desk, in my straight, knee-length skirt when a PC ran his hand up the inside of my thigh and grabbed between my legs. An Inspector was stood by me while I was pointing out a location to him on the map, and another PC beside me was on the phone. Neither of them was in a position to see what had happened.

A red mist descended and I turned around, punching my assailant with both fists and kicking him repeatedly. He threatened to report my attack on him. I offered to go and see the Detective Chief Inspector forthwith to put in my allegation of indecent assault. Apart from the Inspector asking me if I was OK the subject was never mentioned by a supervisor or my assailant; nor did I ever have any more trouble at work.

Caroline (Traffic Div) 1990s

Two officers made my life an absolute misery. I'd rejected a pass from one of them who was married, and he got the arse and bullied me along with his short sidekick. I had photocopies of female parts put in my tray, the nickname they called me in front of every one was 'Split' (referring to female genitalia). They also called the one black officer on my relief the 'BIF' – black ignorant fucker. Nice. They tried to stick me on for not wearing a bra under my white job shirt when I was on the motorbikes. I obviously had the yellow reflective jacket on over the top so no public could see I was bra-less – and in those days I didn't need to wear one. I was in tears and terrified of them.

One officer, a hugely obese idiot, was a pompous twat who thought himself a bit of a poet. He penned a poem entitled 'Storm in a D-Cup', which he posted all over the traffic garage.

I was humiliated and really upset. A more senior officer – male of course – was a wet fart and did nothing, so I decided that I would do something that I had always thought was a sign of weakness and go for a sex discrimination case via the Federation. One sergeant stood with me: the only one at the garage to do so. The threat of the case was enough for the horrible sergeant and the idiot sidekick to stop, which was all I ever wanted. I HATE bullies.

Mary (M Div) 2000s

Today's generation often can't conceive that things like the station-stamp were allowed to happen. I was told I'd be gone in four years once I'd found myself a husband, and was frequently marginalised. I fear that even today there are still a few dinosaurs with outdated views or practices, but women are more generally respected and accepted. As an Inspector it was much easier for me to set the tone, and I always aimed to include everyone.

> A sergeant with whom I worked in my early career was reputedly a lesbian, although I was so naïve I would never have recognised her preference, and would not have thought the less of her if I had. She was certainly very professional in her working life, and so it was only when she transferred to another station that I heard talk of her sexual tastes. Looking back now to the early days of the Women's Police Service it is clear that two of its foremost pioneer members, Margaret Damer-Dawson and Mary Allen, were in a caring relationship in which they preferred a more masculine uniform than was customary for the times. Maybe their desire to storm the male

bastion of the Metropolitan Police was one way of them proving women's worth in a world then unquestioningly dominated by men? Lesbianism, unlike male homosexuality, has never been illegal, and it seems likely that the nature of the Job did attract many lesbians to join the Police Force as pioneers and champions of the right of women to be whomsoever they wish to be. They have not always been accepted as readily as perhaps they should have been.

Jenny

Marion (C Div) 1960s

I was a young, innocent nineteen-year-old when an older, female colleague who 'batted for the other side' pursued me for months. She would corner me in the ladies' loo, trying to grab and hug me. She was always on my case, wanting to take me out. The fact that I was straight and not interested made no difference. It didn't help that both the sergeants and the Inspector were also gay. She was eventually promoted to sergeant and transferred. Many years later she wrote to me trying to explain her behaviour. By then I was married with two children.

Gina (G Div) 1970s

I used to play Met Police badminton. On an overnight trip away from London, playing at the Nationals, a woman on our team came to my room at night saying she'd locked herself out of hers. So I made up a bed for her on the floor. She complained of being uncomfortable, but I said a single bed was too small to share. I woke up in the middle of the night with her in my bed. In the morning I had a great big red mark across my neck. A friend explained that the girl was a predatory lesbian and I'm like, 'Eeuw . . . no more Met Police badminton for me.' She actually wasn't a horrible girl; just a bit needy and desperate for a relationship, and saw somebody who was vulnerable. Someone's sexual orientation is irrelevant unless they are predatory, but that is what this girl was. In hindsight I should have complained.

Karen (C Div) 1990s

From my earliest childhood I always wanted to be a police officer; there was never any other option. Yet I left the Police Service because of serious homophobic bullying that in the end put my life in danger. I remember sitting in the dining hall at Hendon Training School and having someone put a lemon on my plate. I did not realise it was a reference to me being a potential lesbian.

I believed that to be gay in the police was illegal, as it was in the Armed Forces back then, so I was never going to admit my sexuality; it was going to be my secret. However, my appearance made people suspicious, and the comments, bullying and harassment started the very first day out of training school. I was singled out by a senior officer and bullied dreadfully. The harassment was relentless in all the usual ways: having a truncheon shoved up my skirt, or a hand to check whether I was wearing stockings or tights etc. It was a massive part of the culture. One time I was told to go to Lambeth with a box which contained a human hand and to get it fingerprinted. I was scared but was prepared to do it . . . but it was a 'joke'. Another time I was told I had to fly to Glasgow to pick up a very dangerous prisoner who was to be handcuffed to me on the flight back. I had never flown before and my senior officer knew that. It caused me a huge amount of anxiety. Again, it was a 'joke'.

One particular female officer took me under her wing and encouraged me to make a complaint, which I reluctantly did. However, the female officer had an ulterior motive, and was also gay. She actively pursued me for some time and I ended up in a very secret relationship with her for about eighteen months. Having her backing made life easier, although the shift I had left continued to leave vile things in my drawer and the word 'dyke' was scrawled on my locker.

Later I started a serious relationship with another female officer, and we had to ask permission to live together. Although we never 'came out' as such, the bullying got extremely serious. Our radio communications were cut out, we were not booked off duty together on many occasions, and we were put on opposing shifts. It was dangerous, as well as being bullying. The final straw came one night with a serious disturbance in Leicester Square when I called for urgent assistance. My radio was cut-over by the comms operator . . . and nobody could find me. I drew my baton and hit two men who were armed, before some bouncers from a night club came to help me. No police colleagues arrived because they did not know where I was. I felt that my life had been in serious danger that night, and my partner told me to go home as it was getting out of hand.

I cried inside for years after I was forced out of the police. My mental health deteriorated, I didn't trust a single person and I found myself on the wrong side of the law. My life fell apart and it took a long time to put it back together again. The police was my life, and I was so lost for so many years.

7

PLAYING COPS AND
ROBBERS WITH THE MEN

I was still a serving officer in 1970 when the Equal
Pay Act became law. It forced the Met to assess the
work of women officers as the prelude to the full integration of women into the Police Service. Soon afterwards a decision was taken to abolish the specialist
department of Women Police and finally – and fully
– integrate policewomen and men.

Before that happened, however, I found out I was
pregnant. In May 1974 I left the service and so was
never personally affected by the integration process,
although I knew that full equality seemed a desirable
goal. Women would be fully integrated into the Job
with equal pay and equal conditions. All doors would
be open to them, all opportunities for advancement
and access to all sections of the Police Service would
be available. Ah . . . but nothing is that simple, is it?
A statement 'making us equal' did not qualify us to

be truly equal in the minds of some of the men we worked with.

Some former colleagues told me that many women police felt abandoned and feared that more than half-a-century of specialist female expertise was being thrown away overnight. Station Sergeants found themselves having to cope with jobs that had previously fallen to women, and new girls joining the Job no longer received specialist training. It was many years before the problems this created were properly addressed. We still had a fight on our hands, but the pioneer spirit remained alive in the hearts and minds of the indomitable female officers.

Jenny

Gina (G Div) 1970s

Girls who went to Central London Divisions went straight to work on relief, just as the men did, but we weren't then integrated at Hackney where I had been posted. That left me still in the 'Women Police Department', dealing with things like missing persons and indecency. I insisted that I was going to resign unless they put me on 'relief'. It took six months, but in the end they put me on. I can't remember there being a big fuss, but some other WPCs didn't want to do it. They were a bit agitated when I did.

Once I fully joined the men I was never treated badly; but it was made clear if you wanted equal pay then you had to go out and walk the streets of Hackney . . . on your own . . . on night duty . . . just like the men had to. They were reluctant to put me on the Area car, and I can remember one call at Hackney for 'suspects on the railway line'. It was on my beat and I said, 'Yeah, I'm making my way there.' The cars were all screeching to a halt and it was, 'Gina, you look after the cars.' I can remember feeling disgruntled, but then they were all screaming at one another over the radio as the two lads they were looking for came flying over the hoarding towards me. Of course all the blokes were miles away on the railway lines by then. I was alone on the street.

I shouted over the radio, but no one listened. Because I was young and fit – probably fitter than the blokes as well – I ran after them. They were all shouting at me, 'Go on, Gina.' That was absolutely, totally, the turning point. I'd demonstrated, in their opinion, that I'd got some skills and that, albeit I was small and may never be fantastic in a brawl, there were things I could do. It didn't take me long to feel valued, not discriminated against, and part of the team.

They would always send me to noisy parties because I'd go in and say, 'One of your neighbours has complained,' and they'd all say, 'Do you want to come in and have a drink?' And I always managed the situation. We all had our own skills in that team and I definitely felt that I was used for sorting out, you know, lairy blokes. I would go in with my hat on the back of my head and say, 'Excuse me, please.' They didn't want to hit me, you know, whereas blokes might have gone in a bit more heavy-handed.

Lorraine (S Div) 1970s
I was the only female Special at Hendon but was happy walking on my own. We had no radio, merely a whistle in those days. I used to come in every Wednesday night and was often used to relieve the Station Officer. One time, a bus driver came in to report an accident. I remember thinking, 'I can't do this', because everybody had said that anything to do with London Transport was always difficult. The Desk Sergeant was

looking at me, and I thought, 'Oh he's going to wait for me to fail.' So I took the book out and said, 'Sarge, I think I know what I'm doing, but would you stand with me and correct me if I go wrong?' He went, 'Yep,' and stood with me, correcting me a couple of times as I went through the book. Afterwards the sergeant said to me, 'I didn't think you were going to ask for help . . . I was waiting for you to fail.' He was my best friend after that, and used to take me out all the time.

Having a female Special was a new concept for them but, because I was willing to work, I was accepted. I have a sense of humour and I used to bring in a bag of sweets for the relief. I went wherever I wanted to go including some of the council estates; not that it was a particularly rough area. There was a taxi driver who would say to me, 'You know you're the only police officer we ever see.' And, because I was walking, he'd give me more information than the home beat officers got.

Margaret (N Div) 1970s

When I was a 'specialist' before full integration, it was mainly missing person enquiries, searching or escorting women prisoners, hospital observations and care proceedings. I did resent the notion that I was a baby-minder. I wanted to do more exciting things and go and play cops and robbers with the men. I loved night duty when I could go out in the back of the RT car [the main car with radio transmission capabilities] and do 'real' policing. For that reason I welcomed integration.

However, with hindsight (isn't that always a wonderful thing?) I can see that the Job chucked the baby – no pun intended – out with the bathwater. Once I was promoted and transferred I realised that male officers didn't have a clue about care-and-protection issues. What's more, they weren't really bothered about them either. Cases of clear cruelty or neglect, which were criminal offences, aroused their ire, but the more nuanced cases such as 'proper development being impaired' stayed under their radar.

Several things were lost as women no longer had specialist training to recognise care-and-protection issues, to conduct thorough and continuous missing person enquiries or take statements from women witnesses. Most importantly they were not trained to gather information properly and keep good records. I'm convinced this led to a lack of protection for children and young people.

We had always been meticulous about sending Form A4(5) to juvenile index. That was a brief form that simply reported that a juvenile had 'come to notice' and what we had done about it. If you saw a young person at two in the morning, not doing any particular harm, but just 'out', you'd usually have a word to find out why they were wandering around in the middle of the night. You might even run them home. Then you would send an A4(5) off to note it. These forms became vital if a subsequent care/protection issue arose because you had such a wonderful trail of evidence. Male officers never 'got it' and, try as I did, I could never get the ones on my relief to complete these forms when they encountered, but did not arrest, juveniles.

It was like the Job saying, 'We don't need the CID any more,' and just abolishing it with no replacement of the expertise learned by doing the work and the specialist training. I didn't enjoy my several months in the CID. I was a real victim of discrimination then as no police system knew how to cope with women doing the same job as the men. I was a Temporary Detective and, had I been a man, I would have had a regular partner with whom I would be expected to be out patrolling the streets and arresting people. They did have unwritten targets that they were expected to meet. As I was the only woman CID officer on the Division, there was no partner for me and, because I was not allowed out on my own, it meant I could not deal with major crime book entries. Therefore I was little more than a telephone minder.

One day I took a call that required immediate action, and one DC said he'd come out with me. We got the 'body' and it turned into a really good arrest with a lot of clear-ups. The DC and I found that we were quite soulmates and began working more together. I have to give some context here and say that a senior woman officer had advised me to find one person on my first posting to CID and stick to them for advice, rather than taking advice from several people. He was married and I had a fairly new boyfriend who I was besotted with. Nevertheless, the rumour-mill started and he ended up being transferred. I was then left back minding the telephone.

I did do a few months on a Murder Squad. Guess what my job was . . . office girl! I had to go through all the statements and create a card index of all the key points and similarities. It was interesting, but I was never asked to go out doing door-to-door or to take statements. Integration coincided with me passing my sergeant's exam and I decided to return to uniform duties.

Susan (P Div) 1970s

I had one major problem at Bromley. I didn't drive and it was a massive ground. I actually was no use outside, so I was put in the reserve room a lot. I was moved to Catford which was a grim station, with a much more varied ground where it was easier to get out without being able to drive. I was out on foot patrols, often doubled up in a Panda, and after a few months I was posted operator on the Area car. This was unheard of.

Some people didn't like it, saying that if they needed help they wouldn't want a woman turning up in the Area car, but after a while it was accepted that I could actually be a good operator.

Relief work was a 'horses for courses' type of job. There were the thief-takers, the plodders, the ones who avoided work, and certainly ones that avoided paperwork. I fell in the middle. In spite of integration the year before, women police were still needed to do 'women'-type work such as searching of women prisoners, suicide watch on a few women in the cells, obtaining statements from victims of sexual assault, domestic violence and so on. There was no longer any special training. We were to be treated exactly the same as the men, but – in addition – were expected to deal with so much more.

There was still a women police office, complete with comfy chairs and a desk. Often there would be a PC asleep in there on night duty. The locker room was tiny with only four lockers. I found the other women officers were extremely supportive of each other. After nearly two years I moved into the women police hostel in Catford which made the travelling easier. Canadian Avenue was a large Edwardian house with ten bedrooms, two bathrooms, two receptions, including a panelled dining room, large kitchen, conservatory, laundry room and a lovely garden. We had a cleaner and a gardener. I absolutely loved living there.

During my probationary two years I had attachments to a lot of specialist departments to learn a little of what their work involved. There was traffic, CID, Beat Crimes, Crime Prevention Office and Juvenile Bureau. As soon as I had completed my probation I was given a five-week standard driving course at Hendon. This was an intensive course for non-drivers. We learned how cars worked, to change a tyre in about three minutes, and also the theory. It was a wonderful course.

At the end of it we took a driving test and I returned to the station qualified to drive Panda cars, General Purpose cars and small Sherpa vans. I remember, however, driving a new Inspector round the ground for several hours and then having to give him the keys because I couldn't find reverse gear to park it. 'There must be something wrong with it,' I said. He condescendingly asked me if I realised it was an automatic car. Oops.

Sometimes women officers were posted to Juvenile Court to act as matron. It was boring and we would sit in court beside the Court Inspector, and take care of any juveniles during the proceedings. Yet I also worked a lot in plain clothes during my fourteen years' service. I did licensing, vice, obscene publications; I visited clubs with a male officer and prepared court cases. I worked in the Juvenile Bureau with a Detective Inspector dealing with all the 'non-accidental injuries' on the whole Division; a forerunner of today's child abuse teams. I worked closely with a team of specialist social workers. I still loved relief work and I think I was very lucky to have such a varied career.

Wendy (G Div) 1970s

I joined under the old system of a separate Women's Police Department and was posted to Hackney. It was brilliant, really lovely, the men looked after you and if you wanted a lift then you'd blag a car to take you on your enquiries. I'd double up with another WPC on patrol; we never patrolled with male officers. We did missing person enquiries, 'Alien enquiries' to verify a person's status to stay in this country, and sometimes matron duties at Old Street Magistrates' Court.

I didn't welcome integration; I was brought up as a WPC. Most of the other, old-style WPCs went on reliefs as soon as the new system came in, but I moved to City Road because my lovely, lovely Superintendent didn't want me to be integrated, he wanted me to do missing persons. And then in 1978 a job came up at Juvenile Bureau and he told me to take it because he couldn't protect me from integration forever.

I had been in Juvenile Bureau for less than a week when they found out I was cohabiting with my husband-to-be. I got called in by the Commander who said, 'We can't have your cohabiting to slur the name of Juvenile Bureau.' My husband-to-be was an Inspector, you see, although he wasn't on the same Borough. I was thrown back onto relief at City Road where everyone knew my history. I hated it. It was such a horrible part of my life. I don't remember a lot of it after I got put back to reliefs.

One thing sticks out in my mind: one night duty I was put out on my own. It was really, really cold and the sergeant and Inspector were driving round in their warm car. It was so cold I had my hands in my pockets, and they said, 'Get your hands out of your pockets.' I did, but then went through the flats where I thought I was safe. They were waiting for me on the other side of the estate and, of course, I had my hands in my pockets. And they said, 'We'll stick you on [report your conduct] if we see you doing it again.'

I got pregnant fairly quickly after I got put back to reliefs. I went to my GP and said I was pregnant. He was an old school doctor and he said, 'You're a police officer, very dangerous, you could get kicked in the belly.' He signed me off sick, so I was sick for nine months until I had the baby.

Carol (R Div) 1970s

I was in the Job during the integration upheaval of 1974/75 and did not totally agree with it. I still feel the Job lost an enormous amount of common sense and expertise. If memory serves me correctly we were given no extra training and were expected to just slot in. There were a number of us who wrote to *The Times* newspaper explaining our frustration at being thrown in at the deep end. This did not go down well with the hierarchy.

My first call as a street Panda driver was to a dead body in a domestic situation; something I had never encountered before. I had already requested the Communications Officer to treat me as knowing 'little or nothing', and he had agreed, bless him, to not advertise my inadequacies to all and sundry on the radio. Instead he kindly talked me through it. The reliefs though were brilliant. At no time did I feel discriminated against. I found a lot of the women who joined after integration lost the respect of some of the older coppers because they tried to sound and behave like the men.

Cheryl (Q Div) 1979

When I went onto relief in 1979 there was still a feeling that the women were there to deal with women and children and make the tea. There was a lovely WPC on my relief called Avril. She was not happy with the changes and was more comfortable in her old role although, to her credit, she always gave it a go.

Pet (Q Div) 1970

I came out of training school and went straight onto a relief at Wembley in January 1974. It was fine with me because I liked working with the older men who were ex-servicemen. They hadn't worked with a black person before, let alone a female officer, and it was good. The very first day on my probation I walked down Wembley High Street with my 'parent' constable, who we went out with for the first two weeks.

The shock! I'm 5'4" and a bit, and black . . . and female. All the way up to Wembley, people were stopping to look; it was an eye-opener. I had a man one day who drove down the wrong side of the road just staring at me. I have to say I had black people wanting to shake my hand. Where I worked black people did not have a good relationship with the police, but you know one thing that was never mentioned? The Police Force employ so many black people, so the black people working for the police had a good rapport with them; I saw it as a very happy thing. It was good fun. I did my fair share; being older, I thought, 'I'm going to pull my weight.' I took calls and I went out. If there was a thing to do, I was always there. Nobody did anything for me that didn't happen to anybody else. I never ran away from what had to be done.

The separate Women's Department eventually joined the relief . . . but it was harder for them. Some of the girls were a little bit lazy; they had done a specialist job for so long and, all of a sudden, they were exposed. I was lucky because I joined not knowing what the other side looked like, even though I reaped the benefit of their knowledge and expertise; how to do a statement and all various things. They were pushed into a change-over period where they weren't initially as active as the girls who came straight out from training school, who didn't want to be separate WPCs. We were one of the guys. I gained tremendous respect from the guys, I used to play snooker with them and I could take all the nonsense and give it back. I tell you what was good? The Area car driver would rather have me as his passenger/operator than many other officers. Sometimes they don't want women . . . but I was a worker.

Mary (P Div) 1980s

While the men were away dealing with the miners' strike and Greenham Common, the women held the fort: and very well too I might add. I remember going to a knife and bottle fight that only WPCs attended. The fight stopped and the combatants asked if we fancied a party. My sergeant at Thamesmead once put on my report, 'She gets on well with her male colleagues.' That was just as well as I was the only female at the station and had to share the toilet facilities. We had to ride bikes, but they only provided male bikes and I still had to wear a skirt. The locals, normally not keen to see the police, would come out to watch me trying to mount or dismount the bike.

One PC refused to patrol with me as I was a liability; he did not want to have to defend me as well as look after himself. That was until I was posted driving one Friday night. I took him as a passenger and our first call was to a fight. I was out of the car and had the aggressor on the ground before the PC had got out of his seat belt. Our next call was a stolen car which we chased until two decamped – I caught mine and my male colleague lost his. Funnily enough, he was OK with me after that.

In 1986 I got accepted for the Crime Squad. I had a good arrest rate, had done a lot of work with the CID and had two registered informants. On my first day a reception committee told me I had only got the job because I was a woman, and they would not be working with me. After ten months I asked to come off. My DCI knew what was going on but liked the fact that I'd stayed and tried. Of my former Crime Squad colleagues at least two have since ended up in prison.

Lyn (V Div) 1980s

I left the Job when I had my son as there was no part-time option in those days.

I was sad to leave, but looking back on my time in the Job, it was probably the best thing that ever happened because I loved every minute. It wasn't politically correct in my day. You just got on with nicking the shit and throwing the key away. You had 100 per cent backing from your colleagues because you were doing the job you loved and had great satisfaction. There wasn't any need for counselling because you all went to the pub and were there for each other. Great times, great memories . . . and great friends.

Mary (R Div) 1980s

I was told that it was safer not to let WPCs have truncheons because they could be taken off a woman and used against her. We were, however, still required to patrol alone. An older WPC told me to put ball bearings in my gloves (I didn't).

The fashion of the day was stockings and suspenders. In the female changing room they festooned the pegs and women had an extra £2.08 in their pay for 'stockings allowance'. Women were not issued trousers. I later received a pair that could only be worn for night duty, or in the winter months, as per the Instruction Book. Oddly the trousers had a plastic gusset; did they think we were inherently incontinent?

Deryl (P Div) 1980s

When I was posted to the sectional station of Sydenham I didn't realise that several other women had been posted there but had only lasted a few weeks. Suddenly PCs who had always been perfectly fine with me would not talk to me, including one who lived in the section house with me. He came up to me there to say, 'No hard feelings but I just can't break the agreement at work.' I told him if he wasn't going to talk to me at work then not to bother talking to me when I wasn't. Happily, as I lived on site, there was always someone to talk to at refs [refreshments].

I soon realised that the undoubted instigator of any dodgy calls I took, an experienced PC, was often hanging around, but when I needed help they all piled in and the 'Coventry' died a death. I then spent some happy years there. They even got me a calendar with naked men, to sit alongside their one with naked girls.

During my service there was increasing acceptance of women in all roles. They repeatedly thought we couldn't do things . . . and we repeatedly proved them wrong. In 1993 the last separate warrant number was issued to a woman officer. We became fully integrated with the men when they lost that individual warrant numbering system.

Sue (W Div) 1990s

When I became a uniform Inspector at Battersea they hadn't had one before, so they made room for me to get changed . . . in the stationery cupboard. But actually everyone was great and the Chief Superintendent became my mentor. Once, when I was in the custody suite, I felt someone grope my bottom. I didn't think twice about it and immediately turned round and punched the groper in the face. It was a drunken prisoner. Later he apologised to me.

Helen (L Div) 1990s

When I resumed after my career break I went back onto a response team where, although I only did two days a week, I worked full shifts and never expected any favours for having children. It didn't take me long to prove that I was every bit as hard working as my full-time colleagues, and I never used the excuse of having child care issues which dogs many part-time women who insist the job owes them, not the other way around. There seemed to be a certain amount of ill feeling towards women who, apparently, had to be accommodated because of their issues.

Debbie (Y Div) 1990s–2010s

I was always given every encouragement and support from my line managers.

When I joined in 1980 I was going to be the first female Commissioner (well done, Cressida) but after sixteen years' service and already a DS, I decided to have a family. I have two fabulous kids and I wouldn't change a thing but after they were born, they became my priority. I couldn't have balanced the study, work, child care and the amount of 'overtime' and general 'kiss-assing' you'd have to do to get management support and pass the exam. Those women who do achieve rank (and there are thankfully now lots of them) often have to make a sacrifice elsewhere in their personal lives. Sometimes senior female officers can be less understanding than their male colleagues, almost as if they are trying to show how tough they are. I have also met some fantastic senior female officers who have stayed the same despite achieving high rank.

I became the DS Federation rep at Haringey, more out of default than a deliberate choice. I had worked at complaints, and once back on Division I helped someone with advice about a complaint. I have always had a strong sense of fair play, and I dislike bullies. I like helping people who are in trouble. All qualities that make you want to be a police officer. I also have always been able to speak out (constructively) if I thought that something wasn't right. And I found that as a female officer and the senior DS, I'd also often be the first port of call to male colleagues and junior colleagues when they had a welfare problem so it was a natural progression.

When the uniform Borough rep left his role, I stood as the Operational Command Unit rep for sergeant. I was the first female Detective Sergeant to stand, in my own right, on the Sergeants' Branch Board. That is, not as a detective, and not as a reserved women's place.

Ellie (B Div) 2000s

When I joined in 1989 all the women left when they married – it wasn't an option then as it is now. Having children and remaining in the Job is commonplace now.

We do our best to accommodate their needs. It very much depends on who you are, what rank you are, what skills you've got, as to where you can then be positioned. You can't have a blanket rule. We have a business to run, it's a business that operates 24/7 but if someone comes to me and says, 'I only want to work, Mondays, Tuesdays, Wednesdays 8–4' then I say, 'I don't think so.' If they are working just 50 per cent of the hours, they also need to show they will work 50 per cent of the weekends, and find a block of nights they can plan for in the course of that year.

You can normally negotiate with anybody if they have children or are a carer, or whatever; but they need to come to me with a realistic proposition. If they do then I'm more likely to grant it; they have to manage their own lives. I have to arrange my life around my commitments. I understand children get sick suddenly – I get that, it's no different from your mother falling over; you want to be there, but because you've got children you should not expect to have a special exception. There is a fine line between those that really know how to manage the system and those that don't. What I've always found is if you negotiate a compromise then usually you get 20 per cent extra effort out of that employee.

Not so much now, but maybe ten years ago, the organisation went too far in the direction of the individual, to the detriment of others. I was fed up working every Christmas because I didn't have kids. Sorry, what's that got to do with it? I think when we started flexible working we almost pandered too much towards individual needs; now we have a much healthier balance. It's like me working at Tescos' and they want me to staff the tills from 11 to 3; I've got to be there. And Marks and Spencer's ... if you can't drive a lorry or check out people's groceries at the till they'll just dispense with your services. I think we offer an awful lot, I think there are so many different aspects for your career in the Met that you can actually, to a large degree, pick and choose. A friend of mine is now an Inspector in the Mounted Branch. She has three children and, because her husband works mainly Monday to Friday, she does mainly the weekends so they can manage their child care. People have to remember the type of organisation we are: we can't just put up the closed sign and all go home.

Dee (Q Div) 2000s

I loved my probation, doing a sometimes very hard, serious and heart-wrenching job. I had to earn my place in the team and the trust of my colleagues in the same way as my male colleagues. This I did through hard work, as well as passing a couple of tests. When I say tests, one of those was dealing with a sudden death. No officer will be fully accepted onto the team until they have dealt with their first sudden death. I have no idea why, but that was the way it was then. You cannot wait to be asked to do it; you need to volunteer for the call when it comes out.

So one night duty (it had to be a night duty, didn't it!) I heard the call. I got to the address, and some of my team had turned up and were waiting outside to witness the young probationer deal with a dead body. Dealing with dead bodies is very much part of police work. What my team did not know was that, having worked in nursing homes prior to joining the police, I had seen dead bodies before.

As I walked up the communal steps to the front door of the flat, the smell hit me. I went weak at the knees but I was determined not to show it. Some of my team were giggling quietly. As I reached the door, I was pushed into the address and the door closed behind me. I was inside facing an elderly man lying on the floor. He had died peacefully in his sleep but had fallen out of bed owing to the weight of maggots coming out of his face. I could see and smell that he had been there for a while. You do what needs to be done, like calling the coroner, bagging up valuable items and so on. It's only afterwards that you think about the sadness.

My team were disappointed with my lack of reaction. I think they expected me to scream. Compared to some stories I heard, I think I got off lightly. I look back on that time with great memories. I learnt a lot, laughed a lot and sometimes cried.

Megan (K Div) 2010s
You get a standard kit and then have a number of 'points' with which you can buy parts of your uniform. The amount of times the baton falls out of the holder or it doesn't work or it doesn't open. I was involved in a police collision on duty where the baton on my belt swivelled and the baton went into my spine and I got nerve damage and it's permanent now.

With the utility belt, Met cam and everything else you have to wear, you end up looking like Michelin Man.

Ellie (B Div) 2010s

The Met vest still squashes your boobs after all these years – and that's a serious consideration as we wear them all the time. And also the menopause; we have never really looked at that until now because all the women left before that started. Women didn't survive into the menopause when they were working in the Job. I had women coming in and they were literally soaked and they just didn't have enough uniform. So I said, 'Right, order some more, it's on me.' And then you make them wear a Met vest on a hot summer's day and you wonder why they're melting or can't do their job properly. But it's still the best job in the world.

8

WHAT DO YOU MEAN, WOMEN CAN'T DRIVE!

One cold January morning in 1970, I passed my driving test. Not having a car of my own, I didn't really drive after that for some months until I started a Class 5 course for the police. I was not the most confident driver although the instructor was good and very patient. I passed the course, but being in the women's department and not part of a relief gave me few opportunities to drive. Then one night the Duty Officer threw me the keys to the General Purpose car and said, 'Come on, you can drive me round.'

Grateful, but a little nervous, I got in the car, did the checks, tyres, engine compartment, petrol, rear view mirror, wing mirrors, clear vision . . . and we were off. Leman Street was a new building with an underground car park but I had no problem there: up the ramp and out onto the midnight streets without one single 'kangaroo hop'.

We headed for Wapping which in those days was a series of narrow, cobbled streets, poorly lit and sometimes awkward to manoeuvre. Nevertheless I soon settled into the whole, 'chauffeuring' the Inspector, who complimented me on my careful driving. He said I was not like 'the lads' who would skid round the cobbles and spin on a sixpence.

As Night Duty Inspector he had a radio, and while heading down a narrow street towards a sharp left-hand turn, he got a call requesting his return to the nick. That's when it all went wrong. I did an immediate three-point turn, misjudged the space and hit the wall; saw my mistake, crunched the gears and reversed . . . straight into a set of railings. The Inspector blinked his disbelief but remained calm.

'Just start the engine and get us back to the station,' he said. I don't know what he told the Traffic Officer who turned up to look at the damage, but I heard no more about it.

No one ever asked me to drive a police car again.

Jenny

Eve (Traffic Div) 1970s

I was one of the first three women to join the male bastion of the Traffic Division. It was a challenge, and I wanted to show the men that I could do this, too. I went to Hendon Driving School to learn about the mechanics of a car and traffic law. It was another stiff learning curve and I was learning with men, so, as women often do, I had to go the extra mile. I did really well. When I joined my garage, one or two of the older bike riders complained that women were not required to ride motorbikes. Some became quite petulant about this. However,

I didn't set the rules and I doubt that I would have joined the department if I had had to ride a huge motorbike.

I loved driving the Rover V8 3.5 litre cars. They went like a rocket and I remember being the driver when a shout came up asking for a car to take a kidney urgently from Harefield hospital to Westminster. It took me between 20 and 25 minutes, which was a really fast time. Nearing my destination, I drove the wrong way down a one-way street with blue lights and siren going. As far as I know, the transplant was successful.

Jennifer (H Div) 1970s

One late turn I was asked to return a young woman who had escaped from a secure mental hospital in Epsom. I wasn't the most confident of drivers but, not wanting to appear unwilling, I drove while a fellow WPC sat in the back with our patient. By the time we reached Epsom it was twilight. We drove through the huge wrought-iron gates and towards the main building – only to be told we had to go to another block somewhere in the rolling landscaped grounds. By now it was dark with few lamps dotting the complex, and the path on which I was driving seemed to be getting narrower. I had nowhere to turn around, but thought that if I just carried on we'd somehow find the entrance to the correct building.

Then my colleague saw a sign. We veered off the road towards a Victorian brick building and up a ramp. To my utter dismay I found myself driving along a veranda: white railings and pillars to my left, French windows to my right, and not a fag paper between us. Looking to my right I saw a male nurse pause in his effort to close the curtains. His mouth dropped open. I tried to look nonchalant, as though it was an everyday occurrence to see a car with two uniformed officers drive along a veranda in the dark.

My colleague hadn't expected a white-knuckle ride, and was now as silent as our patient, but a lot more frightened. I didn't know how it was going to end – the veranda I mean – but luckily there was only a slight drop to the grass, followed by a roller-coaster ride over grassy knolls before we finally hit the road again. We deposited our passenger and drove back to the nick. Not a scratch or dent on the car, although I can't say the same for my colleague's nerves . . . or my ego.

Sally (V Div) 1980s

Women weren't allowed to be operators on the Area car. They said it was 'an important car', and the one that deals with all the real emergencies from Scotland Yard. I said, 'But the Panda car can get there before the Area car so what's the difference?' I asked about it when I had my yearly interview with the Superintendent and, because of that, and a few others who complained, they changed it so we could drive the 'important car' after all.

Jo (Traffic) 1980s

Several years into my service, I applied for Traffic and found there were nine males alongside me as candidates. I thought I did well on my board but all the men got the traffic postings they wanted . . . and I failed the board. I knew I could do the job. It was blatant discrimination. Fortunately I had a very supportive Superintendent who helped prove that I was worthy of traffic by letting me join the traffic team at Heathrow where I was based.

I worked hard on every course, including the Vehicle Examiners' course which was known as the 'Nuts & Bolts' course. I remember one instructor telling me I would not amount to much because I did not ride motorcycles as a hobby. So I was proud to get Class One status, which led to me being seconded onto motorcycle surveillance. That was hard work, but thoroughly enjoyable.

Sue (B Div) 1980s

My husband, who had the same service as me, had three driving courses. I didn't get any. There was certainly a reluctance to 'waste' an RT Driver course on a female. It was thought we would marry and leave.

Angela (Y Div) 1980s

I had to fight to get a driving course to become an Area car driver. Men with less service were getting the courses before me, but I complained bitterly and eventually got a course. It terrified me because of the speed at which they drove, but after good instruction I could drive well – and at speeds up to 140mph. Other male colleagues said the course scared the hell out of them and failed to drive that fast. I did at one time, in 1996, drive the Commissioner's car.

Linda (Recruiting Office) 1980s

In January 1983 I was posted to the Recruiting Office and became the first woman police officer to gain an HGV licence so that I could drive the articulated Recruit Truck. We had a civilian who used to drive it but he kept letting the team down. I said, 'Well, how about me having a go then?' and the Chief Inspector went, 'Linda – you're a woman.' I grinned and said, 'Well spotted sir. And why can't I drive a truck?' He said, 'Well, I don't know really.' So he rang the driving school: 'I've got this constable who's been in the job for seven years, got a class 5 Panda licence, and never had a "polacc" [any accident involving a police vehicle]. Is it all right if I put them up?' At no time did he mention I was a woman.

They said, 'Yeah, yeah.' So the papers went up to driving school and apparently there was an almighty row going on between the HGV instructor and the chief of the school.

Fortunately a friend of mine heard the row and said, 'What's the problem with you two?' and they said, 'Recruiting want to put a woman on the HGV course.' So my friend goes, 'Who is it?' and they go, 'It's some bird called Linda.' He said, 'Oh I know Linda. Let her have a go, she'll be fine.' And they couldn't believe he actually said that.

I actually did my course with a sergeant from B11 who drove the prison vans and he was more frightened than I was, although the biggest problem I had was reaching the door handle to get in. There was always someone around to help me if I had a bit of trouble. So I completed the course in nine days instead of the usual ten. I was driving a Ford Fiesta at the time and somebody said, 'How can you get out of a Ford Fiesta and drive a truck?' I said, 'Because you tell your brain, you're not in a Fiesta . . . you're in a truck.'

The story about my driving the truck got into the papers – page 3 of the *Evening Standard* – and soon after I was driving up Tottenham High Road in heavy traffic and a guy directing lorries in and out of one of the factories there came running out. 'I didn't believe it when I read about you,' he said. 'They've actually allowed a woman in a truck?' It was still very new in the 1980s.

I was driving the truck along the North Circular when an Area car came bombing alongside me, looked up, saw it was me, put the blue light on and pulled me over. The operator, said, 'Can I have a ride in your truck please?' There's obviously a lot more women truck drivers and bus drivers these days . . . then it was rare.

Caroline (Traffic Div) 1990s

I was one of a small handful of traffic WPCs who rode motorbikes. The public would do a double take when they saw me on the bike, as did the local slags when I got called down to do a vehicle examination on some shitty car stopped by the local officers. One slag said to me, 'You won't find anything wrong with this, luv,' when I arrived on the bike. His car was examined by me, declared unfit, and he had to arrange to have a total lift for it. He learnt to respect the cloth! The public were fine; sometimes a bit taken aback when I was on a motorbike, but it's more acceptable now.

Annie (Regional Crime Squad) 1990s

There was a lot of leg-pulling about lady drivers, and the bosses always wanted reassurance that you were not going to get married and then leave to have children. They thought it more cost-effective to give driving courses to a man. But I did many driving courses: Advanced Surveillance, Anti Hijacking. It was amazing.

Mary (R Div) 1990s

I once crashed a police car . . . and stopped a riot in Woolwich town centre. I was driving a marked response car into which I placed a prisoner. A fight had started around something he may, or may not, have done to someone else's sister. Certainly there were people still keen to sort the matter out because they were banging on the sides of the car trying to get at him. It was bedlam, with police and public fighting each other in the street. I swung my car round a badly-parked Panda . . . and drove straight into a post. As the offside wing fell off, all the fighting stopped while people burst into spontaneous applause. Happily the Garage Sergeant forgave me for leaving the scene once I'd explained that I was being mindful of my prisoner's safety.

9

DULL IT ISN'T

Trained and ready to go, I first hit the streets of H Division in the heart of the East End in July 1969. My first encounter with East Enders was in the underground ladies' toilets at Aldgate. An experienced officer who was teaching me 'beats' took me down the stone steps into the grubby, white-tiled walls of the main lavatory area. Inside was a small cubby hole belonging to the lady who looked after the toilets. We sat on wooden chairs covered in faded worn cushions while the lady made us 'a nice cup of tea' and told us about her morning clients who were having a wash with a shared bar of soap at the small white basins.

Some of the women were 'methers' [meths drinkers], others were prostitutes – nicknamed 'Toms' by us police officers. At night, they wandered the streets or sat around the bonfire in 'Itchy Park' – real name St Mary's Churchyard. It can still be found at the corner of Whitechapel Road, just up past Gardiner's Corner, a landmark building now long gone after being burned down by arsonists.

To this day I can recall the aroma of Izal, carbolic soap and body odour which mingled with the smell of tea and greasy hair like a thick, fermenting broth. In the cramped room, sitting round the table, the lady told us how she looked after 'the girls': women who had nowhere to go and were open to abuse, physical and verbal, from all. The East End provided a harsh life for many, but out of that grew some truly genuine people.

In those early days of my service school crossing duty was a bane, but our Woman Inspector insisted we did it. Us being visible out on the streets was a good advertisement for the role of women police officers. It was just a short walk from the nick, but in winter it was desperately cold standing there with the chance that the Inspector might drive by at any time to check on us. Woe betide you if you weren't standing straight with your uniform neat and tidy.

One bitterly cold day, when I was at the crossing, a kind man carrying a cardboard tray loaded with polystyrene cups of tea for his mates, dropped a cup in my hand. I didn't know what to do with it.

'Drink it,' you might say; but what if Ma'am drove by? She might 'stick me on' – not that she was that harsh. So I put the cup on the windowsill of a building by the crossing . . . and stared at it until it went cold. Then I left it there. To this day I still feel guilty – the man might have returned and noticed I hadn't touched it. If by chance you're reading this . . . I do

*thank you for your kindness and hope you will forgive
a shy rookie's seeming ingratitude.*

Jenny

Maureen (V Div) 1940s

Kingston was a busy town and we still had the men Specials
working with us from the war. I was standing with one of those
Specials outside a building one day when someone asked us
where a particular local pub was. Well, I didn't know pubs at
all, and nor did he, so neither of us could help. Only when we
got back to the station did we discover the truth: we'd been
standing right outside it all along.

When I was in uniform I did quite a few escort duties. I once
went on an escort with a CID officer, Ray Purdy, who sadly
was murdered in Chelsea. I didn't really know him, but if you'd
gone out with somebody for a job, you'd say, 'Hello' if you met
them again. One weekend, I got off the train at Wimbledon
and there was Ray waiting to get the train to go home for the
weekend. On Monday he went back on duty and was murdered.
He was in his late thirties and had two children. It's a silly
thing to say, but it's something I'll never forget; it really shook
me up.

Mary (D Div) 1950s

I used to stroll slowly along with my hands clasped behind my
back, trying to look authoritative. I remember a man put a
banana into my hands and . . . for one horrible moment . . . I
thought the worst. To be fair to him, I was always being offered
sweets and once was hauled up to Scotland Yard to be disci-
plined because the wife of a senior officer saw me eating sweets
on traffic duty and complained.

Daisy (E Div) 1950s

King's Cross was a wonderful area. The work was varied, and
so was the population. There was the railway station which we
patrolled because the Transport Police had no women officers
at that time. Opposite the station was the 'Black and White
Café' where runaway girls would congregate. We made friends
with the two lovely lady attendants in the underground toilets
at King's Cross. If we were looking for anyone they would tell
us if they had been around.

One day another WPC and I were patrolling when someone said 'please come quickly' as a young woman had given
birth . . . and the doctor wouldn't come to help. Sure enough,
this girl had come home from work at lunchtime and had
given birth on the bathroom floor. She was about nineteen
years old and her parents had no idea she was even pregnant. I
went over to the doctor's surgery, but found he was in no hurry
to oblige. So I took out my pocketbook and pencil, and
prepared to write. I had no idea what I was going to write . . .
or what good it might do . . . but on this occasion it worked.
The doctor immediately decided he would come back with
me to the flat and attend to the girl.

How things have changed! In those days, police could only
ask for an ambulance if an accident happened in the street.
Only a doctor could order an ambulance to a private house. As
always, there were ways to get round such rules; I recall an
incident when a lady fell inside her house and broke her leg. I
made out she had fallen in the street just so that I could phone
for an ambulance.

The famous Chapel Street market was on one of our beats.
Here you could get your bag stolen at one end of the market . . .
and buy it back at the other end. There was an occasion of
cock fighting in Chapel Street which was dealt with by

uniformed officers in plain clothes, but it was almost impossible to get close because women hanging out of the upstairs
windows were keeping watch. Betting in the street was illegal,
and I recall going on a job in Chapel Street where the lookout
had only one leg. The Inspector took his crutch away to stop
him running off.

Margaret (H Div) 1960s
The thing I remember about Aldgate East was Woolworths
which used to be down on the main road. One cold November
I was called to arrest two alcoholic shoplifters. It was sad and
tragic. As I walked them up the road, I remember the tall one
saying, 'I'm sorry about this miss but I need somewhere to be
at Christmas.' He was arranging to be in the nick so that he'd
be somewhere warm and dry for the holiday.

Carol (Z Div) 1960s
Whilst on duty on Gypsy Hill front desk, a somewhat elderly
lady dumped an enormous selection of carrier bags on the
desk and proceeded to get excited. She didn't speak a word of
English so I called the Duty Sergeant who fortunately had
been an army officer in India. Very patiently he extracted from
this woman the fact that the bags were full of Green Shield
stamps. She was under the impression she could exchange
these to allow a relative to come to this country.

Lyn (F Div) 1960s
One Sunday on early turn I asked my sergeant if I could use
some of my overtime to have the last two hours of the day off.
She said I could, providing I was able to conclude an enquiry
which had been going on for several weeks. 'Easy,' I thought. I
found the house and met an elderly gentleman, dressed in his

outdoor clothes and a dressing gown. He obviously could not see very well, and it took a while to explain who I was and why I was there. It turned out that he was hoping we could help him move from his cold, dark flat.

Well, time was passing and I needed to get back to the police station to take my time off. I tried to get away, but 'No', I couldn't leave without seeing his wife, Cissy. In spite of my protestations, he went into the bedroom and I heard him telling his wife all about me. Then this delightful little lady, who looked like a china doll, came into the room and repeated everything . . . and more . . . that husband Harry had already told me. By now my time off had gone out the window, and as I gently tried to extricate myself, Cissy told me that Harry had bought himself a musical instrument to entertain them both . . . and she would love me to hear it. I knew I was sunk when I heard her say, 'Harry, take the young lady into the front room and show her your organ.'

Cissy and I sang along as he played *Once in Royal David's City* and a rousing *Land of Hope and Glory*. They wanted to continue, but I told them that my dreadful sergeant would be looking for me. When I returned to the police station, I had to give a full account of my 'adventure'. Several colleagues started giggling, but when I got to: 'Harry, take the young lady into the front room and show her your organ,' the office was in hysterics. We had to take the phones off the hooks as we couldn't answer them. I didn't get my time off that day, but I felt my time had been well used and hoped my report to the local authority would help the couple get a better flat.

Terri (C & H Div) 1960s–1970s

I had my fair share of odd and funny experiences. One involved a drunken lady who, on seeing me, threw herself between two parked cars and hung onto the bumpers. It took well over half an hour to dislodge her. In the morning she apologised and told my fortune as she had 'the gift'.

Down at the Tower of London I once arrested a budgie after being told by a burly lorry driver that this poor bird was under his lorry. We managed to catch it and I toddled back to the nick with the bird safely trapped in my hat, only to be told by the Station Sergeant that I was improperly dressed with no hat on. He didn't believe me when I said I'd got a budgie in my hat until I took my hand away and the little bird flew out and landed on the lights. Luckily one of the lads rescued it and ended up adopting it. It lived happily at his place for many years.

I was on patrol with a colleague walking along Bow Street and we went to a house where we were regaled with tea and cake for about an hour. (Always good to get to know the people on your beat and have them get to know you). Our radio went and our sergeant said that as it was raining so heavily she would come and collect us. Shock, horror . . . we hadn't even noticed the rain . . . but luckily the lady of the house let us pop, fully dressed in our uniforms, into her shower and get beautifully wet. We then went outside and stood dripping under an awning awaiting the sergeant's arrival. From the look on her face she knew exactly what we'd been up to, but never let on. I'm sure, however, that she kept her eye on us a little more than was necessary over the next few days. Overall I was very lucky to serve with some lovely female officers and they were all, without exception, a credit to the Met.

Annie (E Div) 1970s

It was so unusual to see a patrolling female officer so I was often followed by members of the public and have had coaches stop in the West End to take pictures of me. I found the public would quickly come to your assistance in those days. In public disorder situations, a lot of yobs thought you were the weakest link. They also thought they could verbally abuse you without any consequences: again, they were put right and found themselves in the charge room.

Quite often I found that male criminals reacted very differently to me than they would if a male colleague attended. I can remember stopping a huge bloke in the West End who was acting suspiciously in the backstreets. I knew he had been trying to steal a car and had a set of 'jigglers' [thin metal strips to open doors] on him. I also knew there was something more to this. I nicked him and told him he had two options: walk with me peacefully to the station, or I would summon a few of my 28,000 colleagues to help me. My team was gobsmacked when we walked into the charge room. Enquiries revealed that he was over the side from prison, where he was serving a life sentence for murder!

Janis (D Div) 1970s

I've cried and hugged the battered survivors of domestic violence; talked to a potential suicide victim and felt huge relief when they aborted the idea; held babies and small children having a rough time at home; laughed at the drunken female singing at the top of her voice that 'All coppers are bastards'; sat outside a shop door, sweating and out of breath having tried to catch a suspect of burglary . . . and failed miserably; directed traffic on the Marylebone Road enjoying the rapport with the lorry drivers as they drove past: all just the sort of tasks that a police officer does in the course of their day.

Ann (M Div) 1970s

Once I stood for a whole shift below a building that had been badly damaged in a severe storm. I was there to prevent members of the public from walking under it: only much later did the irony strike me.

Margaret (N Div) 1970s

Nothing can truly prepare you for foot-patrolling on your own and facing Joe Public while you are still inexperienced. The public treated me much as they did the men. If they were 'upright' citizens then I would be treated with respect; if they were being stopped or arrested then I'd be treated with derision, curses . . . or both. It's the case that if someone seems to be in charge, the public will respond by complying. A uniform helps, of course, but it's your attitude and demeanour that's important.

Jennifer (H Div) 1970s

I first saw Eleanor perched, cross-legged, on the charge room desk when I was called to Limehouse to deal with a female prisoner. She bore all the signs of a meths drinker: red-rimmed, watery eyes and skin wrinkled like a pickled walnut. Cigarette in hand, spouting foul language in a very cultured voice at the police officers and sergeant, she swung an accusing arm if they came too close, questioning their parentage, particularly that of their mothers and suggesting what the officers should do with themselves. Not being contortionists, they declined her offers.

Sometimes seeing a female officer can have a calming effect, but I got my full share of the name calling. As she quietened and the men lost interest in goading her, she told me about herself. She had been married, happy and with a good career. But as her children left home and emigrated far afield she was left alone and had started drinking heavily. She seemed to be a lonely, intelligent woman with a death wish. She didn't care if she sold her body as long as she had her drink and could sit with her street buddies. More than one of those women would be murdered on the streets by one of their fellow drinkers. I remember being shocked when I heard of the death of Barbara, a regular fireside drinker of Itchy Park, who was murdered in a brawl.

Shirley (Z Div) 1980s

When I was a Home Beat Officer at Norbury, a senior officer asked me if I had a spare stocking that he could use as a fan belt on his car. I got the stocking and went to his office with it draped around the back of my neck as I sashayed provocatively into the room . . . only to find he had three other senior officers with him. Luckily they saw the funny side.

Sue (P Div) 1980s

We had the famous Professor Cameron as pathologist at the post mortem of a murder victim. He asked me if I smoked . . . I didn't. He showed me a bucket of non-smokers' lungs looking all pink: then a bucket of smokers' black lungs. On another occasion a PC came with me to the mortuary to fingerprint a dead woman to try and identify her. My colleague showed me how to straighten her fingers out by breaking them with a truncheon. There was a £10 extra payment for doing that horrible job.

On a far happier note, there were a lot of jokers on relief. Sunday early turn would see one of the PCs go down the cells with his shirt on backwards, like a dog collar. He would open the wicket gate and ask if the prisoners wanted to confess. Believe it or not some people actually did! One day, the

Bromley Area car driver fiddled with the 'two tones' on our car. We found ourselves on a call down Lewisham High Street, sounding like an ice-cream van and with everybody on the pavement staring and laughing. We got our own back by putting a gerbil in his car. We knew the driver hated them.

Our relief would have a big meal during the early part of the night-duty week. One of the men had been a chef in the Merchant Navy, and I would help him make these beautiful meals. We would unlock the kitchen side of the canteen, and use the equipment. One memorable night we were sitting eating, along with the odd glass of wine, when the Chief Superintendent walked in on a visit. I'm not sure who was more shocked, us or him. He turned and marched straight back out. I think the relief Inspector got words of advice, but nothing else was said.

Lorraine (S Div) 1980s

The worst night I experienced was a Friday when we had a triple fatal car crash. I was out with a PC. We had stopped at a set of traffic lights when a person told us there'd been an accident down the road. We could see this Mini in the middle of the road and – just as the lights turned green – it burst into flames.

All the occupants were burnt to death. If we had gone through the red lights and got there we might have been burnt as well because it went up, literally, as the lights changed. You think how long you're at traffic lights; it's not long, is it? We may have got to the car just as it exploded. The other car, a Rover which had caused the accident, was in a tree. The passenger in the car was a girl. It was her engagement party. Some bloke who was drunk decided to drive her home. He killed these three but survived himself.

The Fire Brigade asked me if I'd help to take the girl down. A fireman asked if I had ever dealt with a dead body, and I said, 'No.' It was a bit daunting. The skipper came up afterwards and said, 'Are you all right, you're very pale?' It was the smell, and everything else. One of the boys in the car was a PC's son and we had the job of going to the family's home.

Then I got back to the police station and a woman came in. I'll never forget this; it was 5 a.m. and she claimed she'd been sexually assaulted. I was going to go home, but they said, 'Lorraine, could you interview this woman?' I ended up dealing with her as well and didn't leave till gone 7. I literally went home, showered and went back to work. I was shattered.

Kim (R Div) 1980s

One late turn I was sent with another PC to a flat near Bellingham railway station. A nasty smell had been reported and the occupant hadn't been seen for weeks. Opening the letter box, that smell of rotting flesh hit me. There was a small fanlight window and it was decided that, because I was the smallest, I would be the one to go in. I opened the window and balanced on the sill before easing myself into the blackness.

As I gingerly slid down, my right foot found something semi-solid to stand on and then I realised it was in something slushy. My colleague shone his torch through the window and I managed to get off the bed on which I had landed and get to the floor. I found the light, ran to the front door, opened it, hung over the balcony and threw up. Taking deeps breaths we both re-entered the flat and found the elderly occupant deceased on her bed. My foot had gone straight through her stomach. Explain that at Coroners Court! I can still experience that slushy feeling and the smell and the flies. I threw my shoes away and could never go to that block of flats again.

My nineteenth birthday was spent on my first night duty attending a fatal accident involving two teenagers on a motor scooter, a parked VW camper van and a lorry. The male rider was sitting against a garden wall with only half a leg and his female pillion passenger was on the road with her head completely flat. Apparently the scooter driver overtook the lorry on the nearside and hit the back of the camper van. The pillion passenger went underneath the back wheels of the lorry. The Traffic Officer was very professional and said I was not to accompany the body to the hospital, because it wasn't a good thing for a young girl to experience. I was grateful for his thoughtfulness, although I am sure that in this day and age some people would think this was sexist.

I then had to inform the deceased girl's parents. She was fourteen years old. I grew up that night by being catapulted into the realisation that, through stupidity, life could be snuffed out in a second. Birthdays were a time for the buying of cream cakes for the relief, and early that shift, I had bought in a large strawberry gateau. To this day I can't look at a strawberry gateau without thinking of my nineteenth birthday.

Sue (B Div) 1980s
Some of my friends dropped me like a stone when I joined the police. My immediate family were baffled but supportive. I am from a working-class background and my extended family were dismayed that the first one to go to college had joined the police. Generally they viewed police as stupid, corrupt and lazy.

I remember taxi drivers and members of the public stopping to give me a lift to urgent calls. But sometimes, even as a sergeant or Inspector, the public would defer to my male colleague. People seemed to think that I was partnered with a male driver to keep him warm on night duty. We just used to laugh about it. I never felt that I wasn't in charge. Sometimes I would deliberately take a backseat – for example when interviewing a Muslim male victim – because I would find they'd be a little hostile or feel they were being disrespected. This wasn't the case with all Muslim men, of course.

Cheryl (Q Div) 1980s

I got a wide range of attitudes from people from all walks of life. I remember going to a call at the house of a woman singer-songwriter who had a hit at the time. When she didn't get the service she expected, she said to me, 'Do you know who I am?'

I replied that I didn't. She was very cheesed off. Off-duty, most people were intrigued and interested in my job. My mate and I went to Bailey's in Watford for a night out and – to avoid being quizzed about our jobs – decided that if we were approached by any prospective males we would tell them that we worked in a shop. We did get approached by a couple of lads: it turned out they were PCs! Oh how we laughed.

The toughest thing I had to do? I attended an RTA when I was twenty-one years old. The middle-aged driver had had a heart attack at the wheel. A crowd gathered as I tried to drag him out of the car to give him CPR, but not one person stepped up to help me. I did my best, but he died. I was then told to do the 'death message'. Unusually, I called at the neighbour first to ask about the lady who was about to learn she was a widow. I was told the woman had angina and that I should find where her tablets were *before* giving her bad news.

As the lady opened the door, I barged my way in and asked where her angina tablets were before sitting her down to tell her. As expected, she started gasping and holding her chest but the tablets, already on standby, did the trick. I then had to tell the dead man's mum, who also lived there. She fainted. So I laid her on the floor with her legs up on the sofa. At this point . . . cue the son who walked in to this mayhem.

When I told him, he picked up a dining chair, and cracked it across my back, shouting at me for being 'a lying bitch'. The mum was worried sick I was going to nick the son. After everything had calmed down I left feeling drained, angry and guilty that I had not been able to help the husband/son/dad. The next day the biggest bunch of flowers was delivered by the family. I was touched that, in the midst of all their grief, they even thought about what I had done the previous day.

Julie (L Div) 1980s

Just after the Brixton riots, while tension was still high, I became the Engagement Officer (known then as Community Officer) acting as the go-between when black youths were arrested. At the time there were a lot of knifepoint handbag robberies, so when I saw this young male running down Streatham High Road, carrying a ladies'-style bag, I tried to stop him. A chase ensued, which resulted in a crowd gathering when he was eventually stopped on Mitcham's ground. It became a good team effort with more units and dogs called in to back me up while I performed the search, and the crowd got hostile. In the bag I found . . . a Bible. He'd been running for a bus on his way to Bible study and hadn't heard me challenge him to stop.

After it had all calmed down, the youth walked all the way back to the local police station to report that the 'stop' had been professionally carried out and that he was sorry for the confusion. He'd wanted to thank me for being considerate and professional. Maybe he thanked me because I was female?

Kim (R Div) 1980s

When the Brink's-Mat robbery happened another woman officer and I were looking after the wives of two of the suspects whilst they were being interviewed. Every day the women were allowed a walk around the police station yard, handcuffed to one of us. The huge wooden gates were closed and there were dogs and dog handlers in the yard as security. We were told they were high security and there was a possibility that there may be an attempt to have them 'sprung' in order to stop them giving evidence. Enjoying the sunshine and fresh air I was cuffed to one of the woman when, all of a sudden we heard shouting and someone scrambling up the high gates. The dogs went mad and we women were manhandled into the corner of the yard, ending up on the ground with a dog and handler standing in front of us as protection. Tension was high as you can imagine and my blood ran cold. A head appeared over the gate and a cheery police constable shouted that all he wanted was to 'come and have a dump' . . . bless him. We were relieved and, eventually, so was he.

Helen (V Div) 1980s

With a new probationer I went to a call about an elderly person not seen, milk on step, etc. We knocked on the door, got no reply and so gained entry through an open window. We knew we were at a sudden death, and it was just a case of where the body was. This was a very dilapidated Victorian house on three storeys. We searched every room up to the second floor with no luck. When we got to the top floor we saw an elderly lady lying on her back on a bed with her mouth dropped open, looking very dead. There was a little Jack Russell terrier on the bed with her which, when it saw us, started to bark.

The 'dead' lady shot bolt upright in her bed, opened her toothless mouth, and shouted at us. We stumbled backwards in terror: the corpse had come to life! It transpired she was a bit of a loner who had decided to spend the day in bed rather than do what she usually did, and the one day had become two. She was absolutely fine. Once we had explained what had transpired she was grateful, but it remained a comical, yet frightening, moment.

Jane (Z Div) 1980s
Whenever I walked down Croydon Market the shout would go up . . . and everything on sale became 50p. It was their code to let the other traders know police were about.

Janet (Y Div) 1980s
I arrested Father Christmas. It was December 1989, and I was still in my 'street duties' time at my new station. I came across Santa selling rolls of Christmas wrapping paper from a shopping trolley; no evidence of a sleigh . . . or reindeer. My enquiry, asking him if he had a trading licence, was met with a very un-Father-Christmassy attitude. He refused to tell me his name or address, and as such I arrested him under what was Section 25 of PACE for trading without a licence. A local Panda turned up and I escorted Mr Claus to the custody area. I was never allowed to forget that I was the woman who had arrested Santa Claus and nearly ruined Christmas.

Around that same time I stopped a driver going the wrong way up the street. At that point in my life I was still quite naïve. I very politely told the man that he was going to be reported and he might go to court. He was in his late forties and equally polite. His wife came over to us, became very irate and said that he was a magistrate at a local court. Of course me being new and not wanting to be seen to bend the rules, I repeated – politely – that my report was still going in. Another probationer

PC had also come over at this point, but he did not speak, other than introduce himself and say that he would have to stand by what I was going to report. The man was calm and quite resigned to what I was doing, having accepted his driving had been dangerous . . . but the wife was shouting angrily as they drove off.

Ten minutes later I got a call telling me that the magistrate I'd just 'stuck on' was dead and his wife was kicking off. She was saying the police had killed her husband. Shortly after he'd driven away from me he had suffered a heart attack, driven into some railings and died. They were a black couple and it was coming up to an anniversary of the riots on the Broadwater Farm estate; a time when relationships with the black community were not good. My Superintendent was concerned to calm down the situation before the cries of the woman purporting that police had killed her husband could cause a repeat of a riot situation.

Eventually there was an inquest at which the death was deemed natural causes and I was cleared of all suspicion of having an overbearing attitude towards the man. I was sad that the man had died, but I was assured that my behaviour was not something that caused the death. This didn't make me cry – but I was astounded that someone would lie about me and my actions.

Jane (H Div) 1980s

After about ten weeks on Division I went on a Street Duties course. The idea was to work in plain clothes and garner intelligence. My colleague learned that drug dealers were working from an address in a block of flats. She got the warrant and we headed over there around 7 a.m. We put the door in, as there was no one there. Searching the flat my friend found a small tin on the mantelpiece, which had white powder in it. She was chuffed that she had found such a large drugs stash, until I pointed out there was a name on the tin ... it was actually someone's cremated remains.

Cressida (C Div) 1980s

I felt I was slightly marked out because, firstly, I had a funny name; secondly I was on the graduate entry scheme, and thirdly I arrived with my own set opinions as I was older than some beginners. I remember one day bringing a *Guardian* newspaper in to read. It never occurred to me that there was anything odd about that; I changed my newspapers every day; I read anything and everything. But I remember people saying, 'Oh my God, look what we've got here.' The good thing was I got on very well with my colleagues very quickly. I liked my work and I liked them, and they seemed to like me in the main, but I was conscious that it was quite tough for some people in 1983.

I don't want to dwell on this because it has nothing to do with being a woman officer, but not very long after I got there some members of the team I joined made allegations against other members, which resulted in a trial of 'conspiracy to pervert the course of justice'.

I was a very young officer looking at this huge furore going on all around me, with the team absolutely divided, as you can imagine. That stood me in good stead, I think, seeing how people respond when they are upset, angry, when they feel attacked, how teams can be. It was interesting and difficult as a very young person to see how leadership and management was done in that situation. It didn't affect my future because – although it was a fractured team – somehow or other I managed to carry on learning, getting on with everybody wherever they stood on these sorts of issues and navigating my way through. Looking back there were one or two people who I will thank forever who probably saw the police officer's role differently from mine but nevertheless thought, 'She's all right, we're going to make sure she stays all right, we'll look after her.' And they did.

Having had a relatively sheltered life as a youngster, going to Soho in the days when it was very seedy – you patrolled by yourself in Soho, Mayfair – was a shock. You had your beats and you walked round them and all sorts of things would happen, whether it was ambassadors getting arrested (and of course, they had diplomatic privilege), or celebrities, or big protests, lots of shoplifters, criminal damage, all the daily stuff but with the West End vibe to it all through the night. It was a fabulous place to work.

Mary (R Div) 1980s

There had been problems at a nightclub in Woolwich and we had information that gang members with firearms were going back for retribution. The decision was to close the club and disperse the disaffected revellers. I was posted driving the van and had a sergeant as my passenger. We were on an industrial estate alongside the venue to block anyone who might think it could be an alternative location for an impromptu rave. As we stood having a crafty fag about a hundred youths came streaming down the road. Without really thinking we ran towards them. Several paces in, I reflected on the wisdom of this, so I turned back to the van. Mick kept on running and his relief was palpable when I drew alongside with all lights blazing and sirens blasting. Thankfully this was enough to turn the tide.

Linda (S Div) 1990s

I was policing the Kenwood concerts in Hampstead Lane and, all of a sudden, these two black limos double-parked outside this house. I said, 'Sorry gents you can't do that because we're going to get busy shortly because we have a concert going on.'

And they said, 'Oh, but Mr Brosnan won't be long.'

So I pressed the buzzer on the gate and out comes Pierce Brosnan, looking absolutely gorgeous, and I go, 'Excuse me Pierce, but do you think your two cars could come into the drive and wait until you're ready?'

'Oh, officer, of course.' And I put my hand out and said, 'It's Linda,' and he said, 'It's nice to meet you, Linda.' I just looked into those blue eyes and wouldn't let him go.

He said, 'I won't be long. I can understand why you didn't want them double-parked.' As I was walking back to Bishop's Avenue, he came alongside in his limo. The window wound down and he said, 'Thank you Linda, thank you very much.'

Sam (P Div) 1990s

I've spent my career laughing really, though sometimes the laugh was on me. During my first few weeks on patrol a double-decker bus was stolen, and I saw it coming along the road. I leapt on to the back of the bus thinking, 'Got him.'

But a moment later I realised, 'I can't get to the driver.' It was the old-style Routemaster with a separate cab for the driver. There was me and my handbag, getting chucked round this bus, 'ding-dinging' the bell to make him stop and thinking, 'I've cocked this one up.' I put it up on my radio where we were going. He just ignored me, racing round in this double decker, and then he took it to Catford bus garage where I finally arrested him. He said, 'I just like driving buses.' Apparently he was known for it. He'd always take the bus back; he wouldn't just dump it somewhere.

By contrast I answered a call to the house of an elderly lady who hadn't been seen for a while. I broke in and found that she had fallen against her burning gas fire and hadn't been able to get up. She had been there for days. She had been burnt all across her back and legs but it wasn't your typical burn: it was more like she'd been cooked like a chicken. The poor soul was still conscious and very confused. I chatted to her while we waited for the ambulance and can remember looking at her and thinking, I didn't know burns like that could happen. I didn't know if she could survive as the doctor said she had 90% burns. I visited her in hospital but she passed away after a few days. I found it very upsetting when I found her, although obviously didn't show this in front of her.

I was also called to another address where a man had set fire to himself while his wife and family were away. He had left suicide notes downstairs, taken pills and drink and gone upstairs and set fire to himself. The neighbour came in but the man was so badly burnt his arm came away like a sleeve when the neighbour tried to save him. It was the first time I'd gone to a burnt body and what got to me was the smell – a real sickly-sweet smell – and the distressed neighbour. How do you get over that? It was a terrible way to die. I've also seen shocking situations with children and elderly victims that make you sad, but the camaraderie and support of fellow team members always got you through.

Janet (Y Div) 1990s
I once went to a call at a public house and a group of men there thought I was a Strip-a-gram. They were good-humoured though, and we had a laugh when they realised I was 'the real thing'.

Jane (H Div) 1990s

There was an occasion in an interview when both the PC I was with, and the suspect's solicitor, actually groaned out loud at my naïvety. I grew up in a small village and was quite shy. I had arrested someone for assault, and asked him to tell me what happened that evening. He started telling me, and I was writing it down. He told me, 'Then I said "See you next Tuesday . . ."' I stopped the interview and said, 'Sorry, I don't understand? Why are you saying you hate each other and then arranging to meet next Tuesday?'

My colleague groaned and the solicitor looked surprised. The prisoner said, 'No love, "*See you next Tuesday*".'

I patiently replied, 'Yes I heard you, but I don't understand?' He then rephrased it in a much less polite way. I had never heard this phrase, so had no idea this was the 'polite version' of the 'C' word.

Mary (L Div) 1990s

I liked being a Custody Officer at Walworth. One night I processed twenty-four prisoners single-handed. With the 'drunk and disorderlies' I would always read the evidence to them before releasing them. Only once did I fail to get an apology.

Cressida (W Div) 1990s

On my first posting as a young sergeant I had this older, very experienced, bachelor Inspector, very capable man, rough-tough northerner, and I thought, 'What on earth is he going to make of me?' He was a bit squizzical [sic] to start with but he decided he was going to make the most of whatever he could of me, I suppose, and he trained me very well.

On my second night out with him we had a call at about 1 a.m. to late-night drinking and shocking behaviour going on at one of the pubs he had to check under the licensing laws. As we walked in through the back door he said, 'We'll catch them.'

I don't know what they were thinking; they were bound to be found out. They'd got this strip show on, like Strip-a-grams, and the Inspector and I emerged either side of a completely naked woman who was just at the vital moment of the strip show with all the punters sitting in front gawping at this girl . . . and then these two police officers appear . . . 'Hello.' I'm sure they thought we were part of the act, but luckily the Inspector could be very serious and took control very quickly.

Mary (R Div) 1990s

In the days before video recorders were common I was on patrol and saw a fire in some garages with maisonettes on top. Flames were licking up the sides of the maisonettes and I took the walkway up to them and knocked. A woman opened the door and smoke came pouring out. I said, 'The garages are on fire, let's get everyone out.' She said, 'I thought the floor felt hot. Would it be all right if we finished watching *Corrie* first?'

Cressida (L Div) 1990s

I was amazed and also appalled at the way some people ended up actually living their lives, in terms of the sheer amount of aggression people would put up with. As an Inspector I used to go out on patrol by myself a lot, both walking and driving. I happened to be driving when I received a call over the radio at about two or three in the morning. I was nearest so I went. There was a woman on the floor and her husband had, it turned out, stoved in her head with a claw hammer. I was the first on scene and called a couple of people to help me.

The husband had made off so, once we'd done the initial thing as Duty Officer, I got back in the car and came across him walking down the hill, about three-quarters of a mile away. He was covered in blood. Nowadays there'd be a whole great big thing about cross-contamination . . . but I just nicked him. The woman survived, thank God, and he was charged with attempted murder and GBH. He eventually went to court for GBH.

I got to know her quite well as a victim in fact, even though I was an Inspector and CID dealt with the case. She did not want to give evidence at all. I remember driving her to court and she said she didn't want this to go ahead, she didn't want to give evidence. The judge said, 'This is not Mrs Smith against Mr Smith, this is Regina versus Mr Smith, and we're going ahead.' She didn't give evidence, but he was convicted and served about three or four years.

As an Inspector I'd seen a lot, but I remember thinking, 'How awful, how extraordinary to get in a position where you loved somebody so much that even though he'd put the claw end of the hammer through your head, you still want to live with him'. It was never clear to me whether she was completely unable to work out how she could live without him financially, physically, or in every other way. Of course, we know this is not at all uncommon; it was just an extreme example.

The odd thing was, the night it happened, I dealt with three or four other incidents, two rapes and goodness knows what else. Peckham in the early 1990s was a busy old place. I remember going home and having an hour-and-a-half sleep and then going to my close friend's wedding at Camberwell Registry Office, only about a quarter of a mile from where this had happened. I stood there thinking, 'These two are getting married, and four hours earlier I was with those two who'd got married fifteen years before'. Policing is just strange. It's extraordinary the things you deal with.

Pauline (L Div) 2000s

My biggest enquiry was Operation Seale into the murder of
Damilola Taylor, a ten-year-old Nigerian boy stabbed to death
in Peckham. I was the Family Liaison Officer. There was more
than one trial but by the time of the last one I had retired from
the police. I'm pleased to say that myself and the Taylor family
had always got on well and so I was invited back to assist with
the family. We stood together in The Old Bailey, holding
hands as the guilty verdict was given. We all wanted to jump
for joy, but we didn't. I felt that the family would now hopefully have some peace in their lives. It gave me closure on my
most difficult enquiry in my thirty-one years of service in the
Metropolitan Police. I could enjoy retirement.

Kate (K Div) 2010s

I received a call to a self-harmer. When I arrived a male had a
knife to his neck and ambulance personnel were fighting to
get the knife before he sliced his throat. We managed to get the
knife . . . that's when I realised he had sliced his stomach open
and his intestines were on his lap, along with the two bottles of
bleach he had drunk. He survived, but every time I smell
bleach this memory comes back to me.

10

'LOVE,' SAID GRANNY ... 'LOTS OF LOVE'

I was called to a house . . . well, it was the ruin of a house . . . just across from the nick. It was one of those places where you wipe your feet on the way out. I didn't know where the garden ended and the kitchen began. Dog faeces lay on the floor, barefoot children played amongst it, laughing, happy, and filthy; the parents equally so. The children were well fed and loved. Social Services and I agreed, while we would not live in those conditions, that the children were in a loving home and should not be removed. A little hygiene education was called for so I willingly handed that task over to Social Services and left the house scratching.

Women police officers have always been charged with a particular responsibility for children and I like to think that police powers to safeguard children – and women – have increased since my day. For my

*female colleagues who preceded me in the early part
of the 1900s the situation must have been even more
challenging and distressing.*

Jenny

*If policewomen were available for making enquiries,
many of us think there would not be so many cases of
children assaulted and even murdered, while their
assailants remain undiscovered. Policewomen in
Hyde Park have helped in the prevention of crime
against children and the public have therefore a right
to demand that policewomen be attached to all police
forces, both to prevent and to detect these crimes.*

*It cannot be denied that the little girl's natural
protector is the older woman who understands her
difficulties and dangers, and who possesses an instinc-
tive watchfulness and power of observation where children are concerned, and it is this older woman with
the power of the Law behind her – the policewoman
– who is required if the new Children's Act is to fulfil
its purpose and make further and better provision for
the protection and welfare of the young.*

Edith Tancred (Chairman Women Police
Committee) 1930s
Metropolitan Women Police Association Archives

Mary (D Div) 1950s

We occasionally had to go along on brothel raids to look after
any children found on the premises. In fact a lot of my work
involved looking after kids in custody. Many of them were young
villains who were always full of bravado if they were facing an
appearance in court but who, behind the façade, were just

young kids. I would take them back to their care homes. One thing that seems particularly poignant is that I remember their grip on my hand would always tighten with nervousness as I took them towards the door. I'm not surprised about that now . . . knowing what went on in some of those care homes in the past.

Shirley (Z Div) 1950s

While at Tooting I witnessed a young child who had been run over on the pedestrian crossing. I went into the nick and saw my woman sergeant. I was very upset, and stated that I was no good if things were going to make me cry. Her reply was, 'The day you can't cry, get out of the Job.' How true that statement was.

Diana (H Div) 1960s

I arrived for night duty one dark November night to be told to go to a house where a woman was giving birth. The baby had just been born, the mother didn't know she was pregnant, there seemed to be just rags on the bed, nothing of conse-quence to keep the baby warm. There were two men hanging about so I told them to boil some water; what for I had no idea. The ambulance men arrived, but couldn't cut the cord. The mother had not birthed the placenta, so the ambulance men were worried. Once the water boiled they cleaned the baby's mouth and I put my jacket over the baby to keep him alive. Eventually the doctor arrived, snipped the cord and left. The ambulance men, the mother and me carrying the baby trying to keep him alive, went off to the hospital. Sadly the baby ended up in a children's home. Not a happy story.

Kathy (C Div) 1960s

The crypt of St Martin-in-the-Fields was a place that runaways frequented. On this particular occasion I stopped a girl and took her to the police box in Trafalgar Square. The conclusion was that she was an approved-school absconder. I called for the van which arrived, but I had to walk to it with her. It was a big lesson that day as this young girl had an open tub of single cream in her bag, and tipped it over my head as we were walking to the van. The cameras of the tourists were going ten-to-the-dozen and I felt very foolish. What's more, I hate cream! I always remembered to look in bags after that.

Sandra (T Div) 1960s
A local girl of six or seven years old went missing. Along with a dog handler and a goodly number of uniform officers we blitzed a local park looking for her. We had been searching for some time and had got to the point where we were re-searching areas that had already been checked. We retraced our steps and, underneath a shrub, we found the little girl. I can't tell you how gratifying it was to see her big smile as she crawled from her hiding place and took my hand.

Sandra (F Div) 1970s
I was called over to Brent one morning to help deal with a mentally ill mother who wouldn't let the child-careworker treat her injured baby. The baby had been hit in the face by the mother, and its poor little tooth had been knocked out. I remember kneeling beside her and just talking quietly and soothingly until, eventually, she put the baby in my arms and I handed it over to a very grateful careworker. Some months later one of our new recruits, Ruth, was up at the Yard on a Junior course where my incident with the mother and baby was quoted as being an example of how a WPC should handle a situation like this; sympathetically and without any injury. Well – to say I was pleased to hear I had done good goes without

saying, but if Ruth hadn't been on that course I would never have known.

Shirley (L Div) 1970s

I had been called to a basement flat to deal with a man whose common-law wife alleged he had gone berserk with a hatchet and knife, and was threatening to kill their four young children and himself. He had just been released from a local mental hospital and was informed by a neighbour that 'she' was having an affair with her real husband down the road while he was in hospital, so he had thrown her out and made the threat.

The common-law husband ended up crying on my shoulder, while the PCs got into the flat by the back entrance. The flat was filthy. Twin, six-month-old babies were sucking bottles of curdled milk, and the other two little ones, three and four years old, were in a sorry state. The fireplace was used as a dustbin, the table had newspapers piled up on it as a tablecloth. They all slept in a double bed with old coats as coverings. I dealt with the children as in need of care. Sadly, one of the twins died in hospital. At Juvenile Court the magistrates gave me a commendation for my actions. The Superintendent called me into his office, threw the report in a tray and said, 'It won't go anywhere.' I must admit I was hurt and disappointed.

Margaret (J Div) 1970s

When I transferred to Barkingside I had a lot of dealings with Child Protection. There were some terrible cases. I was called to a case of physical abuse of a little boy locked in the cupboard under the stairs. I remember his name and everything. There were policemen crying when we found him. His parents were completely bonkers. It was awful, because you know those people who are not very well mentally and who trudge about. This couple dressed oddly and walked about being really miserable ... but we didn't know they had a child. He was about five or something when we found him; he'd been in this cupboard under the stairs for all that time. Christ knows what he turned out like. Very sad.

Carol (R Div) 1970s

Care and Protection was our main job, but one sticks in my mind. I was in the Orpington area so I must have been at St Mary Cray. A woman had been picked up drunk by the ambulance crew and I was called to her house as there were five little ones on their own; no adult present. The house was the worst I had ever seen. No furniture, only mattresses on the floor, and all the children were filthy and soaking wet with urine and faeces. Every cupboard in the kitchen was full of old milk bottles and they all contained urine, there was no food. There was no electricity and I had to keep leaving to get fresh air as it smelt really bad. We used to employ a police photographer in those days and he had to set up spotlights to take the snaps. I asked if he was using colour film and he said there was no need as the black and white showed it up better. Those pictures were used for years as a graphic to illustrate Care and Protection cases.

Kim (R Div) 1980s

Two young children were reported as being in a flat on their own, mum having 'gone to work'. I was requested because WPCs had to be present when children were involved. The flat was on the second floor and had an iron-railing-type security door which no one could open. We called the Fire Brigade with an extending ladder to access the flat via one of the windows, and I was then told to go up the ladder too. Firstly I'm petrified of heights, and secondly, at that time, WPCs only wore skirts. With a number of firemen and policemen at the bottom of the ladder awaiting my ascent I wondered what washing I was going to show! After explaining my fears a kind fireman said he would walk up the ladder behind me. I started my ascent with the kind fireman following. My legs started to shake . . . and the ladder began to shake and I froze. Kind fireman climbed up, putting his arms either side of my waist, and calmed me down. We went up slowly, and finally two huge great arms grabbed my skirt belt and hauled me into the lounge of the flat.

The children were OK, thank goodness, but not living in the best of conditions. One was aged five and the other was three. Both children were taken down the ladder and taken into care. It was then left for me to climb back down. My kind fireman ascended the ladder again and helped me down by literally cuddling me. Nearing the bottom, someone shouted that they liked my red knickers. When on the ground, the sergeant handed me a safety pin and said all WPCs should carry one to clip the bottom of their skirts before flashing drawers. I saw the fire crew a few times after at various incidents and apparently my 'knickers name' – their words – was 'Red'.

Sally (T Div) 1990s

While helping out at Brixton, I came in early one morning to assist the Night Duty CID who had a young lad who appeared to have been attacked. Basically he was late coming home, got on a bus, didn't have any money and was kicked off by the bus driver. The lad was only ten years old. He was walking up the road from Brixton Hill to Streatham and got dragged down an alley to a shaded car park area and attacked before somebody looked out of a window and shouted down and the attacker ran off.

A substance found on his arm turned out to be semen and I had to take a statement from the boy by play-acting, with puppets and things, to try to get him to explain it all. The boy had his head thrown down during the attack, had bitten his tongue and had nearly passed out. The boy remembered the guy had a digital watch on, which in those days were quite new. We also managed to get a photofit of the subject, but our enquiries did not lead to an arrest at that time. About two years later I received a phone call from the Brixton CID. While conducting a murder enquiry on a young boy they had found the photofit from my case and eventually made a connection to *my* young boy. They managed to get some DNA from their suspect which confirmed the link to the other offences. A digital watch was found in his possession. He did get charged, and was convicted for murder and for the attempted murder of my young lad.

Louise (G Div) 1990s

We came across a lot of children aged thirteen or fourteen, mostly runaways, young girls daft enough to come to London because the streets were 'paved with gold'. They were usually cocky and arrogant, 'I can deal with it . . . I'm all right.' But the girls were way out of their depth, more cocky than streetwise. Most of them became prostitutes to survive, and most became drug addicts. It was organised crime, network crime probably, as quite a volume of money was being turned over. Invariably the madams were prostitutes who were a bit old for it, has-beens. Once the drug addiction had taken its toll on them physically they'd lose the high-end market and they'd go further down the food chain. The pimps would be running a protection racket around them and some were classed as their boyfriends, because 'they loved them really': that old chestnut.

Linda (S Div) 1990s

It was the first time I realised how nasty paedophiles were. A message came in one day: a caretaker from one of the council blocks of flats had been called to the lift because there was a black plastic bag in there. When he opened the bag he found a murdered little boy. I'll never forget this little boy's funeral. They had a coach and black horses and, because I was one of the Home Beats, I led the procession from the house down to the crematorium. I cried all the way to the chapel. He was only five. He was just playing out when this paedophile released from prison picked him up. The paedophile was caught and convicted. It was horrible, evil.

Mary (R Div) 1990s

One Sunday I took a call to an abandoned baby. A teenage boy had found a baby in a plastic carrier bag. The baby was in a yellow babygro that had the feet cut off and was wearing a white knitted cap. She was so cold she looked purple. It was obvious that she was newborn, her umbilicus crudely cut. I went with her to hospital and got to cuddle her once she was warmed up a bit. She was admitted onto the neonatal ward where she looked huge – most of the other infants were premature, but our girl was a healthy seven pound plus. Once she was cleaned up and fed I gathered three of the nurses together. I explained that it was my job to try and find her parents, so I'd value their expertise. As one nurse looked to be of African heritage, one Asian and the third Oriental, I felt we had most bases covered. We stood looking over her for a while until the

African nurse said, 'Honey, till she's walkin' and talkin' you just can't tell'.

We gave her the name Aisha and for the next month I, together with two PCs and a Detective Inspector, tried to find her parents. No stone was left unturned, but we concluded that the mother was probably a teenager who had a concealed pregnancy. As we wound up the enquiry the DI and I both wrote her a letter; mine described how she was found and all that happened to her on her first day, my DI's explained all that we'd done to try and find her parents. We felt it was important to give her a history.

Just before her second birthday I went with the social worker to visit Aisha with her adopted parents. The words of the nurse came back to me because it seemed certain that Aisha was of West African heritage. I took her the two letters, the clothes she'd been found in and a replacement plastic bag, the original having been destroyed during analysis. As we sat drinking tea and chatting the social worker commented, 'Blimey she's grown – what have you been feeding her?'

'Love,' said Granny . . . 'Lots of love.'

Ellie (G Div) 1990s

In 1997 the government brought out a White Paper proposing a Sexual Offences Register. What it didn't do was say how to do it. I was an Acting Detective Sergeant at the time and I was asked if I would set up the unit for Hackney as the new legislation was coming in and we would have the 'Dirty Dozen' paedophile ring coming out of custody that year.

They were christened the Dirty Dozen as they were all part of a paedophile ring of twelve relating to the Jason Swift and the Mark Tilsley murders. I was simply given the White Paper and told, 'Create something.' I had to create a system and get partners on board. That was when partnership was not part of the Met.

So I had to set it up, get the partnership working and deal with high-profile paedophiles within a year. This meant dealing with probation officers, getting into jails and meeting these people who were due for release and coming out of custody. This was the setting-up of the Sexual Offences Register and what I created became basically what we do now; it became the model of excellence. I studied the group I was going to be responsible for. They'd never had a female officer deal with them so I always made sure I had my hair done and make-up, you know, had feminine clothes on, always shook their hand. That really threw them. Female officers didn't exist in that world.

They were coming out of prison no matter what we did, so we registered them when they came out to our protective custody. Not to protect them, but to protect the public from them.

Jane (SCD5) 2000s

When I was the operations Detective Chief Inspector for the South East I remember reading a review about this young lad who couldn't tell his parents what had happened to him, so he wrote them a letter. I could feel myself sitting there getting quite upset, it was so harrowing. His parents had to read that and think 'that's what my son's been through'. I think the abuse happened in a school, but it was how he managed to let his parents know that really got to me; even after I'd been doing the job for some years.

As DCI I took on the partnership side of child abuse which involved Female Genital Mutilation. We did a lot of work around FGM because, as far as I am aware, there has not yet been a conviction in this country. We were really trying to change communities' way of thinking and to improve how the NHS might inform us. That brought on a lot of problems for the NHS because they were being told things in confidence. There are actually some straightforward guidelines but, if you give that information to the police, you could potentially have someone who will stop coming to see you – and a person's health is paramount. Women don't see a correlation between what happened to them as children and some of the medical problems they have as an adult.

The women who were supporting it were often victims themselves. We said there's nothing written in religious scripts about this, and it was interesting talking to the men. It was a bit of, 'Oh my gosh.' We had men saying, 'What do we need to do?' It was enlightening people and I found that work was fascinating.

All FGM cases came through us to be then dealt with out on Borough. We were arresting people at airports because there was stuff found on them to do with the whole process and ceremony of FGM. There was some good work going on. In France they regularly medically check children at the age of five, but we don't do that because we don't have routine checks of children's welfare.

Janet (CAIT) 2000s–2010s

Some of the arrests I did as part of the Child Abuse Investigation Team were pretty significant, especially one where a trial resulted at the Old Bailey and the guy was found guilty of several counts of rape and indecent assault on his twelve-year-old daughter. Many of the arrests may not have resulted in convictions, and sometimes the people [victims] didn't necessarily want to go through the ordeal at court, but I felt that helping people feel that they were being listened to and taken seriously was worthwhile in itself. The lack of staff and high workload within the department certainly took its toll on my anxiety and levels of stress, and I had to see my GP regarding this. I eventually went to the Police Rehabilitation Centre. The doctor there placed me on sick leave; something I had been reluctant to do for fear of the stigma and how I would be seen by my supervisors and colleagues. By the doc making the decision, it was taken out of my hands, and reduced my feelings of inadequacy and guilt.

11

LADIES OF THE NIGHT

On my Division in the 1970s, women officers weren't allowed to patrol alone after 10 p.m. There was usually only ever one WPC on duty at night, so I often went out in the police van or a Panda car with a male officer. We would frequently see the two regular prostitutes hanging around the corner of Canon Street Road at the junction with Commercial Road. There was a tiny all-night shop there called 'the hole in the wall', where they would smoke their cigarettes, chat to the owner and keep a look out for customers and the police. The shop was popular with police too because not much stayed open past 11 p.m. in those days.

Both were sturdy middle-aged women, one brown-haired, one blonde, both chatty, and both flirty with the police. They would wave and shout friendly abuse at the PCs, offer them their services, and ignore me completely. The officers returned the chat, but drove

away with a wave after the small talk. There was a
friendly camaraderie amongst those who inhabited
the streets in the early hours of the morning.

On those dark nights it was easy to imagine that
little had changed for such women since the days of
the First World War; a time which proved the worth
of the fledgling Women Patrols in dealing with prosti-
tutes and vulnerable young girls. The experiment of
using women to try and control prostitution was such
a success that the then-Metropolitan Police
Commissioner agreed to employ one hundred such
patrols to continue their work under his auspices and
with the sanction of the Home Office.

Arrest and raids on brothels, however, stayed as the
almost exclusive domain of male officers until well
into the 1980s. Only evolving attitudes, along with
the full integration of women into the Police Service,
changed this.

Jenny

'I do believe that the scourge of prostitution may sometimes be better dealt with by women than by men, in
whom it is difficult to eradicate the sex instinct –
unless they are religious fanatics, the worst type to
deal with that form of vice.'

Nevil Macready (Commissioner) 1920s
Metropolitan Police Archives

Margaret (D Div) 1950s

Some of the 'Toms' [prostitutes] were pretty much poverty-
stricken, but they weren't all helpless, downtrodden women.
There were those who had made good money and looked after

it wisely. Some owned several flats and had kids at private boarding schools. I remember one who used to ask me if I would be kind enough not to show that I recognised her in the street when her kids were home from boarding school in the holidays. The money she earned as a prostitute paid for the kids' education, but she was paranoid they would find out where the money was coming from.

One prostitute was so wealthy that when she heard I was getting married she offered to let me have one of her flats for my new husband and me to live in; an offer I had to refuse.

Daisy (E Div) 1950s

King's Cross was a well-known red-light area. We dealt with a lot of working girls; the regular 'Toms' who appeared in court time after time. Some of these girls had fallen on hard times and needed money, and it was all they knew. As a woman officer one of my jobs was to search the prostitutes who had been arrested and brought into the station each night. I remember one Tom who was quite old, probably about forty, and who turned up regularly wearing a tightly buttoned jacket. Tucked in-between the buttons I kept finding individual ten-bob notes [50p] which I had to count and record as her property. It didn't take me long to cotton on to the fact that I could tell how many clients she had 'serviced' that night by the number of ten-bob notes I was finding. She became affectionately known as 'the ten-bob tart'.

In fact, you got to know the women well, and there was a regular routine to deal with them as they came before the magistrates at Clerkenwell Court. The men made the arrests, but as a woman officer I dealt with a lot of the paperwork, filling in all the forms before the girls went to court.

Mary (D Div) 1950s

I always had a lot of sympathy for the 'Toms' working the streets around Paddington Green where I was stationed. Most didn't choose to become prostitutes; some had a hard life and were always at risk of venereal diseases. I had to search the girls that were brought into the cells but, amazingly, we were never even issued with rubber gloves to deal with them. I remember one of my Inspectors telling me just to make sure that I washed my hands after the searches. We got to know the prostitutes pretty well because they were the same women being arrested all of the time. They knew that being arrested was part of the price of doing their job, and that if they behaved they would be back out of the streets later that night . . . sometimes twice a night if they were busy.

Francine (F Div) 1960s

When I did a brothel raid at Hammersmith I was asked to list all the equipment that was found there. Being rather green at the time I really did not know what things were called, though the shapes should have told me something. I put 'hairdryers' down and I was never allowed to forget it!

Hammersmith was really the happiest station ever. The women bosses were fantastic, the work interesting, and we covered Notting Hill Gate which was an eye-opener. Prostitutes had to be given three cautions before arrest, or else asked if they wanted advice on changing their ways. I had one of the latter requests. I think it was the first, and probably the last, prostitute who ever asked for help in this way. I tried to advise her but I have never been sure if she was serious with me or not. I was quite surprised by how many prostitutes were married and sent their children to private schools.

Kathy (C Div) 1960s

While patrolling in Soho I stopped a teenage girl, an approved-school absconder. She produced a razor blade and started to swipe at my face. I had to duck and stand back to miss it. From out of nowhere, four prostitutes that I had looked after as matron jumped on her, grabbed the razor blade and sat on her while I waited for the van to arrive. I think that was probably my proudest moment when they said, 'You don't do that to *our* WPC.' Happy days . . .

Lyn (F Div) 1960s

Although I was thirty when I went to my first posting at Notting Hill Gate, I was quite green where 'Ladies of the Night' were concerned. One very classy lady, a rarity I can assure you, beautifully dressed with a real fox fur round her shoulder, worked for herself as a call girl for very wealthy clients. She had been arrested as part of a CID enquiry. My job was to persuade her to make an appointment to see someone from Social Services who would try to get her to go on the 'straight and narrow'. As I tried to explain what this appointment was all about, she suddenly said to me, 'Do you own a car?'

'No,' I stammered.

'I have a Daimler,' she said; then, 'Do you go abroad for your holidays?'

'No,' I stammered again.

'I go to the South of France three times a year,' she said. Short pause, then, 'Do you have a fur coat?' Again my answer was in the negative. 'Well, I have two full-length fur coats as well as this,' she said, indicating the fur wrap. She never said another word . . . and I just left her to it.

Kathy (C Div) 1960s

The 'Toms' in our area were a likeable lot and happy to share their stories. I was asked if I wanted a cuppa by one of them who I knew quite well – she actually taught me to knit one night duty when I was matron. Never refusing a cuppa I went into her place of work. She had two cupboards with crockery in, one for her clients and one for her friends. Luckily my cup came from the friends' shelf. She showed me her wardrobe full of nurses' uniforms, school uniforms, high heels and fishnet stockings and suspenders and other paraphernalia. She even offered to buy my uniform. I asked her about her clients. She described one man with a beard who was always her last client. He had some odd requests! He asked her to save all the durex used that night. He would ask her to lie on a glass table so that he could lie underneath it and see her all squashed up. He would then ask her to put a plastic bag over his penis and pee into it; if she could defecate he would give her more money. His finale would be to drink the contents of the durex while she watched. I was retching from my socks up having visions of his beard . . . Yuk.

Jennifer (H Div) 1970s

Police officers are great storytellers. Walking the night-time streets with an officer in and out of the narrow dark alleys and streets of Wapping and Shadwell where there were many open spaces, bombsites, not yet built on, where lorry drivers parked up for the night and slept in their cabs, my male companion – who walked at the irksome policeman's pace of slow, slow and slower – told me his favourite tale of one of the regular prostitutes who serviced the lorry drivers in their times of need. The driver was hard up but needy; the prostitute equally so. He persuaded her to give her services for the princely sum of half-a-crown [25p]. The deed done, the driver whisked away into the dawn light. The Lady of the Night surveyed her takings and realised that her half-a-crown was, in fact, an old penny wrapped in silver foil. Incensed at the deception, she attended the local police station to allege rape, because he hadn't paid the right amount for her services. When the police pointed out that wasn't rape, she demanded that he be arrested for 'pecuniary advantage'.

Another prostitute, Pauline, was a bandy-legged midget who stood on dustbins to service her clients. She was quite vocal and aggressive but in much demand apparently, straddling, besides the dustbin, the East End and the edge of the City to accommodate her clients.

Lyn (C Div) 1970s

On night duty you'd nick a 'Tom' and take her to court in the morning, which earned you overtime payments. Then, in about 1977, Court Presentation Officers were introduced to deal with court cases and to stop officers getting overtime. That's when the men decided to stop arresting prostitutes.

It didn't take long for the word to get out and we got so flooded with 'Toms' that all the Mayfair residents were asking the Chief Superintendent why this was happening. That's why the 'Toms' Squad' came in; and that's why only women worked on it. With no money in it any more, the men didn't want to do it. To cope with the crisis they brought all the women police officers in, even some from the outer stations who were already drivers. Before then, we women were never given a driving course and were told, 'Well, you're not going to stay . . . so why spend the money on you?' Then, suddenly, driving courses started being offered.

We patrolled Soho and Mayfair arresting prostitutes working on the streets. Brothels were different because they came under 'Clubs and Vice'. On the Toms' Squad we knew the women; we got to know the faces, we got to know the streets, we got to know the cars. It wasn't an offence to be a prostitute, but it *was* an offence to solicit, so it was a case of watching if they were going up to the bloke.

We had Soho 'clip girls' who used to take the money, tell their client they would meet them round the corner, and then not turn up. We had the prostitutes in Soho and we had the prostitutes in Mayfair. They were all very busy and after two or three cautions they were arrested and went to court. Sometimes we'd ask the blokes to come to the station; we didn't need their evidence because we knew what the girls were doing . . . but it scared the men off for a while.

Susan (P Div) 1970s

I was involved in the infamous Cynthia Payne brothel raid. Cynthia was the 'madam' who became famous for using luncheon vouchers as a currency for men to pay her prostitutes at orgies. This was a major operation as there were all sorts of high-ranking people using her services. I assisted while the Obscene Publications Department interviewed her. Later she sent flowers to me at the police station. She said it was 'Thanks' for not looking down on her. I was flattered.

Caroline (B Div) 1980s

I was dealing with a violent drunk down the Earls Court Road one evening when a few street-girls came up and helped me. I used to chat with them and sometimes buy them a coffee if it was cold and they were standing outside. All these girls, looking extremely glamorous and tarty, with short skirts, sat on my drunk, having a fag and telling him to 'Fucking shut up' while we waited for the van. Members of the public ogled as they went past, and I'm waving them on saying, 'Don't worry . . . nothing to see here.'

If it was a warm evening there'd be about twelve to fourteen young girls in their twenties, along with one or two older women who'd been round the block a couple of times and would look after the younger ones. Some of the girls said their mum had brought them up, and she'd had an 'uncle' who'd interfered with them. Then mum got married to someone else and didn't want them any more. We always nicked the girls, never the kerb-crawlers. They were good informants as well. Most of them were druggies, but they'd let us know about any new drug pusher who'd come into the area. The pimps kept themselves to themselves, but they looked after the girls. It was the punters who beat the girls, not the pimps. Some women would have black eyes, things like that, but they'd say, 'What's the point of going to the police; it's part of the job.' Any allegations of rape they made were put to one side. The CID used to say, 'What do you expect?'

Cressida (C Div) 1980s

There were a lot of street offences on West End Central's ground, so at any one time you'd have a lot of the working girls in the custody office. Because they got arrested so often they would know their way around. I remember being in there with a sergeant when an officer brought one of these women in and I said, 'Oh hello' (I can't remember her name, Marion, or whatever it was) and she said, 'Oh hello Cress, Sarge,' and she just grabbed the charge sheets and said, 'I'll start filling this in, shall I?' She filled it in entirely on her own from beginning to end and then said, 'Do you want me to do the fingerprints?' Off she went and did her fingerprints and then sat down and said, 'Right, I'm going in the morning, am I?'

The sergeant said, 'Well, there's two ways . . .' but she said, 'Before you say anything else . . . who's the magistrate?' He said, 'It's so and so,' (I'm not going to mention his name) and she said, 'Oh I love him, I'll stay then. Do you want to keep me in custody?' She gave me a great big wink and said, 'He's lovely. I think he likes girls like us. He's always kind. I'll be straight back out. So I'm staying in custody. Do you need grounds to keep me in?' She just dealt with everything, from beginning to end.

On another occasion I saw the Chief Superintendent driving into the underground car park. He was just getting out of his car and putting his trilby on as I came down into the underground area. As he was walking in through the back office, this lady came out of the charge room. He raised his hat and said, 'Good afternoon, madam.' And she said, 'Good afternoon.' She walked past me and then she started to speed up.

We walked into the charge room and the sergeant looked round and said, 'Oh my God, where's Julia?' And I said, 'She may have just er . . .' and the Chief Superintendent said, 'Is that the young lady I just said good afternoon to and raised my hat?' And I said, 'Yes it is sir.' And he said, 'Well, what was she in here for?' The sergeant said, 'I've just charged her with soliciting. She's supposed to be staying in custody.' It was a great laugh. There was a light-hearted debate about how she let herself out of the door, because in those days they all knew the codes, they knew everything about how everything worked. Pretty much ran the show.

Louise (G Div) 1990s

Amhurst Park in Stoke Newington had a massive red-light area in the early 1990s. The prostitutes attracted a lot of drugs into the area so we nicked a lot of 'Toms' night in, night out. It was a predominately Jewish area and so it didn't go down well with the devout Jewish population. One evening a woman robbed a punter and stole a load of travellers cheques and banknotes. When I went to search her back at the station I thought there was a sanitary towel in her knickers. She pulled them down and there was a big wodge of banknotes, travellers cheques . . . and a cigarette lighter; it was like a handbag's-worth. I try not to think about it . . . but you'd be surprised by the amount she was able to wedge up there. We also had a mother and daughter acting as prostitutes. Mum took daughter out with her when she was working because the younger daughter was prettier. She attracted more punters . . . and mum could get the overspill. Her daughter was fifteen.

When I transferred to the Clubs and Vice Squad in Central London we used to do brothel visits where a madam took the money off the punters and sent them up to the girls. There were no toilets in the brothels, so the girls would urinate in a bowl on the floor. Some would also do 'scatting', where they would defecate on their clients. And then there was the brothel where they specialised in older women – and when I say older women, I mean grandmothers; proper old. I remember going to spanking parlours. There were rows of formica cubicles, divided spaces like in a toilet, with one girl in each. Normally the girls would be spanking the client. Invariably the girls in those parlours were heavily pregnant. In their condition they would struggle to get punters in the normal way. It was £10 a spank.

Most of the street-girls would 'roll' their punters if they could: take the punter's money, do the deed and while in the act, steal from the punter if the opportunity arose. It went with the territory and was mainly opportunist. Some would just go out and take the money with no intention of doing the sexual act, but those were usually the prostitutes who were desperate for drugs and who actually got themselves beaten up as a result. It wasn't clever; it was more drug-led.

12

WHEN NO MEANS NO

I would never seek to defend attitudes which all too often prevailed among police officers dealing with the victims of sexual crime at the time when I served in the 1970s. It was then the job of women police officers like me to take a woman's statement, but the job of male detectives to investigate their allegations. The concept of having dedicated 'rape suites' where victims could be examined and treated with dignity was some way in the future. In my day, a rape victim was likely to be examined in the Divisional Surgeon's room at a police station where the alleged crime was being investigated. It was not unknown for both the victim and their alleged attacker to be examined in the same room, albeit at different times.

How rape victims were treated depended to some extent on the nature of the assault. I was aware that the CID would usually treat cases of 'stranger-rape', where the attacker was unknown to the victim, with the utmost seriousness. The same was undoubtedly true where a child was the victim of a rape or indecent assault. Such investigations may, on occasions, have been flawed, but the motivation to catch those criminals was always both heartfelt and genuine.

Where worse mistakes were made, from the earliest days of the Force through to more recent and more enlightened times, was in the handling of sexual assaults where the victim and suspect knew each other: allegations of what is nowadays called 'date rape', or cases of domestic rape and sexual assault of a man upon his wife. It seems that victims were all too often put in the situation of having to justify their allegations, or to prove that they had not given consent to sex. The starting point always seemed to be that the investigating officers would not believe their stories.

The way police handle all such cases has changed out of all recognition. Victims now have dedicated 'rape suites' where they can be treated with the necessary dignity. The entire process of handling such crimes is far more victim-centric, with specially trained Sexual Offences Investigative Techniques Officers – both men and women – who deal with these cases. A little later a system for dealing with serious sexual offences was introduced and given the name 'Sapphire'. Such units used new criteria governing how these offences were to be dealt with, with the aim of reassuring and assisting the victim.

Most important of all is the change of approach. A victim will be believed, their allegation always investigated, unless or until the investigation disproves the

allegation. This was at one time far from fact; not
least because we women officers did not always have
the voice to question such treatment.

Jenny

Janis (D Div) 1970s

The 1970s were a time when people were even more judge-mental of women who reported sex crimes than they are today; that includes male police officers and those in the CID. They had not then received enough of the sort of specialised training that's necessary to understand and work with survivors of sexual offences.

Because of the integration of policewomen onto the day-to-day reliefs I missed specialised training about sexual offences. That meant that taking a statement from my first rape victim was a real case of 'winging' it. I had been trained to take statements in less serious crimes, and I used that, along with my understanding of being a female to get her, and me, through it.

I hated that at the end of the reporting stage the case was 'no-crimed' – which means that a decision was recorded that no crime had been committed. It was because the victim had decided not to go ahead and give evidence. She was frightened of standing up in court and being judged. She had gone through the most horrendous of crimes and had then decided not to take it any further because going to court was equally as traumatic for her.

Kathy (K Div) 1970s

I had a case of an elderly widow in her eighties who was raped in her home. Her underwear was strewn round the front garden. As well as feeling abused she felt such a sense of betrayal to her late husband who had been dead for many

years. I could have cried with her. I took her to hospital and
had to wait for the inevitable forensics . . . when all she wanted
to do was have a bath. She was kept in hospital because she
was injured as a result of the rape. Apparently she had opened
her front door and was pushed inside and raped. A man was
arrested and dealt with, but what got to me was that he was a
young man with a wife and child. Very, very sad . . . and a case
I won't forget.

Linda (Y Div) 1970s

When I was at St Anne's Road, in about 1977, each relief only
had one WPC on. If you were the WPC on duty and a girl
came in and alleged rape, you dealt with it. We had this lovely
old Female Medical Examiner, an old lady doctor; right old
battleaxe she was. And, at that time, we just examined everybody
in the doctor's room in the police station. I basically stood
outside while a female victim was being examined and then
sat down with the girl and wrote down the whole story. When
I met with the doctor she said, 'I think she tells a good story . . .
but there's no evidence of any sexual assault here at all. In fact
I'd quite happily say she's still a virgin. The poor girl obviously
has no sexual experience whatsoever – I think there was a bit
of fumbling that went wrong and she *thought* she'd been raped.
Because she'd heard that word but there's no evidence of any
assault whatsoever; no marks, no nothing. I can honestly say
that this girl, more than anything else, needs some sex
education.'

So I said, 'OK, you're the doctor.' The girl couldn't tell her
story at all, she had no awareness of anything. She was a very
naïve young lady who didn't know anything, and after the
doctor spoke to me, I had to agree. That's how we were taught
in those days.

On another occasion I had to go to hospital with a uniform sergeant because a woman claimed she'd been raped by three blokes round the back of a pub. He'd been a Detective Constable but had to do a year as a police sergeant in uniform before he could go back to CID to be a Detective Sergeant. I was absolutely appalled, but he basically said, 'Well, tell us the story then.' She told us the story and he said to her – and I cringe when thinking about it – he actually said, 'I think you fancied one of them, and you took him outside and his mates joined in as well, and you didn't want your husband to know . . . and that was it.' I couldn't believe I was hearing this. I was shocked. The woman withdrew her allegation, and that was the end of the matter.

Susan (P Div) 1980s

I was working in Sydenham on a small team of officers dealing with indecency offences. One night, as I was returning to the station, I became a victim myself. I was grabbed and sexually assaulted. The irony was that I was doing a late turn because I had been at the sixteenth birthday party of one of the child victims I had been dealing with. She and her mother had asked if I could go to their family party. They were grateful for all the support I had given.

I was quite happy with my life, but I was floored by what happened to me. The thought that people I worked with would be putting *my* clothes in evidence bags, reading my statement and so on, was just too much. The man was never caught, and to be quite frank I was pleased; I'm not sure I could have gone through the court process. I began suffering with agoraphobia and didn't go out for months. My GP got me counselling with a forensic psychologist and treated me for post-traumatic stress. I never returned to work.

Annie (SPG) 1980s

I was attached to 6 Unit of the Special Patrol Group at Gipsy Hill in the early 1980s when a fifteen-year-old juvenile was arrested for a series of sexual assaults on women. He was also suspected of being responsible for a couple of rapes, one of which was on a woman while she visited her baby's grave in the local cemetery . . . a savage!

Because of his age he was bailed with very strict conditions and a curfew, while evidence was being gathered. However, it was believed that he would strike again, and so he was put under surveillance. A number of the SPG Units were deployed in plain clothes, with us girls as decoys. Each time he was observed leaving the address, we would be dropped ahead of his route in the hope of him striking one of us.

He liked to stake out a particular park, and on the day that I was the decoy, he headed for this location. Dusk was approaching and I was dropped off at the park. I walked around a bit, aware that he was going in the opposite direction to me. I continued on my circuit, when suddenly I could hear he was now coming my way. Heart starts beating a little quicker, and I could hear the raised levels in the voice of the commentator. The next communication was, 'Yes, he has spotted you, Annie, and is having a look see . . . Don't look round whatever you do, don't scare him off.'

I could hear my heartbeat in my ears now. My hand instantly went to my handbag, where my stick was. Then the message came over that he had locked on to me and was following at an equal pace . . . but keeping a little distance. Suddenly, he had quickened his pace and was fast approaching. I thought I was going to be sick. I knew all the guys would be closing up ready to pounce, but that did not alleviate my fear. I could hear his footsteps and braced myself, when without warning he veered off to one side. I heard a skitter of gravel as he skidded off and away . . . then silence. I could feel the disappointment hanging over the airwaves, but could not breathe, let alone speak. Then, 'Sorry, big bird, I think as he got up to you he realised you were at least a foot taller than him.' The coward obviously only picked on smaller women, and I am 5'10". Then I was sick in the bushes. I had flashbacks on this job for weeks, but a few large Pernods with the team in the pub put that to bed.

About a week later he attacked one of the other SPG girls, in a similar scenario. She was a tiny girl, sustaining a number of injuries before the team got to her and dealt with him. He eventually received a custodial sentence at court, and I seem to remember the officer being commended.

Debbie (Y Div) 1980s

From an early stage of my service I was involved in the investigation of rape offences. In 1982 there was the infamous Thames Valley Police interview of a rape victim which was shown in a 'fly-on-the-wall' documentary television series about the Force. The officers were virtually accusing the victim of lying. Suffice to say it, sadly, probably mirrored police rape investigations across the country.

Detective Inspector Ian Blair (later to become the Metropolitan Police Commissioner) conducted research into rape investigations in London. In 1985 he was the Detective Chief Inspector at Kentish Town when I arrived as a brand-new Detective Constable – one of only two substantive female detectives in the office. We were told that victims would be believed, that there were to be dedicated Sexual Offences Investigative Techniques interview officers, dedicated rape suites, comfort rooms and female medical examiners. Everything was being designed to persuade the victim that we *would* take any allegation seriously.

Sexual offences are notoriously easy to make up, for all sorts of reasons – infidelity, revenge, mental health, previous sexual abuse – but they are very difficult to disprove. An alleged victim might be able to tell lies once, but if you ask questions repeatedly, but still compassionately, a witness who is being untruthful will get caught out. However, we were also very careful not to judge any victims. 'No means no', and a prostitute who has consented to sex ten times that evening still has the right to say, 'No' on the eleventh occasion.

For the first time, the Met started dealing with rape that occurred within a relationship or marriage with the same degree of compassion and determination as were shown in other rape cases. Victims must not be judged on their appearance or lifestyle choices.

Linda (S Div) 1990s

I came on duty at 8 a.m. one Sunday and they'd basically got three blokes in the cells, and a girl waiting to speak to me about being raped. One of our boys had been checking round the Strawberry Vale estate, because there were some dodgy people who lived there, when this girl ran towards him and said, 'You're a police officer, aren't you? Please help me, I've just been raped.' He put the shout out as the boys came out of the flat and ran. We arrested three men.

By then we had proper units – rape suites – where we could take the girls. The one I took her to was at Hendon. It took me two or three sessions to get out of her what she could remember. The girl was actually a prostitute in Whitechapel. She'd been abducted off the street and taken to this flat in East Finchley. She said that a number of men had gang-raped her, held her down, did all sorts of things with her, and it was absolutely horrific. Two of the men who had been arrested were not prosecuted. We ended up with only one of them at the Old Bailey, but because we'd got all the evidence, and my statement was brilliant, he got put away for ten years.

Jane (H Div) 1990s

A beautiful young girl who was out clubbing in Central London got a cab home to Bethnal Green. She came out of the club and knew not to get a 'dodgy' cab, but she did get in what she described as 'a nice big, black car'. The driver stopped on route and raped her. She was devastated and I sat with her while waiting for a specially trained officer to arrive. We built up a rapport and the victim requested that I stay and deal with it. I tried to explain that I wasn't properly trained, but she began crying. Anyway, I worked with the SOIT Officer and we took a brilliantly detailed statement.

The car was stopped and the driver was arrested. However, he was a diplomat and could not be charged. It was one of the first times I really felt like the police had let someone down. The embassy sent him home in disgrace. A couple of weeks later I was called to the Superintendent's office and told that the diplomat had stepped off the plane at the airport and had been shot for bringing disgrace on his country. At least the girl knew she would never face him again.

Sam (P Div) 1990s

One Christmas Eve I was called to a horrific rape scene. There was blood everywhere. The victim, a young woman in her mid-twenties, had cuts to her chest and wrists, and a bite mark on her chest. She said she had been a victim of 'stranger-rape' where someone had broken in through the back door. She had been taken to one of the rape suites which we had then, but something didn't ring true and there was some doubt in my mind. There was no evidence other than the crime scene, the blood and the bite mark. And there was one thing . . . she wouldn't come in for the bite mark to be photographed. Then it came out that her boyfriend had left her in the days leading up to this.

Eventually, it was looking at her injuries that gave her away. I met her and put it to her. It took a bit of time, but she eventually admitted that she'd very carefully and convincingly staged the whole scene. She'd cut herself on her chest and she'd bitten herself; she'd cut her wrists and had used her menstrual blood to smear round the scene. She had no history of mental health issues but was unhappy coming up to Christmas and wanted her boyfriend back.

Operation Minstead was the investigation into a series of horrendous rapes on elderly women in South London. I was still at Catford when it started in the mid-1990s, but it was ages before the man got arrested. I remember meeting one of the ladies who had survived but had some terrible internal injuries. These women were all so elderly. His first victim was a ninety-year-old lady who lived with her sister. He would case their houses and disable their lighting by removing the light bulbs; it makes you go cold thinking about it. One of the ladies said she had not had relations with a man since her husband died in the war, until this guy breaks in and rapes her. But she still said, 'I am not moving out of my house.'

As part of that enquiry I had to visit someone in the sex offenders' wing of a prison. His MO [modus operandi] was identical, although I knew he could not have committed these offences because he was in prison. However, I spent a day talking with him, getting the mindset. He spoke quite freely, and I couldn't believe what he was telling me. He had done exactly the same thing: going round casing old people's homes, breaking in and removing light bulbs so they couldn't see him. He would go in and ask them where their money and jewellery was. If they lied to him, even though he'd already searched the premises and already knew where these items were, he'd rape them. He was just so matter-of-fact about it, it was horrible. He'd started off as a 'peeping tom', and blamed it on the fact that he was raised by his mother without a father figure. He was quite personable, and telling it like there was no problem with it.

We had the offender's DNA but had nothing to compare it with. It was the biggest operation in London at the time and we weren't getting anywhere until they had a massive push, putting lots of police officers out there and he was finally caught. It turned out he was a married man with kids.

Caroline (T Div) 2000s

As Custody Sergeant at Heathrow I accepted a prisoner to be booked into the rape-evidence suite. As he walked in and I looked at him, I felt a chill. I can honestly say I immediately thought he was pure evil. He had been found hiding, naked, in his loft in his council house in West Drayton. I booked him in and eventually charged him with six counts of rape, holding charges as he was being investigated for other offences. That man was Levi Belfield who has murdered at least four girls, including Millie Dowler: a truly evil man who hated women.

Debbie (Y Div) 2000s

A new ethos arose nationally to deal with rape. It felt good to be part of something new to support women and vulnerable children in response to the woeful detection and conviction rate for rape offences. That was at a time when the Met became obsessed with performance data.

Ever since its inception, the new Sapphire Units have found it hard to recruit experienced detectives. I think it's not seen as 'sexy' policing by the male detectives, especially those who are seen as the best 'thief-takers'. The units have often been staffed by female officers, along with male officers who have child care commitments. At one time more than half their staff were flexible or part-time workers. Good detectives, of course, but it does mean that investigations are fragmented and passed from one detective to another.

I have a good friend who has just left a Sapphire Unit as a Detective Sergeant. She is a part-time officer who was supposed to job share, but she says that didn't happen. She could be supervising anything from 60 to 120 rapes, and all but one of her team was part-time.

Detective Constables carry about fifteen rape crimes each: is it any wonder that mistakes get made in the investigation? The investigating officers and officers specially trained in dealing with sexual offences are burnt out, exhausted. Sickness and stress levels are sky-high. The Met is now hundreds of detectives short because no one sees the CID as an attractive career. How did they get themselves in this mess?

I dealt with two rape complaints which highlight some of the difficulties in this kind of investigation. The first involved the rape of an African woman, and highlights the problems of investigating crime in London when the persons concerned are from diverse communities around the world.

The woman lived in a multi-occupancy house and, while her husband was out, a man from the Ivory Coast raped her. She told her husband and reported it to police. Neither of them spoke any English, and when the suspect was arrested we found that he could not speak English either. Through interpreters we learned the victim's story and heard that the suspect was denying having intercourse with her. After swabs had been examined for forensic evidence he was eventually charged with rape.

The Old Bailey court case was a logistical nightmare with the need for interpreters. One of the dialects spoken has very few interpreters in England. The suspect then claimed he had lied about having had intercourse purely because he did not understand the law in the UK and had been scared. He was found to have been arrested before, and was sentenced to ten years' imprisonment and deported. The victim was delighted with British Justice.

I was the investigating officer for another case involving the alleged rape of a prostitute. At 5 a.m. uniform police were called by a milkman who had been doing his early delivery. A young woman had come running and screaming out of a nearby house claiming she had been raped and nearly murdered. She was half-dressed, barefoot and her clothing was torn. She had bruising on her throat and petechial haemorrhaging in her eyes. She pointed out the ground-floor flat she had escaped from.

She was immediately taken to a rape suite and forensically examined. She explained that she was a prostitute who had picked up the male and agreed to have sex with him for £15. She had willingly gone back to his flat where they had consensual sex with a condom, which she had put in the kitchen bin. She began to get dressed. She said that the male then wanted to have sex again, without a condom, but she refused. She told officers that he got angry and punched her. He ripped her clothes off, tearing her knickers and top. He put his hands around her throat and began to choke her. She could not breathe and thought she was going to die. She passed out unconscious. She came to, to find him on top of her, having sex with her. Scared for her life, she said that she pretended to still be unconscious. He ejaculated inside her and went to the bathroom. She quickly ran out of the house, straight into the arms of the milkman.

Officers arrested the man who was interviewed, but admitted only that they had consensual sex and that she had agreed to sex without a condom. We searched the flat and found the first condom in the bin exactly as she had described. Her boots, tights and coat were still in the flat. Because of the apparent wealth of evidence, including her injuries, the state of her clothing, and the forensic evidence, he was immediately charged with rape.

The suspect was a foreign national and Interpol confirmed he had a criminal record in his home country. He was kept in police custody to appear at Highgate Magistrates' Court the following morning with a recommendation that he was *not* a suitable person to be granted bail, and should be kept in custody. The bench of magistrates, in their wisdom, granted him unconditional bail. Guess what? He left the UK.

Ten years later, he was stopped on a routine vehicle matter and the 'fail to appear warrant' was discovered. He was arrested and, this time, was kept in custody. We managed to find the woman, who was determined that he should face justice for his alleged crime. Unfortunately the milkman – our witness who could give evidence of early complaint – had by then, sadly, died.

The trial went ahead at a Crown Court with the lowest conviction rate in the country. Not a good start.

The defence tried to exclude the evidence of the milkman. In circumstances such as these, when a key witness has died, the court has the discretion to allow their evidence to be read. They did this . . . but a 'read' witness report is never as impactful as a 'live' witness giving evidence. The woman gave her evidence well, but defence counsel made a big deal out of her 'profession', her drug abuse, and the fact that she had consented to sex the first time. The defendant said he had only left the country because of a family problem and didn't know he should have stayed. He wasn't running away; he thought the matter had gone away because she was a prostitute.

The trial lasted a week and at the end produced a hung jury. A retrial was considered but the Crown Prosecution Service, taking all factors into consideration, decided a retrial was not appropriate. He was acquitted on the direction of the judge.

Jane (A Div) 2000s

About 2009/10 I took promotion and went to what is now the Specialist Crime Directorate as Detective Chief Inspector but for sexual offences. I covered the South East Area operationally for sexual offences and was based at Lewisham. I had Greenwich and Bexley, Lewisham and Southwark. I found they hadn't calculated just how many offences there were going to be; it was just a phenomenal workload. My job was hands-off. It was about the reviews: reviews of high-profile cases or those where there were a number of victims.

There was a lot of gang stuff in Southwark. It was interesting to see how some of the young girls' attitude to being victims wasn't what I had expected. If I had been a victim of rape I would have been horrified, my mother and father would have been horrified, but we had girls who weren't being supported by mothers or parents and their approach to it was just not as horrified as I would expect someone to be. I think it was an attitude in schoolchildren, and also how they were being used in gangs as part of an initiation and things involving girls and having sex with them. Or you'd rape a girl belonging to another gang sort of stuff. I had a victim of multiple oral rape and, the comments she made were not what I expected. I thought she'd be more traumatised but, as we know, everyone deals with things in their own way. So maybe it was just her way of dealing with it. But I was just quite surprised at some of the attitudes really.

I then went over to dealing with 'havens', medical examination suites attached to designated hospitals and dedicated to the care of victims of serious sexual assault. That meant working in close partnership with the NHS. It's always difficult when you've got two different organisations working at different speeds, but I think we genuinely wanted to get to the right place together. That was having access to all communities, and all communities having access to the services we could provide. We really worked hard together to improve the service in the Met, on the NHS side and our side, and I think we made some significant inroads.

Mary (Dedicated Rape Unit) 2000s

I had eight suspects in custody for rape. I was going round asking each suspect if they would consent to intimate samples being taken. One obliging man responded, 'Sure luv, do you want me to knock one out now?' I thanked him and then explained how samples were traditionally taken.

Jacqui (East Area Safeguarding Hub) 2010s

I work in the East Area Safeguarding Hub, which covers the Child Protection Team and the Community Safety Unit as well as the Rape Unit.

I have dealt with many rapes, but two in particular have stayed with me. The first was a rape on an eleven-year-old girl, and the other a rape of an elderly lady.

This young girl had just started at senior school from where she caught the bus home every afternoon at 3 p.m. On this particular day she noticed a man had been looking at her on the bus. When she got off she realised she was being followed. She kept crossing the road, back and forth to avoid him. When she crossed the last time it was by the park near her home.

That was where he dragged her into the park and raped her. It was a cold September day and he kept her there, naked in the freezing cold, for several hours.

I was on night duty and went to the hospital in South London where she had been taken. I spoke to one of the doctors when he came out to see me and I said, 'I know you're busy, doctor, but can I talk to you? I just need some background because I'm obviously not going to talk to this child today.' And he asked me, 'Have you had children?' I answered, 'Yes'. He said, 'That child had twenty-two stitches.' I dropped to the floor; that really got to me. She was a naïve eleven-year-old child from a close, loving family. When you looked at her she looked about nine, she was tiny.

Because it was so bad our Detective Inspector went straight on to be interviewed on the BBC News. This happened on a Friday and the rapist was found on the following Wednesday. The effort put into that was huge. He was picked up on CCTV on the bus, and her blood was found on various items of his clothing. I interviewed her on a video recording that was presented at court. I'd never really done an interview as intense as that. It took about four hours to get very little from her. That was horrible.

The case went to the Old Bailey and he was found guilty. This is one of the jobs I took home with me in my heart. I couldn't sleep for days. I didn't look at her as a victim, I looked at her as my child.

The second case was of a deaf, elderly lady of eighty-three who was bedridden and living in a care home. Somebody was able to go in there during the day and rape her. The sheltered accommodation where she lived was a place where people had varying degrees of disability; she shouldn't really have been there, but when you have no family and no voice, you have no choice. The doors that opened were designed to allow wheelchair access. As a result they closed slowly, allowing a lot of vagrants and drunks to hang around inside because they could get in. This was a random, opportunistic attack.

The elderly lady was a virgin. He couldn't fully penetrate her, but where he had been holding her she was so frail that the bruising on her body was shocking to see.

The staff nurse and the doctors at the hospital were crying; everyone who saw her was crying. She was the height of a seven-year-old.

Trying to get her account of what had happened was difficult as, owing to her age, she didn't use the sign language that was current at the time. The person who interpreted for us was really good, but the old lady wanted to talk about things that had happened in the past. It was awful. She was in shock.

The suspect, although we didn't know it was him at the time, presented himself as a significant witness. He came to the station, describing somebody he claimed to have seen. His description was of somebody of a different ethnicity from his own. As the officer asked his name, I looked at him and said, 'It's him.' He goes, 'It's not him,' and I said, 'I'm telling you, it's him.'

It's really bizarre. It was his eyes, the way his eyes were moving; he just looked suspicious. We found that the name this man had given wasn't his own. We got his DNA which we matched to DNA found in her room. He was twenty-two years old, of slight build, and he looked childlike.

He was convicted at Wood Green Crown Court. I thought it would kill the lady concerned, but I'm happy to say she's still alive and kicking today.

13

THE TRUTH, THE WHOLE TRUTH, AND NOTHING BUT THE TRUTH

Giving evidence in court can be an ordeal for any police officer. One occasion that still sticks in my mind is the case in which some colleagues tried to get me to change my account of what I had seen during an arrest. The case involved an assault on a woman police sergeant. I was in a CID 'nondescript car' one late turn when the CID officers and my woman sergeant who were with me stopped the car to question a man. The next thing I knew, she cried out . . . and the man ran off down the road. The sergeant was holding her hands in pain and my colleagues told me that the suspect had bent her fingers back in order to get away.

We started searching and I spotted him soon afterwards. The crafty devil had doubled back and, instead of running away, was sauntering casually towards us with his coat slung over his shoulder. I shouted, 'That's him!' This time he didn't try to flee but instead claimed that we had the wrong man: we all knew it was him.

As we wrote up our notes in the canteen it was suggested that I must have seen the prisoner bend the female sergeant's fingers back. I said that I hadn't seen it and couldn't write that I had. I was not popular . . . but I was adamant. Later, outside the court room, there was another attempt to change my mind and encourage me to testify that I had seen the incident. I declined. I couldn't lie in court, under oath – I couldn't and I wouldn't.

I duly gave my evidence, sticking strictly to the truth that I had not witnessed the actual finger-bending assault. In his summing up the judge stressed his belief that the case had been strengthened by the fact that we had not all said exactly the same thing. The accused man was found guilty, I was vindicated . . . and the judge commended me on the way I'd presented my evidence.

Jenny

Daisy (E Div) 1950s

I loved the work at Clerkenwell Magistrates' Court. My first 'care or protection' case started there one afternoon when I found two little children aged three and five who had been abandoned by their mother. They couldn't tell us where they lived, but it turned out they lived in a block of flats off Farringdon Road. A PC and I broke into the flat and I remember him saying, 'Don't switch on the light.' He was worried that the mother might have put her head in the gas oven and any electrical spark could cause an explosion. However, she wasn't there and the conditions they lived in were dreadful. There was no food at all and not enough bedclothes to keep them warm. The case went to Juvenile Court and was proved. It was three weeks before the mother was found and brought back to the Magistrates' Court.

There were times when we acted as matron in the cells at the court and one day I was in charge of a woman who had been before the court and had been remanded to Holloway. She persistently called to ask what would happen to her when she got to Holloway. I told her that she would have to have a bath and change out of her private clothes into prison-issue clothing. After several times of being told this, she said, 'Well, I had better tell you . . . I'm a man!'

Shirley (Z Div) 1950s

Croydon Juvenile Court has beautiful wooden panelling. I was Custody Officer when the decision was made to send a girl to an approved school. She raced around the courtroom trying to escape, but met me. We ended up slammed against the panelling. She was escorted to the detention room. When I returned to the court to retrieve my hat, the chairman of the bench called out to me, 'Is the panelling all right, officer?'

Marion (C Div) 1960s

A PC arrested a woman suspected of having drugs in her possession and I was told to help the PC by searching her. She became violent and abusive and we fell to the floor in a heap. I ended up astride her middle, with her head behind me, while the PC was holding her legs. She sat up . . . and bit my bum. It hurt!

She didn't have any drugs on her, so they had nothing with which to charge her other than an assault on police. That meant I had to go to court the next day in full uniform with the PC. Thankfully, she pleaded guilty. The magistrate then asked the PC, 'What was the nature of the assault?' He replied, 'The prisoner bit the WPC on the posterior while she was being searched.' The whole court fell about laughing. I beat a hasty retreat out the door.

Terri (H Div) 1960s

I arrested a huge man down at the Tower of London for some sort of disturbance. Having locked him in the police box and got transport for him, we duly went off to court in the morning. He then told the whole court I had hit him! The magistrate peered over his glasses and said in a very loud voice, 'My man, she would not have reached to your knees. You are guilty and will be fined ten shillings.'

Diana (H Div) 1960s

Hostels for the homeless would turn women out of the building at 9 a.m. During the cold months I would ask the meths drinkers and other down-and-outs if they would like to go to court and then to Holloway Prison for warmth. It was one month for being drunk, or three months for 'drunk and disorderly'. I didn't feel it was an abuse of the system; the local bomb-sites were no places to be.

Annie (E Div) 1970s

I had high arrest figures because I was particularly good at both detecting odd behaviour and remembering vehicle index numbers. In giving evidence in court, I found that juries were generally more ready to believe evidence given by a female officer. They did not associate us with *not* telling the truth, and it was a barrister's mistake to try and attack you in court; the jury did not respond well to that. The magistrates used to call you, 'My officer,' back then, which was endearing.

Eve (C Div) 1970s

Marlborough Street was a fun court and the main magistrate, St John Harmsworth, loved his WPCs. I remember attending to give evidence in civvies as I had been on 'shoplifter duty'. I was wearing a rather grand, bowler-type hat and Mr Harmsworth passed a note down to me asking where my horse was? He also took a dim view of prisoners assaulting 'his' WPCs and would hand out a sentence with that smile on his face, which we all knew meant that he had found the accused 'guilty'.

Another WPC, Kathy and I, arrested three men trying to con tourists with the 'three card trick' scam. We had to sneak along Shaftesbury Avenue without their lookouts spotting us. Then we slipped into the rear entrance of the Playland slot machine arcade. When we emerged from the front entrance on Piccadilly Circus we caught the men red-handed.

They were so surprised to be caught by us that they came quietly to be charged. I remember us walking up Regent Street with our nicked bodies and their manager saying, '£10 and a body to plead in court.' We said, 'No.' The manager wanted us to swap his best men, the ones we had arrested, for another to go to court in their place. He persisted. '£20 and a body to plead . . . £30 . . . £40.' In the end one of us told him, 'if you get to £50 – you are nicked!'

That was big money in our day, which just shows how much the gamers made. When we were in court, many of their 'friends' had come to see who had caught them. Mr Harmsworth peered over his glasses and they were fined, and probably shamed at being caught out by us.

Bow Street Magistrates' Court is one that always makes me laugh because I was required to give evidence on my day off. Being rather immature and stroppy at the time, I decided that if I had to go on my day off, then, I was not going to wear uniform. I would go in civvies! I wore green suede hot pants and a yellow and orange, sleeveless T-shirt . . . and to finish off, flip-flops. Because the case was adjourned I was never called to give evidence . . . but was I in trouble the next day. Ma'am Reid, our Inspector, called me into her office to tear a strip off me. 'How dare you go to our Queen's Court dressed like that?' Ah, well . . . it's been an enduring story and one that I am reminded about by several of my friends.

Sandra (F Div) 1970s

I will always remember one female shoplifter. Her husband, a very wealthy man, told me she was a kleptomaniac and had terminal cancer with only about six months to live. She obviously didn't need to steal, but it was her illness. Well, I sent off for her file, which was so thick it was almost too heavy to hold. The poor woman had been in and out of prison for most of her life. She even had one sentence with 'hard labour', but still she couldn't stop – I'll be honest, I cried when I saw that. I can still see her face vividly in my mind's eye, even though it was over fifty years ago. She was so sweet . . . and she was dying. I really spoke up for her in court and the magistrate agreed and gave her a conditional discharge.

Kim (R Div) 1980s

There was a London magistrate who would stare at our boobs every time a WPC went into his chambers to give evidence for a warrant. I got my own back one day by staring at his crotch. He smirked . . . and I never had the boob stare again.

Jane (H Div) 1980s

When I was a probationer my warrant card was stolen in a night club. The case went to court and the defence barrister tried to make it seem like I was a drunk 'party girl' and had merely lost it. At this time, women police officers had to wear hats in court, and I was wearing mine. He asked me to remove my hat in order to help the jury visualise what a party girl I would look like when out of uniform. I was nervous and a bit sweaty as I removed my hat . . . to show a hairstyle which Ken Dodd would have been proud of. The barrister literally 'harrumphed' and told me to put it back on. Definitely not the bimbo look he thought I'd display. I had a judge's commendation for that case. He commended me for my professionalism (which was nice to get after the Ken Dodd impression).

Mary (P Div) 1990s

A Detective Constable and I were all that was left of a team on a case in which Robert Napper had been charged with two murders and a series of rapes. It was left to the DC and I to take him to court. We decided that the male PC would drive the van . . . while I would be handcuffed to this killer-rapist, Napper, in the back. I can't think who, if anyone, did a risk assessment . . . but I lived to tell the tale.

I once gave evidence in No 1 Court at the Old Bailey. It was a case of 'Arson with Intent to Endanger Life' and 'Indecent Assault'. I was the victim of the assault, as he grabbed my breast just before arrest. I was awarded £100 . . . which was not enough compensation for all the ribbing I got after the case appeared in the papers.

Sam (P Div) 1990s

I've been at court a lot: long trials, good baddies, clever barristers, but normally very successful for us. I once took a guy called Guy Fawkes to court. He'd changed his name by deed poll. I can't remember what I nicked him for, but I bailed him to court for November the 5th. Oh yes.

Jane (SCD2) 2000s

A woman sex worker was raped in her flat by a 6' male who demanded her bank card and pin number so that he could take money from her bank account. The attacker prevented her getting access to her phone and left for a while to get the money. She was Brazilian and she tried to alert passers-by by writing the Portuguese word for 'HELP' on a beer mat and placing it in her window behind the curtain. Then she managed to raise the alarm anyway, and the attacker was arrested when he returned.

In interview he denied raping her and gave a plausible account. Though we had seen the beer mat, the significance of it being covered in what just looked like blue scrawl had been missed. Once we understood its importance, we obviously returned and located the beer mat to strengthen the evidence against him. He was duly charged.

In court, the lady was just the best witness. She would answer the barristers' questions, then place her hands on the witness box, lean forward and repeat it all again for the elderly judge who was hard of hearing. The jury unanimously found the accused guilty. There is nothing better than conducting a good investigation with a successful outcome. As we left court the defence barrister said to us that if she ever needed help she would ask for me and my colleague to undertake the case. Praise indeed.

14

WOMEN – OF NO
VALUE TO THE CID

*As a WPC in the 1970s I did not meet any women
detectives: not a single one. I felt that the detectives I
did meet gave short shrift to women officers in
general. My CID attachment during my probation-
ary period did not alter that view.*

*I cannot make a judgement about all CID officers,
of course, but the ones I met seemed typical of that
era. It was a time when CID officers were fond of
saying, 'To catch a villain you have to think like a
villain.'*

*Well . . . they certainly drank like them. The pubs
of the East End were alive with villains such as the
Kray twins, and CID officers drank and socialised
with them in those same pubs. I spent most of my
attachment in the pub and, as a non-drinker, I was
bored sideways. My opinion of the CID did, however,
change over time.*

When I later returned to the Met as a Scenes of Crime Officer I found that detectives from the 1980s onwards were dedicated, intelligent . . . and totally accepting of women in the police. For many years, women detectives had been thought of as only capable of taking statements; the ones I had the privilege to work with, in all areas of CID investigations, more than proved their worth.

Jenny

'*Women police are of no value to the CID. I am not concerned with welfare work or the work of women police per se. I am only referring to criminal investigation. They should be employed in taking statements from persons of tender age in cases of sexual offences. If the CID requires the services of women they can obtain them from other branches of the Force.*'

John Savage (Detective Superintendent) 1920s
Metropolitan Police Archives

Maureen (V Div) 1950s

In the March of 1950 I went to Tooting as the only woman in the CID, covering the ten stations there. Miss Etridge, our Superintendent, was in charge of CID and she used to have a meeting every month where we all sat in a circle and she discussed issues.

There was nothing of any real interest in the eleven years I did in the CID. I used to get there at 8.30 a.m. and I'd see what they'd got. I'd go out and take statements for indecent assaults and things like that, also Care and Protection cases.

I dealt with shoplifters and that sort of thing. If a man brought in a female shoplifter, they'd say, 'Come and deal with it.' I would usually be the officer dealing with 'Care' cases, but never if a man was the prisoner . . . no, I don't think I ever did. I had no aspirations. I was quite happy to jog along doing what I was doing.

Jan (RCS) 1960s

I was one of the first ten WDCs posted to the Regional Crime Squads based near Orpington. It was a special time for me. I was still quite a junior WDC but doing lots of observations and dealing with larger crimes, rather than local burglaries. On one occasion I was 'tailing' a lady in my own car, which had been fitted with a police radio. She realised that she was being followed, stopped her car and challenged me. She mistakenly thought I was a private detective employed by her husband to check on her movements! Had I thought on my feet a bit quicker, I would have gone along with it and let her go on thinking that . . . but I didn't.

In 1966 I was transferred to the enquiry into the activities of the Kray twins. I took part in the initial 'hit' at 5 a.m., and then spent a year on witness protection duties while the whole Kray job was being prepared. There were two of us with the witness all of the time, sleeping at the address and working twenty-four hours on and then twenty-four hours off. The male officer was armed. I did more than one witness in the Kray case, including one of the leading witnesses from the Blind Beggar pub. I'm not sure that the police ever really thought that someone would attack her, as they were confident that they had broken the gang. It was more about making her feel safe as her testimony was vital to the conviction and she was very scared. She had three small children and had been threatened already.

I also looked after another witness in the Richardson trial (the south London gang). She was a high-class escort and knew quite a few bad people. She was being hidden in a hotel in

Hertfordshire for months. There were just two of us minding her, one on-duty and one off-duty. We spent our days driving around the countryside, playing Scrabble and reading. We slept in the hotel, charged all our expenses and no one seemed to mind. It must have cost the Met thousands.

Another time, they rented a really nice house in Walton-on-Thames and hid a witness there. Again there were two officers on duty (male and female) all the time. She had expensive tastes in restaurants, and sometimes we even had to make secret assignations with her boyfriend. Those were the days, eh? Wonder if such things still go on?

Annie (M Div) 1980s

I worked on the *Marchioness* enquiry, where the boat was struck on the Thames and more than fifty young people lost their lives; heartbreaking, especially being part of the team identifying the bodies and liaising with the relatives. I met Princess Di at the memorial service and she chatted to us for about ten minutes . . . stunning.

While dealing with the death of a young man who had jumped from the twenty-fifth floor, we had the Fire Brigade cooking bacon-and-egg sandwiches from their mobile canteen while we were collecting body parts. It was raining, and as Detective Inspector I was there in charge. I had requested the Fire Brigade to flush the body parts out of a nearby tree. Suddenly I heard a thud on the top of my umbrella . . . you can imagine the horror as I looked up.

Sam (P Div) 1990s

I did two years in uniform and applied for the Crime Squad at the end of my probation. I had a great time. It was fun, the blokes were great, there was definitely no issue with you being female . . . you had to prove yourself . . . but so did the men. The Crime Squad was your testing ground; you had to prove you could go out and find your prisoners and do your early detecting stuff. It didn't matter whether you were male or female, if you wanted to go onto the next rung (the trainee investigator in the CID office) you had to prove yourself on the Crime Squad first.

I'm not sure what sent me down the detective route but it worked really well for me. I went to work in a new unit set up for Serious and Organised Crime. It had only been going for a couple of years and was very covert. We were trying different techniques for dealing with top-level baddies. It was interesting work, so I stayed there for ages. I loved it and stayed a Detective Constable for about eighteen years, because I knew if I took promotion I'd have to leave.

Sally (RCS) 1990s

I was involved in what was then the world's largest seizure of crack cocaine. In the course of a long inquiry, we saw suspects dumping some stuff in a wastepaper bin near Hyde Park. We retrieved bicarbonate of soda paper wrappings from the bin. Bicarb is used as a 'cutting agent' for drugs, and we thought, 'OK, something's happening,' so we hit the address. They were cooking up their crack cocaine. Great triangles, looking like they'd been cut from massive cheeses, were all laid drying in this room.

Debbie (Y Div) 1990s

I don't think there was a day of my thirty-one years' service when I didn't laugh out loud.

I worked with some very funny people. That was the counterbalance to some of the horrific and dreadful things we had to deal with. There was a newly promoted Detective Sergeant on a local Robbery Squad team who needed taking down a peg or two. One evening two young DCs from the same robbery team emptied the sergeant's 'pod' (the portable drawers) from under his desk. They tacked a heavy-duty bin liner to the inside of the drawer, filled it with water and several fish. In the morning the DS found a 'fish tank' in his desk drawers.

Dee (Q Div) 2000s

The male was naked, on his back in his front room with a knife stuck in his chest, and obviously dead. I was called to the scene as the on-call detective. It seemed pretty clear to me what had happened. His housemate was upstairs and stated he had heard a bang. We took him to the station as a significant witness and began interviewing him. In my mind and my partner's mind we were thinking that he was our suspect; he had stabbed the victim.

In the middle of the interview I got a call from the scene examiner telling me that the dead man had taken his own life! He later told me that I had replied: 'Sorry . . . what . . . suicide?'

The scene examiner had found a dent on the wall which measured the same height as the wound. Being naked was also a clue. I learnt that a lot of suicides are naked as the person does not want to cause the trouble of dealing with the clothes. It just goes to show. I will always remember that call.

Louise (J Div) 2000s

We had a detective who was the most chauvinistic arse of a man I'd ever known. He wouldn't even acknowledge me. I was as highly trained in firearms as him, but he wouldn't let me do any of the big jobs. I'm not renowned for keeping my gob shut and keeping my opinions to myself, so I went to the Chief Super and complained about him. He said to sort it between ourselves, so I did. I called him a very bad swear word, told him what I thought and said others thought the same. I sat him down and gave him some home truths; and other than calling me 'love', after that, which was better than ignoring me, he behaved himself. He'd been bullying women all his service and I stood up for myself and the other women. I don't think he was used to a gobby, ginger bird from Essex fronting him out, calling him some quite strong swear words.

15

CHRIST – IT'S A WOMAN

*As a WPC, I knew that some of my male colleagues
were a little jealous of those in the Met's more
specialised squads – the officers tackling the hardened criminals: terrorists, safe-crackers, armed
robbers, mobsters and all-round 'baddies'.*

*Those on squads such as the Special Branch, or
C11 Criminal Intelligence, appeared somehow to
be charismatic figures who were held in high
regard.*

*They were also squads where the gender divide
seemed less important than it was in general policing. When it came to tackling violent and ruthless
criminals such as gang leaders Ronnie and Reggie
Kray, the question was not, 'Are you a man?' or,
'Are you a woman?' but 'Are you any good?'*

Jenny

Margaret (Special Branch) 1960s

I was in Special Branch and loved it. We could do anything because there was no difference between men and women. There was no sexism there, and one of my former colleagues is now a Commander. I was working seven days a week and I bloody loved it, it was so exciting. Our normal hours were 10 a.m. to 6 p.m., but we were only allowed to go home when the Home Office said we could go. If there was a shout at 6 p.m. then we had to wait. If there was some crisis going on, usually something to do with the IRA, then we stayed on into the evenings. On weekends we were often in 'mufti' [civilian clothing] in the crowds at demonstrations.

It was the love of my life, but my husband wanted me to leave because I worked such long hours. He hated it and made my life hell, so I agreed to leave. It made me really unhappy.

Gina (Criminal Intelligence – C11) 1980s

C11 basically gather intelligence on the most serious criminals in the UK. I worked with them ... before the days of computers, I hasten to add. When I joined C11 our priority was investigating the kidnap of any British citizen, or of anybody kidnapped on British soil. In a kidnap situation you go from one scene to another to another and you don't know what to expect; so it's really, really important that we are highly trained in surveillance techniques. We were set up after the kidnapping and death of seventeen-year-old Lesley Whittle. It was thought that there had been infighting about sharing information between different constabularies in the case, so there should be a central department to deal with kidnaps all over the country. We were trained 'in-house', but there were lots of other courses that we did, run by other government departments.

As well as kidnapping, we dealt with 'Demands' such as the supermarket case where they were having baby food poisoned and money was being demanded: that was a C11 job. Nobody's life was under immediate threat but it was a 'Demand', so C11 became involved.

I was involved in the case of the theft, for the third time, from Dulwich Gallery, of a beautiful Rembrandt painting of a Dutchman called Jacob de Gheyn. It was a tiny little painting but was worth millions. It was like a kidnap of a painting with the insurance company held to ransom. An overseas person masterminded it. We followed that person and another guy, to a stately home where I saw them looking at their watches and thought, 'What are they doing that for?' They were looking at their watch . . . chatting . . . looking at their watch . . . looking very interested in a picture, which was also worth millions . . . and then the hand went up . . . and back at the watch. They were timing everything. They'd sussed out where all the security was in this stately home before hotfooting it to their car and back to London.

The same two guys were eventually arrested in the back of a cab. They had the de Gheyn painting with them and were on the way to get some money for it when we ambushed the cab. In the kerfuffle I saw this striped pillowcase sliding along the floor. I thought, 'Shit . . . it's the painting!' They'd obviously tried to sling it before getting arrested. I had this painting in my hand . . . really exciting. We were there to make sure loose ends were dealt with while other people made the arrests. We had to stay out of the limelight because we don't want to be seen at court. Our evidence was mostly given as transcripts rather than from us attending court. Once we're seen we're wasted, because next time someone was kidnapped we'd have no officers to deal with it.

I loved working in C11, my team were great, supportive and we knew we could trust each other; but when a surveillance operation went wrong . . . and I was shot at . . . I knew I had to leave. I believed that our armed back-up had let us down and no longer trusted others outside of my squad. It was in September 1985. I was called at home about midnight to take part in a stake out on a getaway car in Brentwood. It was part of a million-pound robbery. It was a Flying Squad job and so we were a bit suspicious because we were only ever called out to armed robberies when something had been cocked up. We didn't know when or where the robbery was taking place; what we did know was the location of the getaway car.

Anyway, we did our normal thing: we'd go in an observation vehicle and take it in turns, a couple of hours each, to watch the vehicle. Our brief was to follow the getaway vehicle until it met up or, basically, until it got somewhere where the Flying Squad would be able to go in and make the arrests. None of us wanted to be armed, so we were always told that if we were going out on armed jobs we would have armed back-up. You can't be a specialist in everything, and at the end of the day our specialism was safe surveillance. Somebody else would come along and be our armed back-up.

I was first in on watching this vehicle. I was on my own in the back of a little van but at about 9.30 a.m. I needed a break. It's very hard for a woman to pee in the vans. So another vehicle took my place and I was driven off to have a cup of tea. A little later I heard sirens going through Brentwood, and we wondered if it had anything to do with what we were doing. We heard nothing for a while, and the next thing we knew a message was coming over the air saying, 'All units stand by . . . Oh shit, there's two vehicles. We've got about five blokes with "goody bags".' That was our codeword for bag of guns. The men were all laughing, clearly happy with themselves. The vehicle that we knew was the getaway vehicle had a tracker on it so we knew that was going to be OK, but we didn't have a tracker on the other vehicle that we hadn't known about. We weren't really set up to follow two vehicles . . . but we'd do our best.

When we turned a bend we were faced with a road block and, as we braked, these van doors flew open and masked, armed blokes jumped out. One of them came running towards me with an automatic rifle. You sort of register it's happening but it's like it's happening in slow motion, but you're actually reacting incredibly quickly. As he came towards me, I just knew from his body language my end had come. As he opened the door I'd managed to crouch down into the footwell to try to get behind the engine block so if bullets were going off I'd got some protection. As luck would have it he hadn't realised I was female. He obviously saw my female bottom sticking up and he said, 'Christ, it's a woman.' It was like a split second. I was waiting for the gun to go off . . . I could see his shadow backing away from the central consul . . . I'd got one chance.

I don't quite know how I did it, but I uncurled and sprang out of the car, knocking him with the door as I got out. And I ran . . . but it was a country lane with hedges on both sides and I had nowhere to hide. I heard a gun go off and felt a bullet go through my hair. If I had been taking off, instead of landing on the run, it would have hit me in the back, it was that close. Anyway, coming loud over the earpiece I heard, 'Gina is running up the road like a little rabbit.' As soon as I heard that I felt that the best thing I could do was find somewhere to drop. I remember thinking, hedge, there must be a ditch, so I threw myself in that direction. But it wasn't a ditch, it was a bank. There was someone at the end of the road. Pandemonium broke out when he realised he hadn't shot me, and they tried to get away.

I was shocked as much as anything else. I was on the ground . . . eventually they piled back into the van and car and drove down and got to the Eastern Avenue. Everything started to get spaced out, but as luck would have it, by this stage the Flying Squad had managed to come along Eastern Avenue to the end of the road and had managed to ram them. At that point I was completely detached from it. We had to wait to be rescued, but I can't really remember. But I can remember going back to a police station and someone saying, 'Oh women don't stick this job very long anyway, they can't hack it.' And I just went. I don't know who they were, but I just remember thinking, 'How much fucking longer do I have to do? I've done thirteen years, how much longer do I have to do to prove a point?' That did it for me.

Later I had people saying, 'Oh the Commissioner wants to give you a commendation.' So? When you nearly lost your life it's totally irrelevant and totally stupid in my opinion, because actually they're putting sticking plaster on something that needs a lot more than that. And I ended up incredibly angry about the whole thing and completely mistrusting. I couldn't go back and work for the police after that. I wouldn't have trusted anyone. It wasn't just that incident, it was an accumulation of everything . . . and then when someone says to me, 'You can't hack it,' you know they have no idea what you've been through and they should keep their mouths shut. People are incredibly judgemental.

Pet (Criminal Intelligence – C11) 1980s

My girlfriend, who was in C11, said they wanted a black WPC because they had a black guy and they wanted a girl to partner him. I said, 'I can't, not with the kids.' So she said, 'I'll get an application.' She got it and I filled it in, not thinking in a million years I would get it. There were a few single black women by then, so I did have some competition.

I'm sitting there at the interview in front of a panel: little me and these three big males. I don't know what I said, but it was a cheeky reply apparently, and I was selected. I liked the people, I liked the sergeant, but it became impractical for travelling. I moved areas and the sergeant in charge there clearly didn't want a black girl on his team. He made my life a complete misery, giving me all the difficult positions we had to deal with. It was clear I was being pushed out. I resented it and I wasn't performing right, I knew that.

My intelligence gathering wasn't good, but you know when you're walking on eggshells, and you think, 'If you do this you're going to get criticised,' you don't work well. I was appalling and, quite frankly, ready to tell them to stick it and getting bitter inside. I knew I was going back to District, because my report wasn't very good. But three days before my report was due they announced we were going to do a kidnap exercise in East London. Well that day was the saving day. I couldn't believe I was doing so well, picking up a lot of intelligence, and realising, 'I can do this.'

Two days later I went to see the Chief Superintendent who said, 'I've read your report, and before that I've had a meeting with the senior officers who said the report didn't reflect the person who was working. As a result, we're taking you off that team and putting you on another team.'

It was amazing. I went on the team . . . I fitted in . . . I was gathering intelligence . . . it was brilliant, my happiest time. Had they not looked at this exercise I would have left a bitter person. Isn't that fantastic? Doesn't it work? I was still friends with some of the senior officers when I left.

C11 was dangerous. On my first day I was following a known murderer, gathering evidence for the Murder Squad. It was like something out of TV. We did surveillance and intelligence gathering. The guys used to tease us women saying, 'The only reason you get picked for C11 is because they want ugly people. If you're attractive, you'll stand out.' One of the main things is to dress down so you don't look memorable. You have to change your appearance. One time we followed a guy to a bus stop and one of our WPCs felt exposed as a white woman in quite a black area. As a result she came over to talk to me, which was the last thing she should have done. The guy we were following called out, 'You Cassack'; I'd never heard the word before, but later found out it meant 'police'. One of the things these guys are not is stupid; they can smell 'Old Bill'. I started talking Jamaican, making out I didn't know what he was shouting about . . . but he knew I was a police officer. I walked away but it was too late, the job was blown.

Our main role was Kidnap and 'Demand'. We dealt with the kidnap of a Jewish couple from their home in Golders Green. Their parents were wealthy business owners and were sent the cut finger of the husband as a sign they had him and would do worse if they didn't pay up. I was in the house of the kidnapped family with another officer. Our job was to stay in the house to preserve the evidence and watch if anyone came back.

In the early hours of the morning the kidnapped wife was left alive on a bridge. She was amazing; we would not have found her husband if they hadn't released her. The couple had been taken to a lock-up where they were kept in separate areas. It was her information that helped us locate the building. She was blindfolded, but remembered going over a bridge and remembered a clock. We worked day and night for two days and we were able to get him alive. There were two kidnappers; one of them was an ex-worker who had been sacked.

I had the best time in C11, and only left because of child care issues. I still loved the job.

Cheryl (SO6) 1990s–2010s

The bulk of my career was in surveillance. It was like a round peg dropping into a round hole on my course. I absolutely loved it, was top student and seemed to do really well for more than twenty-two years. I was never discriminated against or suffered sexist behaviour. In fact females on a surveillance team were highly valued. Girls on surveillance teams in the early days found it very difficult to balance family life if they were mums. The nature of the job was that you went to work in the morning and you had no clue where you would end up or what time you would finish. You could not tell subjects you were watching that you had to collect baby from nursery! Often we would find ourselves so far away that it turned into an overnighter.

A girl on my first surveillance team (who I am still very good friends with) had her baby and, were it not for her very flexible in-laws, could not have come back on the team. I remember her coming in one morning crying her eyes out because her mother-in-law had bought Ben his first pair of shoes and she had not even noticed that he needed them.

We were one person under-strength when a girl had two children in quick succession and was off for a long period. That definitely had an impact on others with regards to leave and so on. As I had no children myself, I was often called upon to start/finish extra-early/late. I think that part-time and flexible working on surveillance teams has come a long way since those days. I am all for equality and flexible/part-time working . . . as long as others do not suffer the impact of their choices.

Jane (Operation Paget) 2000s

I worked on Operation Paget, the investigation into allegations about a possible murder conspiracy surrounding the deaths of Diana, Princess of Wales and Dodi Fayed. It was a bit of a poisoned chalice, but it has to be one of the most interesting investigations that I've been involved in as a Detective Inspector. I was asked, 'Would you be interested, because we need a DI, and we could do with another female?' We had one other female, a Detective Constable, and a female office worker but, otherwise, yet again, it was a very male-dominated environment.

My role involved speaking to a lot of the princess's friends to try to get some insight into her, and to get their views. I was privileged to speak to some high-profile people. I got the opportunity to travel as well because they weren't all London-based, so I went to the States to see a few people with another officer. We went to France a lot of the time and liaised with the French police and that was great. I was French-speaking, which obviously proved very useful. There was some concern and anxiety to start with in France because they thought we were coming to review their investigation, but we weren't. They dealt with a traffic accident; we were looking at a possible conspiracy, so ours was a much wider investigation.

It was a thing that evolved and evolved. I don't think it was ever really meant to last as long as it did, or to be as wide-ranging, but thank goodness it was, because it did actually get to the bottom of it all and there was some really good investigation that went on with that.

We interviewed the pathologist and all sorts of people. It was fascinating just being able to disprove a lot of the theories, and to disprove them categorically. There were so many stories being put forward. I remember, for instance, a photograph of Henri Paul, who was the driver, with his face lit up, and with Diana and Dodi Fayed in the back. The story was that there was a bright light that flashed and disoriented him as they went into the tunnel. Actually the officers proved that the photograph had been taken outside the Ritz Hotel as the couple were leaving, and nowhere near the tunnel.

Do you know what? The stars just aligned on that day, and if any one of a lot of things hadn't been in there, it may not have happened. If they'd been wearing their seat belts, if Henri Paul was expecting to drive and obviously hadn't been drinking, if maybe the paparazzi . . . you know, I think he may have been revved up a little by the fact that there were paparazzi. There was supposed to have been some sort of comment like, 'Catch me if you can,' and so, you know, he may not have driven so fast. He'd actually had some training with Mercedes; he'd attended a one-day course in driving a Mercedes: that might have been a downfall as he thought he knew how to drive this, and then driving at speed. *All* these things sadly came together with all the other peripheral stuff. Were they going to get engaged? Was she pregnant? 'No' . . . she wasn't pregnant and 'Yes' . . . they were looking at rings.

There were just lots of things to consider. But it certainly *was* an accident.

Sam (Serious and Organised Crime – Proactive Projects Team) 2000s

Our remit is to deal with all serious crime from drugs and gun importation through to kidnaps and contract killings in the

Met, nationally, and internationally. So when we received intelligence that an Indian man was trying to get hold of a gun we took up the investigation. He was a cab driver and had been chatting to the people he worked with about wanting to bump off the husband of an Indian lady. She lived with her mother and father, a brother and her husband, and, for whatever reason he had decided to get rid of her husband.

I was in charge and decided we would do an infiltration operation using an undercover officer. The suspect had put the word out for a hit man, so he wouldn't be expecting an Asian. He met the undercover officer on several occasions and passed over a photo of the husband with a rundown of when the husband leaves the house and what car he had. They'd agree a price on how much it would cost to get the hit done, and then money would exchange hands. We'd be evidencing all this, and at the same time we'd be managing the risk for the family; do we tell them? Don't we tell them?

We didn't tell them.

By using the undercover officer we sort of had that under control and we were happy that he was only speaking to us. In the end he paid half the cost of the 'hit' which gave us the evidence; the cash going over. Then we mocked up the murder scene, which was the first time we told the family what was going on. We basically staged the crime scene at the family home and the undercover officer phoned our suspect and said he'd done it and the suspect's like, 'Great . . . Yeah.' Then he gets in his car and drives past to have a look, sees the crime scene, draws out the rest of the money and goes to pay the undercover officer. He then gets arrested for incitement to murder. He was found guilty at the Old Bailey. That worked particularly well, and that was really from just a throwaway comment about asking somebody for a gun.

Caroline (Special Escort Group) 2000s

I wanted to join the Special Escort Group but didn't think I was good enough to pass the fitness test. Typical woman: I'm saying to myself, 'I can't do that, I'm not any good at this.' Whereas I found with blokes they'd say, 'Oh I'll give it a go.'

But I took my sergeant's exam, and was posted to Heathrow where I had to go on a four-week Firearms course at Lippetts Hill. There were two girls on the course. The other was tiny and totally dwarfed in the body armour; I think it wrapped round her twice. We were just taught the Glock which was the handgun on that course. Then I did my five-day, MP5 machine-gun training at the range just up the road from Heathrow. Because I had my sights set on the SEG, I had a list and was ticking things off. I had three things which I hoped would get me through the paper sift: advanced driver, motorcyclist and the firearms qualification.

I was very proud when I passed the board to become the first-ever female sergeant in SEG. My team was superb, very supportive. I was the only female in the team of eight. We were all armed; everyone is armed in the SEG. We rode motorbikes and drove cars. Every vehicle was armed. Every officer was armed. As a sergeant and commander of the escort I sat in the back of the rear car.

The American President was over, and I was one of the motorcyclists. I was actually riding for a change, as opposed to being in the back-up car. Our job is to clear the route ahead of the cavalcade, riding on the wrong side of the road and stopping traffic, because the wheels on the escorted vehicle must keep turning. We'd all parked up neatly after the run, as the SEG do, standing there having a little debrief, and one of the American Special Agents came over. I had a blonde plait down my back because you can't have your hair in a bun with a crash helmet, but obviously he hadn't seen that because he came over and said, 'You guys, you guys ride. You've got balls.' And I just turned round and said, 'Thank you very much.' And he went, 'Oh Jeez ma'am, I'm so sorry.' Of course all the PCs fell about laughing. He was absolutely distraught that he'd said these things. The lads were beside themselves, and I'm saying, 'Oh thanks, thanks very much,' in a put-on, posh English accent.

Two Asian Muslims were arrested when they tried to blow up Glasgow airport with a car bomb but met a Glaswegian and got hit round the head with a fire extinguisher. One of them was a doctor who was being held at Paddington Green police station. I was the sergeant in charge of the firearms team sent to take him from Paddington Green to the Old Bailey. As such I was responsible for the prisoner. I'm all 'tooled-up', but you could see I'm a female. All my boys are outside, and we've got the police helicopter, 'India 99'.

I start signing for the prisoner when his solicitor, who didn't speak to me because I'm just a woman, spoke instead to the white, male sergeant. 'I'm sorry my client and I cannot deal with this officer, she's a woman.' The male sergeant looked at me and I looked at him, and he said, 'Over to you, Sarge.'

I turned to the terrorist and said, 'Right, this is going to sound really silly and old-fashioned but there are two ways you are coming out of this custody suite . . . both of them are with me. Either, you can get up and I will lead you out as I do with every other prisoner, or I will drag you out by your fucking balls.' And I turned to the solicitor and I said, 'And as for you . . . you can make your own way to court.' And the sergeant on the desk went, 'Everything all right?' and I said, 'Yes, fine. You ready?'

So I led our terrorist out and told the solicitor to make his own way. The armoured vehicle has a seat inside in a box so you can't see out the window, and the prisoner was shackled in. A Detective Constable gets in with him, and I said, 'Hold on tight.' I had assigned my driver that morning on parade. We never assign the driver the day before, just in case he or his family could be kidnapped and he might be made to drive a certain way in order for the escort to be ambushed and get the prisoner out. That day we went through a most long-winded, rather bumpy, route to the Old Bailey.

Sally (National Crime Squad) 2000s–2010s

One of the last jobs I dealt with was a massive money laundering job with thirty-eight prisoners. It was a long two-and-a-half-year operation to put together and took six months at Woolwich Crown Court. It also involved a member of the Fire Brigade who, when we hit his house had literally just come back at 4 a.m. having picked up 120 kilos of cocaine. We went in and there it was. He wasn't happy.

It was a massive job and also involved money laundering. Effectively this guy used to take the English money and change it up for 500 euro notes. English money was too bulky, and by changing it into 500 euro notes they could go from massive holdalls to shoeboxes. For that reason 500 euro notes are no longer available. There were various nationalities involved. They all got convicted. We took one of them to the Court of Appeal because his sentence wasn't high enough. He'd got ten years, and we said it should have been fourteen and that's what he got, along with extra time for the drugs as well. He was a forty-nine-year-old man going out with an eighteen-year-old girl, who was shouting, 'It's not fucking fair. He's my boyfriend. You can't do this.' And we said, 'Don't worry, love, when he comes out he'll be ninety, he'll be dying anyway.'

Caroline (Royalty Protection) 2000s–2010s

As a Close-Protection Officer I worked with The Queen, Princess Anne, Prince Andrew; most of the royal family actually. The Personal Protection Officer will walk behind the Principal and then the Close-Protection Officers will form a flexible ring of steel around them. Depending on where we were, one of us would be up there, one of us over there. But, if you're where perhaps the crowd might be more toxic, we'd be more up-close and personal.

It is very male-oriented – and this isn't sexism . . . it's fact. You're away from home a lot. A lot of the females who are in protection are either single or gay. Blokes come home, put the washing on, and their wife hangs it out. I had to do that myself. I'd come back and I'd be knackered but I'd have to stop at the garage, get the milk, do everything myself and do the washing. So I thought this is not for me.

I'd gone from 'Bobby basic', as it were, to Firearms Officer at Heathrow, then Special Escort Group which was really tough to get into, then Close-Protection, then I went back to uniform. It's the happiest I've been: Static Protection in uniform at Windsor Castle was wonderful. I loved it. When The Queen was out during the week I'd go for a run. When I'd done my armoury duty and Changing the Guard, I'd think 'What do I do now?' So I'd go for a little run. I've run past Frogmore, where Victoria and Albert are buried – just amazing. I loved doing the Garter Ceremony; the pomp and circumstance, wonderful, absolutely amazing. I was very, very lucky to work there at the end of my service. I'm pleased I served, but I'm pleased I'm out.

I often came across the royal family. I used to see The Queen when she was in residence. We have more static points when she is in residence and, as a sergeant, I used to walk round to make sure the officers were in position.

We would stand to attention and salute when we saw The Queen out riding with her groom. She'd stop and talk to us. 'Good morning officer, how are you?' And I'd say, 'Fine your Majesty, how are you this morning?'

'Oh fine, just enjoying the weather. What are you doing today?'

'I'm out on patrol, making sure my officers are in the right place, facing the right way.'

She laughed at that and said, 'I'm sure they always are. Thank you.' And she carried on.

I used to travel up to Balmoral each year as Static Protection Officer again. I almost got knocked flying by the corgis one day. Balmoral has got various points all the way round where the officers stand; it's a huge area. We do work in conjunction with Police Scotland, but it is all Met officers who are on Static Protection. And also at Windsor; we are an oasis in Thames Valley.

I was in full uniform one day, obviously, with a gun and everything, cycling by the River Tay, in the wonderful country-side, going from one static point to another to see the officers, when I see these two ladies walking towards me, headscarves on and surrounded by corgis. I thought, 'Christ, it's The Queen.' I start to slow down to salute her, but the corgis had other ideas and decided to run over and surround me to say hello. I stopped so suddenly I almost fell off the bike; not a very graceful sight for The Queen.

The corgis are a great joy. One day at Windsor Castle, The Queen comes out in her car to walk the dogs. We always keep away, but still keep an eye on her just in case. We could see her indicating to one of the corgis which had gone underneath one of the hedgerows. Then she started turning, looking to where we were, and the PC said, 'Down to you Sarge.' So I walked over to her and said, 'Are you all right, your Majesty?' She said, 'The dog's gone in there and I can't get him out.'

So I'm on my hands and knees in this hedgerow, getting this corgi out. I dragged the corgi out and then she lifts it into the back of the Jag, says, 'Thank you.' And off she goes. She loves her corgis.

I was at the front gate, Henry VIII Gate, one afternoon when William and Kate were still courting, and the phone went and my PC answered it and it was, 'Hello, this is William here.' The thing is, we know it isn't a wind-up, we know it is actually William.

'There'll be a Miss Kate Middleton turning up.'

'Oh yes, thank you sir.'

So sure enough this car turns up and she says, 'Excuse me, I'm Kate . . .' and I say, 'We know who you are Ma'am. He's waiting for you.'

'Thank you.'

'You're welcome.'

At a certain time some of the gates around the palace are shut. I was in one of the tearooms at the top end of the castle when we heard the gate rattling. So I went out with a PC and it's William and Kate. They'd been locked out. He said, 'Sorry, we didn't realise the gate had shut.' They'd been walking out in the Great Park. I said, 'Sorry sir, you can come back in now.'

They are human, a very normal family. I think they've got a good future with William and Harry.

Sam (Serious and Organised Crime Group) 2010s

I am in charge of a team of approximately thirty detectives dealing proactively with Serious and Organised Crime in London, nationally and internationally.

We had a job where we nicked baddies for bringing drugs

and guns into the country, and then one day they bring some people across the channel – Vietnamese children. We don't always know why the children are being brought in, but in this instance it was to look after cannabis. These are like thirteen- and fourteen-year-olds, no life jackets, nothing, in the middle of the night on a RIB, crossing the Channel. God knows how they got them up to Calais. Then these poor kids are just dumped on somebody on the Kent coast and then taken to some house to get on with it. These kids are so scared, but that's the situation. So that's what we see on our job; we might start with a drug importer but they'll be involved in all sorts of things to make their money. If they have a transport route then we get people coming in on the lorries. Then the next time it will be drugs on the lorries.

We don't have enough detectives . . . the management have taken their eye off that. When I started you had Borough-based Crime Squads on which you'd cut your teeth before you'd go to the Area Crime Squad. Then, and only then, would you go to units like the Serious Organised Crime Group.

We'd deal with people bringing guns into the country; then your Borough people dealt with the little oiks on the street dealing a bit of cannabis and class A drugs. But you haven't got those people now dealing with that middle level of crime. They totally got rid of that . . . and so it got totally out of control.

Now they're crying, 'We need this to be dealt with.' So now we have to deal with the lower end of crime, then nobody is dealing with what we should be dealing with.

My officers are experienced, but the last lot of officers I've recruited are not officers I would have taken ten years ago for this role. The reason is I'm now taking them direct from Borough – where they haven't had any real experience. They will get the training when they get here because they will be working with experienced people and get on-the-job experience. But what they don't have is knowledge of the level of criminals they will be dealing with. They're not stupid, these baddies, and it all ends up in the court room at the end of the day. These new officers are not experienced in that, and so that's where it could really fall down. That knowledge base is something you build up over the years, and they just haven't got that experience any more . . . which is a shame. You have to pick your staff as wisely as you can, but they wouldn't have stood a chance getting to a unit like ours years ago.

The detectives carry massive workloads. We had twenty more detectives than I've got now, and there's so much more out there we could be dealing with if we had the workforce. In our covert world, if we don't deal with a crime this week no one will know . . . because it won't be in the papers. By contrast, if you don't deal with the gang problem and there's been another stabbing . . . that does get in the papers. Because of that we are now being moved to deal with that work. The villains know that. They're so much harder to catch anyway, but they just know they're not being looked at. When you look at the amount of bodies out there and the amount of police officers, it's not rocket science. You only have to have something like the Grenfell Tower and the abstraction of police officers sent to work on that and you're taking officers from the same-sized pot.

Now, in 2018, Serious and Organised Crime is about to go through a massive restructuring. They would like it to look like the national model, but they forget the Met is unique. They are looking at bringing all the proactive teams together into four hubs, geographically based around London. They are combining different units with us and we'll be assisting the murder teams and then maybe the kidnaps, but they haven't worked out how it's going to work.

I do a lot of on-call and a lot of overtime, and at my rank you don't get paid for that overtime. I am the tactical command for my team and do regular on-call stints that include tactical firearms. Maybe guns are going to be sold, or there's a kidnapping, and you're going to be called out for ages. It's not like someone else is going to take over your job: you're on-call; there won't be many people left who will do that, as people are going to get fed up with it.

I am still proactive. I'm not an armed officer, but you have to have someone to run that armed operation, and that is what I'm trained to do. You'd have a cadre of tactical firearms commanders and we'd deal with anything where there is a response for armed surveillance on a target we're looking to take out. This is where it's a very risky role; this is where somebody could get shot. Although I am not armed I will be making the decisions as to whether those armed assets are deployed or an intervention goes in. I'm actually out on the ground with the men and the dogs. We've got the dogs now. I have been in the van with all those driving round for hours or just waiting somewhere. It depends on what's going on.

There's not many of us that do that, you have to be a DI or DCI. It's quite a specialist role in our world. The Firearms Unit (SO19) have their own tactical firearms commanders who perform the same role as me. Most of the time now I am office-based directing operations. So out on the ground I would have one of my sergeants running the team, and I'd have a team of Detective Constables out there. We've got two teams Met-wide.

You never really know where you're going to go. I have no women on the squad at the moment. I've never had kids so I've never had to manage that while doing this job. I wouldn't have got to where I am if I had a family. I don't think I could have done it. And the big thing with that is if you've got a family and the phone goes at 2 a.m. you're expected to leave at the drop of a hat; you can't just arrange that if you have children.

I don't know anyone where the man has taken over the child care. It's always been the woman. On our unit one of our female officers worked compressed hours, and we had another girl who had two children and is just pregnant with her third child. She worked compressed hours, which seemed to work, but on a unit like this we need availability, and if you're continually unavailable it just doesn't gel. None of my female friends who have had kids have gone down the route I have. I can't think of anybody in our proactive work with young children.

At the moment I am an Acting Detective Chief Inspector which is purely down to timing. While Hogan-Howe was still in he decided to get rid of the Chief Inspector rank; then Cressida came back and there was a promotion process a couple of months ago. As I have less than a year left to go I decided not to apply, because I could be posted somewhere else for my last year.

I rarely told my parents what I was up to because they'd say, 'What! I thought you were in an office.' I certainly played it down. I was never really scared; you just did it and thought about it afterwards, and then you think, 'My God, I escaped something there.'

I will miss it . . . I will really miss it.

16

A FAR-FROM-NORMAL DAY

*Being a WPC was rarely boring. 'Dull it isn't' was a
favourite slogan among us all at the time. Along with
other members of the emergency services, the police
go on duty as first responders, never knowing what
the day may hold. Even so most duty days had at
least some semblance of 'normality'.*

*Beyond that came the special days when we might
be called on to police a special event such as
London's grand ceremonies of the State Opening of
Parliament, or Trooping the Colour.*

*Beyond that came the far-from-normal days when
mayhem and random disaster could strike.*

Jenny

Sandra (T Div) 1960s

On 5 November 1967 I had finished a week of nights and had
just crawled into bed at the section house when a loud banging at my door roused me. There had been a major train crash.

I was told that as many off-duty women officers as could be found were needed at Scotland Yard; transport was waiting to take us up there.

This was the Hither Green rail crash. We all assembled in a conference room set up as a disaster area. We had telephones, and different colour-coded cards on which we had to write details of dead bodies or parts of bodies that had been found. Other colours recorded details of those badly injured, seriously injured, slightly injured, and so on. There were other cards – white, if I remember correctly – where we would write down particulars from relatives who called in to report members of their family missing or who knew people they thought had been on the train. We had to try to match those details to the colour-coded cards.

As a result of this procedure, the first permanent emergency disaster room was set up to deal with any future disasters.

Terri (C Div) 1960s

The worst demo I went on was the Anti-Vietnam War march, back in 1968. Feelings were running very high that day and the noise from the demonstrators was horrendous. I shall never forget the noise of the horses' hooves as they hit the cobbles outside the embassy. I was in charge of one the coaches parked at the side of the US Embassy, and was told to expect prisoners 'as and when'. The American marines stationed there came to find all the WPCs who were in the coaches and told us that if we needed the loo we were welcome to go into the embassy. An hour or so later one of the marines came rushing out to tell me that the back of my coach was on fire! Luckily it was very minor, no damage, and it was put out with a bucket of water. I went on various other demos, but that one stands out. I was glad to be back to the safety of the section house. The following day the station was inundated with flowers from the public who seemed genuinely upset at the way the police had been treated and that one of the police horses had had to be put down.

Lorraine (S Div) 1970s

We were up in the Strand on duty for the wedding of Prince Charles and Diana Spencer and enjoying a joke with the public behind us. It was a hot day and we had our heavy jackets on. One of the ladies said, 'I've got you a drink.' I thought it was water, but it was actually gin and tonic. I don't drink spirits anyway, but I smelt it as soon as she gave it to me and said, 'No, no, no – I can only have water or juice.'

'Oh it won't matter,' she said.

'It will,' I said. 'First of all there's television cameras everywhere, and secondly I wouldn't be able to walk after having a gin and tonic.' They thought they were being nice to us, bless them. It was little things like that that you remember: how the public are, and how kind they can be.

Sue (P Div) 1970s

The first year of Notting Hill Carnival in the summer of 1975, I had done the Radio Operators course and was posted to the P Division green coach. The carnival had already kicked off. We picked up a young Detective Constable who had been stabbed, and were taking him to hospital when an angry crowd surrounded the coach and tried to tip it up. Another police coach appeared and chased off the crowd. I was frightened, but not enough to think I wanted to leave the job or never do this again.

Pet (Q Div) 1970s

My first carnival at Notting Hill was so great. The men were bodily picking me up, in full uniform. They were so proud to see a policewoman with a black face. It was so embarrassing, but it was good.

Julie (L Div) 1980s

One of the saddest moments was being on standby during the Tottenham riots and hearing of the death of PC Keith Blakelock. I was at Battersea and we were all dozing in the canteen. We awoke to hear officers screaming for assistance. Driving to work the next day the nation was aware of his terrible death; there were placards and protesters outside police stations claiming victory that a 'Pig was dead'.

I now sing with the Met Police choir and, when we perform at the memorial services for police officers, I think of PC Blakelock and others who have selflessly lost their lives in the course of everyday duty.

At the time of the 1981 Brixton riots I patrolled with an Asian PC. He was constantly ridiculed and spat at, but wasn't injured. I was aware, however, that I was wearing a skirt and plastic hat, and was without any Personal Protection Equipment other than a small truncheon. I didn't know the Asian PC, as he was from another station, but we felt like we were two minorities together, which in a way was comforting. I seem to remember that some senior officers were reluctant to send women to these situations.

Linda (Y Div) 1980s

In 1981 I did the royal wedding of Charles and Diana. I was still at Hornsey then and was the only girl from there. My Inspector said, 'She'll be more interested in the wedding, so let her stand where she wants.' So I saw everything. We were told, 'Be friends with your crowd, look after them, have sweets in your pockets to give them,' that sort of thing. I had to parade for 4 a.m. and we were then on our post all day. We could only go to the loo at Wellington Barracks if we got a colleague to look after our post. We weren't dismissed till 6.30 p.m., so I rushed home to get changed and then went out to my first street party with some friends and got home at 3 a.m. I was awake for twenty-four hours . . . full adrenalin.

Princess Diana was just feet from me at the Savoy when I was at a Woman of the Year lunch, and then I was first on the list for her funeral. I saw her from wedding day to funeral day. For the funeral I was just off Horse Guards Parade and was basically looking after the crowd. My bag was full of tissues because I knew what was going to happen. We were all fine until Elton John started singing, and that was it: everyone was crying.

Mary (SPG) 1980s

Special Patrol Group duties involved surveillance, and uniform duties such as the policing of riots at Brixton, Notting Hill and the Broadwater Farm estate. During that disturbance we were called out at around about 7 p.m. and some of us had heard that a PC had been killed. The whole of the SPG met at the old Territorial Army Centre in Finchley. It was quite a sight seeing all the carriers heading along the North Circular towards Tottenham. I was the driver and we were all in riot gear sitting on our carriers for hours, listening to the calls on the radio.

The worst experience was hearing units calling for urgent assistance and saying they were being shot at, while hierarchy were refusing to let us go in and deal with the rioters. It was a scary night, hearing what others were going through that evening, but not being allowed to get involved.

While waiting, I needed to spend a penny, and walked into the yard at Tottenham police station and spoke to someone who I thought was another WPC – bearing in mind we were all in riot gear with helmets on. I asked her where the ladies were, and was shocked when a male voice said, 'I'm sorry, my dear, I don't know.' It was only Sir Kenneth Newman, the Commissioner himself. I'm 5'4", and he was about the same height as me and slightly built . . . so a forgivable mistake methinks.

We were eventually allowed onto the estate at about 6 after all the rioters had gone home to bed. We then spent the next week on twelve-hour shifts patrolling the area.

Mary (M Div) 1980s

I quickly learned that the biggest and most effective muscle in your body is your tongue. When the Wapping Printers dispute was on, I was on a cordon and things were getting lively. There was constant effort to break through where I was, possibly thinking I would give more easily. After a particularly strong surge, whereby a printer was pressed against me, I told him, 'You do that one more time . . . and we'll have to get engaged.' All his mates started laughing and the moment passed. It's harder to maintain anger when you've connected as another human being.

During the Broadwater Farm riots we already had intelligence that there were people out to murder a PC, or rape a WPC . . . even before the sad demise of Keith Blakelock. Most of the team were deployed to the riots so there was only me and the ageing station minder, Don, on duty. He had been directed to close the station and to patrol, so he chose to come out with me. I accepted a call to a 'noisy party' in a tower block. I went up, leaving Don in the car. The music was loud, so I knocked on the door. When it opened I could see the flat was full to overflowing. As I spoke to the householder I could see and hear men behind him saying, 'Get her in. She's on her own. We can do her,' then, 'Wait. There's others . . . it's a trap.' I adopted my best expression of 'Shucks . . . you've rumbled me', and bid them goodnight.

In the stairwell I found Don, who'd come to see what was happening and was deciding what to do for the best. Happily, just seeing his outline had been enough to defuse the situation.

Lyn (SPG) 1980s

In those days we girls in the SPG became close friends. Brilliant times. Shield training had only just started so we didn't have any riot gear. To be honest, I wouldn't want to wear all that. By 1981 we did have to do riot training and again I think we were the first girls that ever took part in shield training. The girls drove the carriers in those days. We'd drive them into the riots, three carriers per unit and a girl driver in each unit. I'd be driving through areas I didn't know and dropping the men off.

We were given a lady's truncheon to fit in our handbag; what was the point of that! I can't remember which riot it was, but we actually had to pick up dustbin lids to protect ourselves.

When I was at West End Central we went to Grunwicks because there were a lot of us WPCs at West End Central; we would do the demonstrations all the time. Normally what happened was all leave was cancelled and the men went to the riots while we girls stayed at the stations to deal with everything there while the men were away.

I wanted to go up on the miners' strike but I was told we 'wouldn't be any good up there'. Actually, let the men go! They'd be a bloody sight better than us. I suppose I'm old-fashioned in that respect. We women do a damn good job in different roles. Men are a different sex. They're stronger than us and always will be ... end of. And that's the only difference really.

When I first started my service we didn't get to go to football matches but when I was at Wimbledon after a football match, a colleague and I turned a corner and came face-to-face with the two gangs of opposing football fans. Because I'd come from the SPG I told them to 'Fuck off.' They were so shocked, they did.

Jane (Z Div) 1980s

I was a very new probationer at the Notting Hill riots in 1988. At that time we had no protection. We only had skirts and handbags, and I remember trying to chase someone and thinking, 'How the hell are you supposed to catch someone holding your handbag and running in a skirt?'

But it all got very naughty at Notting Hill and we were all in a sort of police 'safe area'. Above us on a high-rise block someone had prised this huge box loose. To say it was a window box doesn't do it justice, but luckily we all moved out of the way and it missed us.

Then we had to form a cordon across the road; at that time all we did was to hold onto the guy or girl's belt in front of us. We didn't have any riot training or proper gear for either the women or the guys. We formed the cordon in just our tunics, and it was going off all around us. Certainly our team looked after us women. They would call us 'Doris', and we were called 'Handbags'; but actually they did look after us and always came to our aid.

Linda (S Div) 1990s

At the time of the Poll Tax riots I was a very senior constable and was on that 'thin blue line' at Whitehall. We had a gang of hooligans coming down from Downing Street, and an even bigger gang coming out of Trafalgar Square, and we were caught in the middle when they were about to do battle. They were getting closer and closer, and the Inspector shouted, 'Run for your life!' So I ran into a theatre, the Whitehall Theatre, when I thought, 'Hang about. You have to look after your probationers.'

As I ran out of the theatre a battle was well under way outside and one of my PCs, Barry, was limping badly. I went, 'Barry, what happened?' He said, 'He hit me with a scaffolding pole.' I said, 'Not to worry, we'll go to the first aid post, and then we'll go to hospital.' So we got taken to St Thomas' Hospital, and that's when I did my bit, didn't I? There were all these police-men in there but nobody was taking notes as to who they were, what serial they were from, their injuries, or anything. I said, 'Can I have a clipboard please, nurse?' And I just became liai-son with Scotland Yard.

I went round them all, found out what their injuries were, where they were from, and basically just took over. Then some-one from Scotland Yard came on the radio and said that a Chief Inspector was coming down to assist me. I said, 'Thank you very much – I'll be here.' Just after that message, my mate from the Mounted Branch limped in with his face all smashed in. I walked him into a cubicle and said, 'Nurse, badly injured horse sergeant here needing help.' I held his hand and said, 'You're in the right place now Graham, don't worry. How's your horse?' He said, 'The horse is OK.' Poor old Graham, he was in a state. He was off for a long time and the next time I saw him was when I was on duty at Spurs and I heard this galloping horse. There was Graham, like a knight in shining armour. He came up to me, stopped the horse, leant down and gave me a big kiss. 'Thank you so much for being at the hospital,' he said, 'and for holding my hand, because I don't know what I'd have done if you hadn't been there. It was so nice to see your smiling face.'

Anyway, on the day of the riots I finally got a lift to Lambeth where they were having refreshments . . . and got told off by my sergeant for abandoning the serial. So that was the Poll Tax riots.

Mary (L Div) 2000s

I was Acting Inspector at Walworth on the day that there was widespread disorder at the Macpherson inquiry into the Stephen Lawrence investigation. I was not involved in dealing with that; I was just trying to keep it business as usual for the rest of Walworth. Arrests had been made, and I knew there were two men in our cells who were from the Nation of Islam movement. The events of the day were headline news and The Great and The Good of the Metropolitan Police were ensconced in the conference room discussing all that had happened. It was then that I was told the station was being besieged by the Nation of Islam.

I found that the station was indeed surrounded by phalanxes of imposing-looking men, all dressed in suits and all with red bowties. I recall being impressed by how smart they looked, and how still they stood. As this seemed a situation for someone above my pay grade I knocked on the door of the conference room but was told, 'Mary . . . GO AWAY!'

Away I duly went to assess the security of the station. While we had electronically-operated gates at the back, our walls could easily be scaled and there was no way to secure the front, other than a glass door. A quick head count told me that there were more of them than there were of us. The station officer had wisely vacated the front office and there were only Nation of Islam representatives in there; everyone else had scarpered.

So, I went in and asked, 'Can I help?' After much shouting and gesticulation I established that they had come to free their brothers in Islam. I also gathered that they had bought into the local myth that prisoners at Walworth would be subject to torture. I explained that due legal process would have to take place, but would two of them like to come into the custody suite and visit their brothers? I quickly checked with the Custody Officer that it was safe to do so, and accompanied them in. It was evident that the two arrested men were being well treated, that they'd had their rights, had been given food and drink, and had seen a doctor. As I showed them out I was delighted to see a police officer's best friend – rain. There being little else to do . . . the men dispersed.

Ellie (B Div) 2010s

I remember in the riots of August 2011 handing children over in the corridor because officers were deployed on twelve-hour shifts. One partner would have them for twelve hours and then hand them over to the other as they were going on duty. It wasn't ideal, but it was a compromise. We're not supposed to have them on premises, but if it allowed the cops to do their share and it kept them happy because they didn't have to stress about child care, then that was what I was willing to do.

I have to say when Westminster and London Bridge terror attacks happened, the biggest concerns I had to think about was the twelve-hour shifts because I knew the impact that it would have on people – and in particular on those with families. Some of my officers were actually on the other side of Westminster Bridge coming back from aiding another event when the terrorist attack happened. They helped people coming out of the London Eye for example, and others went to hospital to meet the families and the relatives. Some of those same officers also dealt with London Bridge ... and some of them also dealt with Grenfell.

Last year [2017] for us as an organisation was particularly challenging because you had staff who actually dealt with all three. And you have to be very mindful. With a workforce of seven hundred people including volunteers, cadets and everything else, you can't remember them all; you remember some, but you can never assume you've dealt with them all. I didn't know that a whole group of them had been involved in Westminster, because they never told anyone. They were lost in the system for a whole day essentially. I had been told they'd all gone home and they hadn't; they were still deployed.

So you have to be mindful of that cumulative effect on people. Different trauma and different venues ... but the effect is the same. People get stressed. You can call it whatever you want, but that's what it boils down to. People have seen things in a very short period of time, particularly so last year.

And I think last year also saw a seismic shift in public confidence for blue-light services. It was tangible after Westminster, but after London Bridge it was just reinforced. We were having flowers put on our cars. We were having biscuits handed in at the counter. We were having old ladies popping cards in the post with £20 inside saying, 'Give that to your staff.' When Grenfell happened I remember at the end of the one-minute silence in Kensington High Street a very posh woman wanted to write me a cheque – and that cheque would have been very sizeable. Obviously I couldn't accept that, so I explained how to give to Grenfell, but I think for the first time last year the public really saw how blue-light services had been tested to every degree and tried to do the impossible.

17

HE WAS COOKING PARTS
OF HIS BRAIN IN BUTTER

*Criminals, bad people and people in trouble were
encountered on a daily basis by me and most officers . . . but murder was a rare occurrence. I was asked
to sit in the corridor of the female cells on suicide
watch when a woman was arrested in an alleged case
of murder. I couldn't help feeling sorry for her.*

*She was a Muslim woman, who sat quietly in her
cell, not moving. Unable to speak English she was
doubly trapped. She had children, and must have
been worried sick about them. A police officer brought
down a sandwich for her, which she left untouched. It
was a ham sandwich. When it was pointed out that
she as a Muslim did not eat ham, he removed the
ham and left the bread! Thank heavens we have a
greater understanding now.*

Jenny

Shirley (Z Div) 1950s

During my first six weeks on Division, I and another WPC did a week of night duty keeping watch on a sixteen-year-old girl patient at a local mental hospital. She had strangled her best friend on the ward. CID were having discussions as to what action they could take. As they decided what to do, we were with the patient in a locked side-room, with no key to the door. The only way of attracting any help from the nurses would have been to blow our whistles. All WPCs who did this observation were treated like that.

Sandra (T Div) 1960s

One morning I attended a house in the Richmond area to look after a little boy, whose father had attempted an abortion on his mother and she had died. I took him back to the station and entertained him in the canteen with chocolate bars etc., while all the time he was asking about his mother. He was four years old. It was one of the hardest things I had to do because I knew not only had he lost his mother he was also going to lose his father as they were going to charge him with murder.

Sue (P Div) 1970s–1980s

During my first few months in the job I was told to sit in the cell passage on suicide watch. The cell door was left open, but the door to the cell passage was locked. The woman was an ambulance driver who had killed her lesbian partner. I was told not to discuss the case with her as I would then be involved in giving evidence. I had never met a murderer before, and was actually shocked at how very normal and sad she was. That taught me a lesson which I carried throughout my service, and probably my life. One act does not make you a bad person, and I learned to treat everybody with respect.

Kim (R Div) 1980s

I was posted to a murder incident room to answer phones, make tea and do basic admin. The six weeks I was there felt like a great example of diligent and methodical policing. A mother with mental health issues had killed her own daughter and one of the girl's friends. I escorted the mother from prison to the court for the pleas and direction hearing. I was hand-cuffed to her to walk the short distance from the building to the B11 van while other inmates shouted and screamed at her, throwing cups of urine out of the barred windows. We were both covered in a mixture of liquids. I was advised before I went to take a second uniform: no one told me why, but this was obviously the reason. Another life lesson for me . . . that mental health was to be taken seriously.

Mary (E Div) 1980s

Exhibits Officer was a post you were given as part of your train-ing in the CID. At the time, Kentish Town was running at about a murder a week. The first one I helped to investigate involved a male who had had a bottle thrown at him which had cut the jugular vein in his neck. He had gone home and was so drunk he had held a saucepan to his head, collected the blood and had consequently bled to death. The subsequent trial was in No 1 Court at the Old Bailey and it was quite awe-inspiring thinking of all the famous people that had been in that court before.

The second murder was a youth who had been stabbed at a rave in an argument over drugs. I was Exhibits Officer for that one too. Myself and another officer went back at the end of our shift to have a look around as the murder weapon had not been found. The place was ramshackle with lots of misfitting wooden doors. We found the knife lodged under a door with the victim's blood still on it. A bouncer at the rave was subsequently convicted at the Old Bailey.

Deryl (P Div) 1980s

I was operator on the night-duty RT car when we were called to a possible domestic violence. The driver and I argued on our way to the call as he said it wasn't a call for the RT car. It ended up with me saying, 'Sit in the bloody car. I will go and deal with it.' He came anyway. We got admitted and the man led us through to a woman lying on the bed. I could not feel a pulse. My colleague asked what had happened and the man replied that he had hit her. He asked if we were going to take her to hospital, then realised we were not ambulance person- nel and attacked us.

He was a kick-boxer and at one stage I landed on the body which slid to the floor. Great scene preservation! As the body fell there was a slurping sound and a large cucumber popped out from between her legs. I went to open the door for other units and called for urgent assistance. I got kicked again and burst through a bedroom door. A boy of about five sat up in bed. I said, 'Go back to sleep,' and went back to the fight. We restrained the man and I arrested him for murder. We got a Deputy Assistant Commissioner's commendation. The Detective Sergeant got a Commissioner's commendation for detective ability. Go figure.

Helen (L Div) 1980s

I was plain clothes duty when I approached a man as he attempted to break into a flat where three young girls lived. He attacked me, beating me around the head with his fists. Thankfully colleagues came to my rescue before he knocked me unconscious. Just two weeks later, in December 1988, he murdered a young woman. At the time of his arrest for the assault on me he had already been convicted of a rape carried out when he was sixteen and still in his school uniform. He was bailed to Magistrates' Court for the assault on me but, while out on bail, he murdered the other woman. I consider myself very fortunate to have escaped . . . mostly because I can scream very loudly and my colleagues were close by.

The murder he committed was close to where my assault was. I am told he was handed an extra year for the assault on me – but I was never called to court as he admitted both the murder and the assault on me. As an aside, I remember going into the incident room for the murder on day one and suggesting this guy as a suspect, but for whatever reason he was not arrested for another three weeks. The detectives put themselves forward for commendations but were put firmly in their place by the Chief Superintendent.

Mary (R Div) 1990s

A young mother, Samantha Bisset, and her four-year-old daughter, Jazmine, were found dead at their home in Plumstead; a terrible crime involving mutilation and sexual assault. One acquaintance, who was initially arrested after his hands were found to be stained red, was quickly released when it was proved that his hands were merely marked by a dye from his workplace. I was a uniform constable seconded to help set up the Major Enquiry Suite at Thamesmead Police Station.

I was appointed the Receiver on the case, meaning I had to catalogue and assess everything coming into the office for the Office Manager, a Detective Sergeant, to decide what action to take. A couple of months into the enquiry the DS retired. Normally another DS would have been drafted in, but the role was given to me. I had to deal with a lot of incredulity that, on such a significant case, a mere PC was doing a DS's job. Despite that, I had experience on enough squads to be confident that I was doing a good job.

It was the most brutal murder that any of us had worked on; it was all-absorbing. Most of us were obsessed with the 'who, how and why'. The whole world was our suspect, and we didn't know if he figured in any of our enquiries or if he was a complete unknown. After five months and three weeks of uncertainty I was going through the in-tray when I opened a fingerprint docket. It was an identification on a partial-print taken from the dead woman's balcony. Staring up at me was the face of her killer. One of our team, Jane, had worked on an enquiry to identify the 'Green Chain Walk Rapist' who had attacked dozens of women, many of them with small children. We got out the well-publicised identikit poster and instantly saw the likeness.

At a subsequent trial, Robert Napper was convicted of the murder of both the mother and her daughter, along with rapes from the Green Chain Walk series. From the start we had been mindful of the earlier killing of another young mother, Rachel Nickell, on Wimbledon Common. We had liaised with their squad and followed up leads, including where Robert Napper had been on the day of her death. He had been working at Woolwich Arsenal, but unfortunately all work records had been destroyed in a fire. It took years of continued investigation and advances in DNA before Robert Napper was finally charged with causing Rachel's death. He was convicted in 2008 of manslaughter on the grounds of diminished responsibility.

I received a commendation for 'Professionalism & Leadership'.

Sally (T Div) 1990s

In the CID at Hounslow I dealt with a few murders, including that of a baby who had had its head bashed against a wall by the mother. She got fed up with the months-old baby crying, so she just kept banging its head against a wall and shattered its skull. She got convicted.

Louise (J Div) 2000s

In February 2004, Peter Bryan, a recovering mental health patient, killed his friend, dismembered him . . . and tried to eat him. I'd just come on duty when the call came in. The victim was a forty-year-old chap with special needs, quite vulnerable, and was being exploited by Bryan and his mates who were allegedly using the victim's flat to take drugs. I remember the call came in as '. . . a man covered in blood and believed he may be self-harming'. I had no idea of the gravity of the whole job. When officers from my team went down they found a man in a psychotic state . . . he was clearly in crisis, he was in the premises with the deceased who he'd chopped up, and he was cooking parts of the latter's brain in butter in a frying pan.

I was called down as the 'governor' to manage the scene, but nothing prepared me for what I saw; it was surreal. The body was lying on the floor. I remember seeing his testicles and one leg and no arms; the limbs were stacked like firewood in a corner of the room, like logs. He'd sawn off the victim's arms and left leg and was in the kitchen cooking. On the work surface was what I can best describe as tapas-like little plates of different parts of his anatomy, skin, etc., that he'd been cooking in a frying pan and had offered it to the officers who were there. Oddly enough they declined.

We arrested him in the spotlight of huge media interest and preserved the scene. The overpowering smell of bleach where he'd tried to clean up, and the sight of that kitchen, will stay with me for a long, long time. I was there for hours and hours and hours. I was the governor of the team so I was there to manage the critical incident, gather evidence, make sure witnesses were dealt with, make sure the suspect was dealt with and more importantly look after my staff. Needless to say it was a highly traumatic incident.

I had a sandwich in my pocket. I hid from all the journalists and all the public and, I kid you not, I ate my sandwich; even with all this brain in the frying pan and a dead man lying on the floor with his limbs looking like firewood. I'm only human . . . and I was starving. I recounted this to my sister later and she was horrified: 'You did what?' she said. 'What's wrong with that?' I replied, 'I was hungry.'

All my officers who attended the scene were treated for post-trauma assessments by occupational health that night and needed counselling. Bryan was committed to Broadmoor indefinitely because he'd already committed one murder before this one, and he subsequently killed a fellow inmate at Broadmoor.

Sam (K Div) 2010s

The last murder I dealt with was when I was in Newham. A husband got someone to murder his wife; we never found out the motive. He was quite old; she was a lot younger and had not been long in this country. They had two children, an eleven-year-old and one who was about six, who had just started school. The dad takes the children to school, leaving a communal door to the flats open, and the front door to their ground-floor flat, ajar. The wife's in bed and the bloke who's arranged to kill her comes in. He stabs her forty times and she ends up 'bleeding out' and dying. It was horrendous. She's being stabbed when the eleven-year-old comes home because he'd forgotten his art homework. He hears her being murdered and tries to get in, but he hasn't got a key to the communal door. Eventually a neighbour lets him in and he finds his mother. The assailant has gone.

The husband hadn't actually been that careful. We found a hidden phone that he'd tried to get rid of, and there was the sim card, so it wasn't too difficult. He'd met the killer that morning quite close to the house, obviously to discuss the final planning. The guy who did the murder was a local drug-user. CCTV and phone records helped to link him to the husband, and evidence was found at the killer's house. He and the husband were both convicted.

18

THERE'S THAT EERIE SILENCE THAT FOLLOWS AN EXPLOSION

I was fortunate in never having to deal with acts of terrorism that many of my fellow officers, both male and female, have coped with through the years of IRA bombing campaigns on mainland Britain, and the more recent terror attacks on the streets of the capital. The nearest I came to a bomb was while I was posted to Limehouse police station in the sixties.

I was out in the van when a call came over the radio to a building site in Poplar, East London. An unexploded Second World War bomb had reportedly been dug up. It was actually quite exciting as we drew up to inspect this long-buried device. But that thrill turned to disappointment when the site manager declared that the bomb was a dud and not dangerous at all. My van driver, with all the bravado of a kamikaze pilot, picked up the dirt-encrusted bomb . . . and threw it on the floor of the van between our seats. I queried the good sense of this, but was informed that since it was a dud . . . what was the problem?

We smiled.

The bomb rocked gently, rolling from side to side against the metal handbrake and the seat guide rails.

We laughed.

At the station the PC proudly dropped our trophy on the front counter with a satisfying thud, declaring, 'There you go, Sarge.' A crowd of PCs gathered to look at this new toy-for-the-boys, vying for the chance to pick it up and examine it more closely. A PC came out of the reserve room: 'Sarge, just had a call. The bomb probably isn't a dud. They want it put in the bomb bin in the yard, and they're sending the Bomb Squad to collect it.'

My colleagues, who moments before had been poking and prodding the 'dud', melted away faster than ice cream on a hot day. They left me and the PC to carry it carefully to the back yard and place it in the 'bomb bin', a makeshift ring of old lorry tyres. Hours later the bomb was taken away and duly exploded by the Bomb Disposal Squad . . . and we lived to tell the tale.

Far less humorous in the 1970s was the continuing IRA bombing campaign in mainland Britain. In the Met we seemed to be on constant alert and, although I never had to attend a bombing incident, I and my colleagues were repeatedly warned about the danger of our newly issued 'Storno' personal radios setting off any explosive devices in the area. The radios

improved communications with base when out and
about, but I was told they could be dangerous if used
within about 100 feet of a suspect bomb.

Jenny

Eileen (C Div) 1970s

One evening in December 1974, a time when the IRA were bombing London, I went with two senior officers to Oxford Street. En route I was told we were going to a suspected car bomb near Selfridges. From where we parked we could see the 'vehicle of interest' a little way along Oxford Street. The Chief Inspector told me to stay in our car while he and the Inspector investigated and assessed the situation. That was the last I saw of them for a while.

I noticed a car being driven towards Oxford Street. It mounted the footway to pass our vehicle and I left the car to speak with the driver. On explaining the situation and requesting him to back off in the direction from which he had come, an argument ensued. As he was determined to continue into Oxford Street, I gave him two options: one was a warning that if he insisted on driving into Oxford Street and the vehicle exploded then responsibility for any injuries to himself and his passenger would solely be his; the second option was me having no alternative but to arrest him for obstructing a police officer in the execution of my duty. With the delivery of the second option he backed off and parked about 100 yards away. I then returned to the rear seat of our car.

A split second later, the vehicle of interest exploded, blowing out the windows of Selfridges and surrounding buildings. A lot of glass landed on top of the car I was in, and all its windows disintegrated. The noise was terrifying. I felt the rear of the car being lifted into the air. I understand that as the force of the explosion hit the Selfridges building it ricocheted beneath the rear of my car, lifting it and extensively damaging the exhaust system. The car was a write-off. I left to check on the gentleman and his female passenger. I found him in shock, but not only apologetic for arguing but also concerned for my safety. He was thankful I had put myself in a dangerous situation to save him and his passenger from what could have been, at the least, serious injury.

The Inspector and Chief Inspector returned later. They insisted on carrying me from the car to a waiting ambulance, when I really wanted to walk. However, I was strapped into a wheelchair with the presence of the press taking photographs. I was taken to the Middlesex Hospital, then to the Medical Centre in Hendon and to the Rehabilitation Centre in Hove. I was told by the Chief Inspector that he and the Inspector took a turn for the worse when they saw the state of Oxford Street after the car bomb blew up. Apparently, all they could see were dismembered limbs, decapitated heads, torsos and shredded clothing strewn around the vicinity. These limbs, heads, torsos and clothing turned out to be bits of dressed mannequins blown out of Selfridges' front display windows.

Jean (Special Patrol Group) 1970s

I was attached to 2 Unit SPG at the time of the London IRA bombings. On 8 March 1973 we were told to report for duty at 2 a.m. and drive to Scotland Yard for a briefing with other SPG Units. We were told they had information that four car bombs had been planted around London . . . and we were to try and find them. I think we had the registration numbers, or maybe just the type of vehicle, not sure. So we went out in pairs and started searching the streets. Then the call went out that one car had been found near Scotland Yard. We were to clear the buildings as the Bomb Disposal Squad was going to defuse it. I knew what car it was, and we made our way down the street, knocking on doors and offices, but the next thing I know there was an explosion and I was on the floor.

There is that eerie silence that follows an explosion, and I can still remember that stillness. Then came the sound of falling glass and masonry. I remember lying still for a moment or two until a PC came to see if I was all right. I got to my feet, shaken of course, with blood on my hands and cuts on both knees. Chaos ensued, ambulances arrived, and I went to hospital to be checked over and patched up. I was lucky to get away with cuts to my knees and, once they were cleaned up, I was OK to go. I went straight from hospital to the operations room at Scotland Yard to help with all the calls, and met the then Home Secretary, Robert Carr. I remember it was a very long day before my unit came to pick me up. I learnt then that others on my unit had also received slight injuries.

The sisters Marian and Dolores Price were involved in the bombings and their trial took place in Winchester. Some of my unit went down there to police the trial, and I also went down for a brief time to act as a guard and warden to the Price sisters. They were chatty amongst themselves, but rude and ignorant to anyone else. Funny old world.

Pet (Q Div) 1970s
During the time of the IRA attacks we had to stand watch outside the station, frozen to death. It would be a couple of us on each shift, 24/7, doing an hour on and an hour off for the whole of our duty. We weren't armed. I don't know what we were supposed to do. I have never felt so cold in my entire life. That was the worst part of my police career and I'll never forget it.

Janis (D Div) 1970s

Paddington Green police station was a holding station for prisoners from around London and later on became a high-security station. Whenever the civilian matron was unavailable, a female officer would do that duty. I was posted to matron's duties when an infamous female terrorist, a member of the German Baader-Meinhof terror group, was brought to Paddington to be kept overnight before court. She had long hair, and the most difficult time we had was working out how to wash her hair in the smallest hand basin ever in the corridor of the cells. Quite surreal to share 'girlie time' with a suspected terrorist.

Lorraine (S Div) 1970s

I was out with a PC who was known to be lazy. He'd get in the car, and didn't like getting out again. It was in the 1970s when we had all the IRA suspect parcels and, if you found anything, we had to phone the Bomb Squad. We got called to an incendiary device outside a supermarket in a very small shopping centre which was lit up at the front, but which had a service yard at the back where it was very dark. He said, 'You go round the back, and I'll go round the front.' But he had the car and, if you think about it, a car going round to the service yard with its headlights on would have made more sense than me with a torch. I never questioned it; I always went and did whatever I was told. It was an incendiary device . . . and it did go off as I was walking to it. Someone had planted a firework or something in a bin. I remember they laughed about it back at the station. 'It's typical of him,' they said.

Sue (P Div) 1980s

The night the bomb went off at Catford nick I was meant to be on reserve duty but had swapped with another PC. I was out and about when a voice came over the radio and said there had been an explosion in the station. A young probationer on my relief had found a torch on the front counter in the early hours of the morning. He picked it up . . . and it exploded. He lost his hand in the blast, and received cuts to his face. Several others who were inside had slight injuries from shattered glass and lost their hearing for a time.

This was at the time of IRA activity and the Anti-Terrorist Team took over the investigation and we were all interviewed by them. The wife of one of my friends was the sister in charge of the ward at Lewisham hospital and she let us in to visit during the night. We were all very upset. I cried when I saw my friend lying in the bed with his arm bandaged and his face all cut. Later I was on the Area car when a local yob shouted out that we were 'armless' as a joke. Tension was high and my colleague stopped the car and grabbed the boy. I had to pull him off.

Sue (B Div) 1980s

Chelsea had the reputation of being the most bombed area in the UK. The bomb car was Bravo Charlie 13 (It was ages until I twigged the little joke). I used to volunteer to go on the bomb car because otherwise I was walking everywhere. This was in the days of the IRA and my shift was on duty when the Harrods bomb exploded. I had taken the day off and was actually on a daytrip to France with my boyfriend. I didn't know anything about it until I arrived back at my flat and the phone was ringing. It then transpired that although my immediate family knew I wasn't on duty, most of my friends had heard that a police woman had been killed and they were ringing me all day and all evening. That period was very difficult for me and all those at the station.

Liz (Y Div) 7 July 2005

An almighty bang and a shudder brought the train to an abrupt halt. I was standing with my *Daily Telegraph* under my arm, my rucksack between my feet, and holding on as the lights flickered. The train was busy, but not packed. I'd used the underground before but I wasn't a seasoned traveller. People were moaning and muttering when the train didn't move off. This was at about 8.45 a.m. and I thought I might be late for the conference in Westminster. A lady next to me looked a bit anxious but I said, 'Don't worry, we'll be all right.' Then I heard this shouting from down the train and people were asking, 'Are there any doctors or nurses?' I thought, 'Shit – we've had an accident.' I wasn't in uniform, I was just wearing an anorak but I got my warrant card out and said, 'Let me through, I'm a police officer, I'll find out what's going on.'

As I went through the interconnecting doors into the next carriage people were coming towards me covered in soot, dirty and in shock. They were like ghosts walking towards me in a daze. Newspapers were blowing around and it was all dark and I thought, 'What's happened here?' Lights from the tunnel gave some light, but this carriage was all in darkness and people were obviously hurt. I still thought it was an accident and we'd hit something. A man standing at the end of the carriage said, 'Don't go in there, love.' I said, 'I've got to, I'm a police officer.'

The door was mangled. I had to pull stuff back to crawl through the small gap. It was dark in there and really dirty, with cables hanging down, stuff like that. The smell was indescribable, dirty, you know, dirty, pretty much smelling of electrical burns, nasty, viscous, you could taste it. And I thought, 'It isn't a crash because the carriage isn't squashed, it's disembowelled, it's been blown outwards.'

There was a big hole in the side, the floor and windows were blown out, and then I saw this woman. I thought, 'Why's that woman got her feet up?' She's been sitting with her feet up . . . but her feet aren't there and her trainers are on the sill and her legs are mangled. She looked as if she was sitting with her back to another passenger – you know some people might sit on the train like that – but she hadn't, she'd been sitting normally and been blown into that position, but my brain didn't take that in.

The man sitting up against her had lost his leg. It had gone. His other leg was in a bad way, but he was conscious. Another person was trapped under a load of rubble. Another guy was writhing around on a big piece of metal which had come out of the floor, I think. There were more people further up in the darkness; I couldn't really see because their faces were black.

I'd got a hole; I'd got metal and a ravine. I was standing on a chewed-up ravine of metal with this body underneath my feet. The body was stuck down, minus a head, but I couldn't do anything about the people who were obviously dead. The doors were open and there was a body on the track, which I did nothing about; at least one body. I didn't go down there because I thought, 'If I go down there I'd never get up. I'm not going to start crawling about because I could make the situation worse; if it was a bomb I could trigger something else.'

I thought I'd stick to the people I could help; I didn't want to slide down and land on him, and I've got these poor people sitting here and this woman there and this other chap. My area is not very big and I thought, 'Just concentrate on people you can help and don't become a casualty yourself.' So I put my rucksack down and said, 'Don't worry, I'm a police officer, I'll do what I can to help you.' I took my jacket off and wrapped it round the guy's leg and did a bit of first aid. Then a young man came from the other carriage behind me and said, 'What can

I do?' I said, 'Go and get me some belts, get me some ties. Get me anything you can get off other people. Get me some water.' So he went off and I just reassured the people.

The guy, Andy, said, 'I've lost my leg, haven't I?' And I said, 'Yes you have, but you're going to be OK; you're going to live, you'll survive.' And Martine, the young woman, was conscious but in a terrible state really. She'd lost her legs, they were completely mangled. The chap came back with some stuff for tourniquets and I just held their hands and talked to them, kept them going. Told them who I was, told them they'd be all right. I hadn't a clue what had happened. I didn't know if the front of the train had been blown up but I'd guessed it was some kind of explosion. It could have been electrical. I didn't know it was a suicide bomber.

I had a lady who'd lost an arm. I pulled some metal off her. She was screaming blue murder, so I knew she'd be all right; the more people yell the better chance they have. And then there was Andy and Martine who were next to each other and then there was this other chap further up who I thought was going to be OK. He was conscious and moving. I didn't really do much apart from talk to him . . . but he died subsequently.

Looking through the blown-out window I could see a whole line of people walking past. By that time they'd got the power off. Young people and old people and they could see me. One man threw his tie at me through the window and ran off. They were streaming away up the track and I thought, 'Right, it's only a matter of time', but it was still a good part of three-quarters-of-an-hour before any help came.

They'd been hesitating because they didn't know if there were any secondary devices. In the end a policeman came down and got into my carriage. He said, 'Don't worry, I'm a police officer.' And I said, 'Don't worry . . . so am I.' I'd never been so glad to see anyone in my life as he started doing things to help. By that time I'd probably reached the end of my tether because I'd been down there quite a long time, I'd breathed in all this dirt, you know, I'd had enough of it really, but I didn't want to let Andy and Martine go, I wanted to make sure they were all right.

The policeman came down first and then the Fire Brigade, and then the ambulance crew. I was almost resentful of them because I'd been there all this time, and I said, 'Don't let them die.' I just walked out of the carriage and picked up my rucksack, and my warrant card which I had left with the young man right at the beginning, and who had left them for me down by the door of the carriage that wasn't bombed. A fireman lowered me onto the tracks and I walked away.

I wish I'd stayed, but I thought I'd be in the way by that time as people were there with breathing apparatus and I'd done what I needed to do. I thought there are professionals here now, I'd got no resources, I'm stripped, I'd got rid of all my clothes except for my T-shirt and my trousers. I hadn't got my jacket or anything, I'm vulnerable now, I'm dirty and I've got blood all over me and I've got to get out of here now. So I walked up the tracks and went up the top.

19

SHE SLOSHED HIM A FOURPENNY ONE

What makes a person brave? Do they know they are brave? I've found that you just don't know until you're tested. No one knows how they will react to a given situation until it happens. During my career as a WPC I rarely had to face real danger and if I did, I was not alone: unlike these women who tell their stories in a dismissive way, as though what they did was nothing. Officers do not always know what they are about to deal with when taking a call, entering premises or stopping a person in the street. That in itself is selfless bravery.

Jenny

Alberta Watts, 'Bertie', was a young Detective Sergeant when she volunteered to act as a decoy on Tooting Bec Common. There had been a series of persistent and savage attacks on women walking across the Common at night, and their handbags had been snatched. A few minutes after she arrived on the Common she was struck violently from behind, kicked and flung to the ground, with her arm wrenched. She shouted for help and a policeman came to her assistance. It was with great difficulty that her assailant was over-powered and arrested.

Sir Gerald Dodson, the Recorder at the Old Bailey, complimented her on her courage and said that the arrest was possible only because of her heroism. Her assailant was sentenced to five years' penal servitude after pleading guilty to three charges of robbery with violence. As a result 'Bertie' was awarded the King's Police Medal for gallantry and presented with £15 from the Bow Street Reward Fund. Alberta was the first woman to receive an award from the fund since it was established in 1869.

Alberta Watts (W Div) 1946
MWPA Newsletter, May 1995

The public perception of women officers has partly been crafted through the years by the way they are portrayed in newspaper reports. One article from the 1950s struck me as typical of the time because of the overt sexism it revealed. A courageous deed undertaken to protect a male officer against two violent thugs was commended by the magistrate . . . yet the first thing mentioned in the article was that the woman officer was 'attractive' and 'well-built'. It makes you wonder, doesn't it? I'm sure that had it been a male officer the first words would have been far more likely to be discussing his courage rather than how handsome and muscular he was!

Another case I heard about from that same era showed that the bravery of police women is not a modern phenomenon. A woman officer was commended for arresting a robber after a witness told how she had waded into the suspect and 'sloshed him a fourpenny one'. Not a comment you'd get nowadays.

Just two years later came further acts of bravery by two London women officers which earned them the George Medal, one of the highest civilian awards for bravery. That bravery was mentioned in many of our specialist courses for women police, demonstrating how we were of value to the Service and didn't shirk from danger if it meant protecting others.

A number of women had been attacked by an unknown man on a quiet walkway in the town of Croydon. Investigators feared that the attacks were becoming more and more violent and might soon end in murder. Despite that worry, Sergeant Ethel Bush and WPC Kathleen Parrott agreed, along with other female officers from the local police station to act as decoys to catch the suspect. In March 1953, WPC Parrott was violently attacked and forced to her knees. As she began to lose consciousness she hit her attacker with her torch and ripped his mask from his face. He escaped but not without causing such injuries to WPC Parrott that she was off duty for six weeks.

A little over a month later, Sergeant Ethel Bush saw a man matching the description of the assailant while she was on uniform patrol in the area. Rushing back to the police station, she changed into civilian clothes so she could act as a decoy and went back to the alleyway where other attacks had occurred. With male officers hiding as her back-up protection, she walked alone until a man hit her over the head with a wooden branch. Badly hurt and with blood pouring from a head wound the officer still managed to turn around and confront her attacker. Although she held on to his clothes, he punched her hard in the face and managed to escape.

The attacker was later arrested and identification evidence from many of his victims helped secure a ten-year prison sentence for him.

Learning the details of such cases was an inspiration for me when I became a police officer, but no account of the courage of women police would be complete without mentioning the case of WPC Margaret Shaw Cleland, another recipient of the George Medal. I remember watching the real-life drama of what this policewoman did unfold on television at the time. She was called to a house where a man was perched on insecure metal railings at the edge of the roof, almost 50 feet above the roadway below. He was holding his 22-month-old baby son in his arms and threatening to jump. Inching her way towards him along the roof, WPC Cleland spent more than an hour trying to persuade him to step back and give up the baby.

Despite his absolute refusal, and after seeing him stand up and threaten to jump if she came closer, the woman officer finally persuaded him to allow her to put her coat over the baby to protect it from the cold. Now within reach, she threw herself at the man,

wrenching his little boy from his grasp and simulta-
neously pulling him back from the edge. Other offic-
ers rushed to her aid and the man was overpowered
and brought safely down with his son.

Women officers encounter danger almost on a daily
basis and, along with their male colleagues, continue
to face such threats with courage and determination.

Jenny

Sandra (T Div) 1960s

Two or three uniform PCs had been called to a big old house
in Richmond where a little elderly lady lived alone. She had
been sectioned and was awaiting transfer to Banstead Mental
Hospital. I was about nineteen at the time and not long out on
Division, but I was called to attend as the officers couldn't get
her out of the room. That was because she had an extremely
large knife in her hand. They asked me to go in and talk to her!
The next thing I knew, they'd closed the door behind me and
I was in there on my own with the woman. She put the knife
down and started secreting razor blades all over her body,
including inside her mouth and inside (you can guess where)
underneath her underpants! I talked to her quietly and calmly
because the knife was still right by her hand. She picked up
the knife again so I thought I might as well see if she'd give it
to me, handle first. To my amazement, she did. I opened the
door and told the PCs and the two doctors she was ready to go
to the hospital. Volunteer drivers used to transport mental
patients to the hospital with police accompanying them. I sat
in the back with her to Banstead, razor blades and all. Once
there the first thing I mentioned was the razor blades and
where they were situated.

Terri (H Div) 1970s

I narrowly missed out on a commendation when I stopped a runaway donkey-and-cart from running amok in the market as it was closing. My Station Sergeant said a commendation was not allowed in this case because it was a runaway donkey and not a runaway horse. I was not impressed.

Carol (E Div) 1980s

Assaults were not uncommon but I was never seriously hurt; I just had a possible broken nose from a fractious prisoner, and a couple of dog bites, that was all. What was uncomfortable for us in the 1960s and 1970s was sometimes being ill-equipped. Situations that were classified as dangerous were different to nowadays. In the Notting Hill riots, for example, Molotov cocktails were being thrown in thick glass Coca-Cola bottles and, in those days, we had no specialist clothing. We were in our normal skirts and jackets and with standard issue stockings. When the bottles broke near you they threw up bits of glass and flame which shredded and melted our stockings. An elderly gentleman came out of his house and gave me his dustbin lid, he said my need was greater than his.

It was, I think, the first or second year the Carnival was ever held. We had been told to blend in, not to be provocative, but to keep our wits about us. It was a lovely day and, as now, we were allowed to dance with the crowd. All good until dark when it turned nasty and the Molotov cocktails were thrown. What caused it I never did know . . . it was just bedlam. What I can remember is all us girls being on a bus at the end of the night, looking dirty and tired.

Caroline (B Div) 1980s

I was plain clothes on night duty with another officer, and walked into an argument about the price of food in a local takeaway. We showed our warrant cards and said, 'Now calm down.' And they said, 'We don't give a fuck what you want.' They pushed the male officer I was with and it all spilled out onto the street. I pulled one of the lads off and I was like, 'Calm down, we can sort all this out, just calm down.' And they were effing and blinding at me so I called for urgent assistance on my radio which was whipped out of my hand as they tried to drag me off this lad. They pulled me along the pavement, but I still kept hold of him all the way and someone came up and put their arm round my neck and I saw this boot and saw my teeth fly over my shoulder and all this blood came out of my mouth all over his white T-shirt and he said, 'Don't bleed on me you white fucking whore, I don't want your fucking AIDS.'

It's at that particular point my attitude changed and I punched him as hard as I could, and spat in his face. I broke his hand when I put him in an arm lock. I was in shock and in a lot of pain, bleeding everywhere but, luckily, the urgent assistance got through. There was absolute mayhem. They grabbed hold of the bloke I was holding onto, and I got up and just walked off. I was in complete shock. I was taken straight to hospital with such severe swelling to the face I looked like a Neanderthal woman.

There were about eight lads involved in the attack, but we only managed to catch three because they all ran off. At Southwark Crown Court they weren't done for assault because I couldn't identify them; they were done for affray. One of the defence briefs came up to me when I was sitting outside and said, 'I just want to let you know how sad I am that this has happened to you,' and I said, 'Fuck off.' I knew exactly what he was doing: softening tactics. I eventually get called in to give evidence. I'm standing opposite the jury, the judge, who was brilliant, and the three defendants, all laughing and joking and their briefs. They had sworn on the Bible to tell the truth and they told a pack of lies. From that day forward I never swore on a Holy Bible; I affirmed. I'm not a religious person, but I am a Christian and I thought how could people believe what I'm saying when those people have sworn on a Holy Bible and they've lied.

The defence briefs said the photographs of my injuries were inadmissible and not to be shown to the jury because these lads were being done for affray not assault, and they might prejudice the jury if they saw the injuries to my face. Giving evidence was really upsetting and I burst into tears at one stage. I wanted to carry on but the judge said, 'No, we'll stop here.' There were six women on the jury and they could see exactly what was going on and the games the defence were playing.

They were found guilty, fined £200 each and, I think, had to do some community service. They didn't go inside but they got a criminal record, that's the main thing. They appealed against conviction and sentencing but that all got thrown out. The judge was superb; he turned to me and said, 'I want to commend the officer for her bravery and tenacity, not only today when giving evidence, but also during that dreadful assault.'

Jane (Z Div) 1980s

I may still have been in my probation when I was asked to cover the front office while the officer went for his break. This guy came in and said, 'I want to see a Station Sergeant.' I said, 'Well, can I help?' but he wanted to see a sergeant and then slapped a load of bullets on the counter. I noticed he was carrying a gun, so I went to get the sergeant. When we got back the guy had gone so the Station Officer said, 'Follow him.' Stupidly

I did. He turned on me and said, 'I don't want you, I want a proper officer' and then took a shot at the Area car that was travelling over. He ran off and was cornered by a dog handler in a graveyard. He tried to shoot himself . . . but the gun didn't go off. He had some mental health problems. I got a commendation for that.

Annie (M Div) 1990s

While I was night-duty van driver I stopped two guys in a car acting suspiciously; they had driven down from the North for the Notting Hill carnival. I was alone and during the search I spotted a firearm under the seat. I got them back into the car, grabbed the gun and pointed it at them while I waited for assistance. They had robbed a number of petrol stations on the route down.

I was plain clothes robbery patrol when I spotted a man following a woman down an alley. My colleague and I ran after him and floored him, to find he had knife in hand ready to rob her of her handbag.

20

IN THE LINE OF DUTY

We must perhaps class ourselves as fortunate that
until recent times women were treated with respect
and deference, meaning they were less likely than
men to be attacked. Yet, while many more
policemen have been killed in the line of duty,
women too have died protecting the inhabitants of
London.

Unlike other chapters in this book, these officers
cannot speak for themselves. It is their colleagues and
friends who now speak for them.

Jenny

LEST WE FORGET

Bertha Massey Gleghorn
Died 19 June 1944 aged 33

Police Orders of Tuesday 20 June 1944
C. Woman P.C. 128-423 Gleghorn. Died 19 June as the result of
injuries received from a bomb explosion during an enemy air attack.
Metropolitan Police Archives

When V1 flying bombs – doodle bugs – started the missiles
would suddenly pause, stoop like a bird of prey and glide
downwards. A flying bomb stooping just over the
Commissioner's Office landed on Horse Guards' Chapel
while another following the same track, dropped behind
Rathbone Place Police Station 'C' Division, on a wall which
buried WPC Gleghorn just as she started out on her beat. WP
Inspector Butcher, on her way to visit women police in the
West End, saw the flying bomb check and stoop. She reached
the scene a few minutes later, but all she could do was to hold
Gleghorn's hand until she was freed from the debris and taken
to Middlesex Hospital. She died there a day later. Her name is
recorded in Westminster Abbey, on the Memorial Roll of
Metropolitan Police Officers who fell in the Second World
War.

From *The Memoirs of Miss Dorothy*
Olivia Georgiana Peto OBE
published by the Metropolitan Police Museum, 1993
Metropolitan Police Archives

Among the various wartime casualty lists and Rolls of Honour
found in the archives, Bertha's name stood out as the only
female officer killed on duty. In line with other Air Raid

fatalities, no inquest was held but Bertha's cause of death was registered on 21 June as 'Due to War Operations'. Bertha's death was never recorded in any newspaper of the time and when the Police Roll of Honour realised the historical significance of her death as the first woman officer to lose her life in the line of duty were unable to trace her place of burial. Despite newspaper and family history appeals there remained no trace of Bertha's final resting place until 2014.

When an appeal was made on the official website for the Roll of Honour project for further information, the daughter of one of Bertha's police friends and colleagues, had found amongst her late father's possessions a photo of Bertha in uniform and on the back he had written: 'W.P.C. Gleghorn. Killed at Tottenham Court Road Police Station by a "doodle bug" V.1. Rocket during the war. I was a pall bearer at her funeral at Golders Green Crematorium.'

Bertha's full story can at last be told; enquiries at the Crematorium have found she was in fact cremated there on 23 June 1944 and her ashes dispersed in the Crematorium gardens. No memorial was erected but an entry was made in the Crematorium's Book of Remembrance, her epitaph reads:

'Gleghorn, Bertha Massey / Born 9th October 1910 / Died 19th June 1944 / In Loving Remembrance / At rest in God's garden.'

Police Roll of Honour Trust

Jane Philippa Arbuthnot
Died 17 December 1983 aged 22

On the afternoon of 17 December 1983 at 12:44 a phone call was received by the Central London branch of Samaritans. The caller used an IRA password and stated that there were bombs in and around Harrods. He gave the registration plate of a car but gave no other details about the vehicle. At about 13:21 four police officers in a car, a dog handler and an officer on foot were approaching the vehicle when the bomb was detonated. Six people were killed (three officers and three bystanders) and 90 others were injured, including 14 police officers. The blast damaged 24 cars and all five floors on the side of Harrods. The police car absorbed much of the blast and this likely prevented further casualties.

PC John Gordon survived but lost both legs and part of a hand in the explosion.

WPC Arbuthnot and Sergeant Lane were killed instantly. Inspector Dodd died of his injuries on Christmas Eve.

Met Police Federation website – www.metfed.org.uk

Helen (V Div) 1980s

I really only knew Jane for a short time and only as a friend, I didn't serve with her. Jane was the week behind me at training school. She was obviously an educated individual, very pretty and very confident. As I was one of the youngest in my intake I ended up doing a week of security patrols at Hendon so was posted out to division on the same day, albeit not the same district, as Jane. However we were both given Percy Laurie section house to live in.

I went with her to her home once and met her parents who were lovely people. Jane drove around in an ancient mustard-coloured Fiat 500 which she drove like a mad thing. I remember being with her when she drove the wrong way down a one-way street with the drivers coming the correct way sounding their horns and gesticulating at her . . . her response (to them) was to assume an expression of total innocence and keep going.

We had both moved out of the section house before her

death, she before I as I recall, she had gone to flat share with somebody somewhere, and as a result we had drifted apart. A friend rang me to tell me it was her who had been killed in the IRA bombing of Harrods and I remember feeling as though the world had stopped turning. Jane was a lovely person, she was kind and funny, generous to a fault and full of life.

RIP my lovely friend.

Yvonne Fletcher
Died 17 April 1984 aged 25

I was standing right next to Yvonne when she was shot. We shouldn't have been there but the Duty Officer had asked us to go and do traffic duty for the demonstration about to take place at the Libyan Embassy but we were deployed on the cordon right outside the embassy. We were outside the front by the barriers at around about 9.15 a.m. when the anti-Gaddafi demonstrators arrived. They came from the other side of the square and walked through the barriers in front of us. As they arrived we'd speak to them; we used to speak to everybody. We'd say good morning and they'd say good morning back in broken English; a lot of them couldn't speak English but they were fine, no problems at all as we chatted away to them. Yvonne and I changed places about three, four, five times because that way you get to speak to other people. The reason for speaking to other people was to get a bit of friendship with them, find out if they are going to be potential troublemakers later on.

As the demonstration started they got a bit noisy and started shouting, which we did expect. Our backs were towards the embassy so we didn't see anything behind us. Then about 10.15 a.m. I thought someone had thrown a firework, it sounded like one of those Chinese firecrackers. Yvonne was five feet from me and fell to the ground. It took me a couple of seconds to realise something had happened, then I heard a lot of shouting and screaming and I glanced to the front and could see a lot of demonstrators on the ground as well. Yvonne was writhing in pain and then she went unconscious. I think there were five of us around her. You've got the famous photograph of the helmets and her hat lying on the ground; one of those helmets was mine. The thing I remember in those first two minutes was the silence. In Central London, silence for a couple of minutes, I couldn't believe it. We picked her up and took her through to a little side street called Charles II Street which is just off St James' Square; someone called an ambulance.

She was put in the first ambulance to arrive and I went with her. There were three or four demonstrators in the same ambulance who were badly wounded as well. So they're sitting on the floor, she's on a stretcher and I'm in the ambulance with one of the paramedics. She was conscious and said, 'John, my tummy hurts.' I could see that her tummy was swollen but I still didn't realise she'd been shot. I couldn't see any blood, I couldn't see anything at all but obviously she was in discomfort and she said could I do anything, so I got hold of the paramedic's scissors and cut her skirt at the top to relieve the pressure and she said, 'Thanks very much.' I said to Yvonne, 'I don't know what's happened but I tell you what, I'll find out.' So anyway we arrive at Westminster hospital. I'm put in a side-room and she's taken straight in. About half an hour later a doctor comes in and says, 'Look she's been shot. She was shot in the elbow, it's gone straight through her arm and into her abdomen but we're taking her to theatre now and she'll be fine.'

I thought, 'Oh God, fine, excellent.' Roughly an hour-and-a-half later the same doctor came back, he's in tears, absolutely in tears, sobbing away and said, 'Terribly sorry, she died in the operating theatre. The bullet did so much internal damage, shattered her spleen, all sorts of things and there was nothing we could do to save her.' I was in bits after that to say the least. I was still sitting there when the Detective Chief Superintendent, I think he was Special Branch, came to see me; he might have been Terrorist Branch but I think he was Special Branch. I had to do a written statement there and then, which I did. And the same guy came in and said, 'Right, PC Murray' – they're very, very, formal, they never called you by your first name – he said, 'PC Murray, I want you to go with Yvonne's body to the mortuary.' It was only 100 yards down the road from the hospital – 'The pathologist, Ian West is waiting.'

So I go down there and I go in and she was placed in the mortuary, there on the table and the pathologist, his assistant, the Detective Chief Superintendent and someone else, I can't remember, were there. With due process I was asked, 'Can you identify this body, for continuity?' and I said, 'Yes.' And the senior officer who was there said, 'PC Murray, we want you to stay here while this is carried out.' So I had to stay there and watch it.

You go to a lot of post mortems but, first, this was Yvonne, one of my colleagues, second, four hours earlier we were laughing and joking, that sort of thing, and then, three: I'm watching this.

I went to see her at the undertakers. The coffin was open when the six of us went there and I gave her a little kiss and I said, 'I meant what I said, I will find out.' When we carried her coffin in Salisbury Cathedral I was at the front so her head was by my head and as I'm walking down the aisle I'm talking away to her. Sounds ridiculous. I said, 'I meant what I said, I will fucking find out what happened.' That's why I'm doing what I'm doing, campaigning for justice, and I'm still doing it.

I worked with Yvonne at Bow Street police station. She was twenty-five. We had the job of Parent Constables: taking the new constables out learning the ground. We were also the first two Community Officers for Covent Garden area which meant we dealt with residents, pub owners, restaurant owners, all sorts of people like that; that was our job. I worked alongside her for two or three years. She told me she was lucky to get in the Job because she was so tiny. Apparently she did very well at the interview so they bent the rules slightly. Basically she was 5' nothing. The height for women officers then was 5'4". Yvonne was a great person and police officer, she could hold her own. If we went to a punch-up at a pub, I'd have to say, 'Look, wait outside, let them get on with it, then we'll pick the pieces up.' But no, she'd want to go in.

People would come into the station and ask for her by name because she'd dealt with them in the past; they wouldn't speak to anyone else apart from her. That's the type of person she was.

We had one primary school in Covent Garden, in Drury Lane. We would do residents' meetings in there, we would do assembly, we would do the Green Cross Code sessions, things like that. One particular year we went there and took part in their school play. I wish I had the photograph, but she dressed up as a fairy and danced across the stage. Stupid things like that. That's the way she was, she'd muck in with anything really. She was a delight to work with. She would help anybody and everybody from a smart suited business man to the vagrant lying in the street. She would help them all. Rarely, believe it or not, did we arrest people. We helped them, which is slightly different. We'd point them in the right direction. I mean she'd give a vagrant a quid to get a cup of tea. We used to do that in the past.

Yvonne was actually hit by a ricochet. The bullet hit the road and bounced up, that's why she was hit in the arm. Over the years I still speak to some of those Libyan guys who were shot and I've met quite a few of them over the years. One of them, from Benghazi says, 'I'm purely alive because Yvonne Fletcher took my bullet.' She was standing directly in front of him. He was very badly wounded. There were eleven or thirteen injured, but Yvonne was the only one who lost her life.

John Murray (C Div) – colleague and
campaigner for Justice for Yvonne

Sally (W Div) 1980s

My dad when he was DAC dealt with the death of Yvonne Fletcher. I wasn't involved in the original tragedy but I did go up at Easter in 1984 when it had happened and we had to do a night duty up there. At the end the Inspector came on the bus and said, "Sal's dad has given us all a letter to take home." It said, "Dear colleagues, sorry to drag you out over Easter, blah, blah, blah, please tell your families, thank you very much." My dad had signed it so I took mine home and gave it to my mum and said, "There you are, dad sent you that."

Gail Doreen Pirnie
Died 26 October 1994 aged 42

Collapsed and died from heart failure, having just completed an exercise while undergoing a Baton Training course at the Peel Centre, Hendon.

Police Roll of Honour Trust

Nina Alexandra MacKay
Died 24 October 1997 aged 25

As a member of a Territorial Support Group Nina forced entry to a dwelling flat at Stratford, in order to arrest a violent and deranged wanted man, whereupon she was stabbed and fatally wounded. Posthumously awarded the Commissioner's High Commendation for Bravery.

Police Roll of Honour Trust

I was on duty with Nina when she was killed. She was on the phone in the canteen at Ilford police station, talking to her boyfriend, when we got the call to this address and the person involved was wanted by police in Stoke Newington. He'd failed to appear for an offence of being in possession of a knife. So we were going to effect an arrest for non-appearance.

In the carrier, our transport vehicle, we were talking on the way there about what we were going to do and how we were going to do it. Nina said, 'I'm going to do the door.' She had just done her Enforcer course. An enforcer is a big piece of metal you smash the door in with. It was a Friday night and she had done the course that week. As she had done the course I wasn't going to tell her she wasn't going to do it. The enforcer is really heavy and she carried it herself up the stairs to the door. Her job was to hit the door and stand aside to let us enter the flat with the big shields in front of us.

We did everything we possibly could correctly at the time, and that's the one reason I can live with myself. There were five PCs and one sergeant there. The information we had was that the guy had mental health issues. I remember listening at the front door and hearing noises from the flat. He was playing this guitar really badly. We thought this bloke sounds not too sane. And so we decided we would get more units to come and join us. We called the other officers out in the other carriers. I can't remember all the information at the time but the information we got about him, about his previous was, he's violent, he carries knives. We listened at the door and we said, 'This doesn't sound too great.' I went downstairs to the flat below and knocked on the door and said, 'Can I come in and look at your flat to know what the flat is like upstairs?' We had a drawing of the flat, a mirror image so we knew what we were going in to and we had a full briefing about it.

I could see Nina was nervous; it was her first time doing a door. I've seen people take twenty to thirty hits to knock a door in. So we're all waiting and me and Kev (my partner on the TSG) were right behind her and we said, 'We'll be behind you, we'll be here. If you do the door and get worn out, Kev will take over.' So she had a few swings at it and said she can't do it with this body armour on. She said, 'I want to take it off.' Me and Kev said to her, 'It's up to you.' Her role was, hit the door, once the door goes in she stands to one side, we put two large shields into the door, block it off and see what's going on. She made the decision, she said, 'I'm going to take it off because it's going to allow me to hit the door easier.' In hindsight, I wish we'd said, 'Don't do that.' But at the time the briefing she'd had was, 'Hit the door, stand aside'. We were all lined up at the door and the decision was, 'Let's go', and she hit the door and with the very first hit the door went flying in. I was expecting four or five hits, but it went in on the first whack.

It wouldn't have been an issue 99 times out of 100. It was just a set of circumstances that were awful. Basically she ran into the flat. Nina was a cop, she liked to arrest people, she was a really good cop, to be fair. I think she saw the door go in and thought, 'I'm going to arrest this person.' I think the door going in so quickly led her to think, 'Right, let's go.' I don't know why she ran in – she knew the briefing – but she did. We went in behind her, it was so quick. It was a small flat and everything happened quickly. Between me and my colleague and the suspect in the corridor was Nina. We couldn't get in front of her, get to the suspect before she did, and of course in the corridor she met him. I didn't know she actually got stabbed at the time; all I know there was a massive scuffle in the flat because everyone just bowled in and he ended up on the sofa in the lounge with me on top of him. I was the arresting officer at the scene. Then we went into the corridor and realised that the people behind us had discovered Nina was stabbed.

We didn't get an ambulance; we took her to the carrier and realised she'd been stabbed in her abdomen area. I think at the time we were in shock. We just wanted to get to hospital. We didn't even think about it. She was my friend. She was conscious so we didn't think it was as serious as it was, so we carried her down to the carrier and someone phoned ahead to Newham General Hospital which wasn't far away. We had her across our legs on the carrier and I'm saying, 'Don't you dare die on me.' She knew what we were saying; she was in pain, but I was holding her hand and I'm saying, 'Don't worry, we'll be there in a minute.' We blue-lighted it to the hospital and when we got there people met us with the trolley and we got her straight off the carrier onto the trolley. She was rushed in. None of us went in because we all collapsed on the floor. I remember just sitting on the floor outside the carrier outside the hospital just shocked about what had happened. The next thing I remember is one of the people saying, 'Don't worry, she's with us now, she'll be fine.' I didn't know the severity of the injury. I didn't know how bad it was.

We went back to Forest Gate to wait for an update. I cannot remember who the person was – I think it was a Superintendent – who came into the briefing room and said, 'Look guys, I've got something to tell you. Unfortunately Nina's passed away.' I couldn't believe it. I went, 'Whoa, whoa, whoa, whoa.' I said, 'Hang on a moment. Are you sure? We took her to the hospital,' and I quoted the bloke, 'He said she was going to be fine.'

Nina was a very good-looking girl and got a lot of attention. She was a girlie girl when she went out nightclubbing. She was a lovely person and gained the respect of everybody. She was a good cop and a really good friend to a lot of people.

It's people like her who have made the job what it is today. Without people like her it wouldn't be the norm that women are on TSG carriers or engaged in public order or engaged in firearms operations and can do just as good a job. It's people like her who went and did things that blokes did and did them as well as blokes, if not better at times. Nina was actually one of the forerunners for female equality in the Met.

Richard (Territorial Support Group) 1990s

Steve (C Div) 1990s

When Nina came to Charing Cross I was one of the ones dealing with her on the Street Duties course. In those days they did the full residential course at Hendon and then came out to Division where they were put out for 'puppy walking' you might say, a term that's been used many times. She was just a really nice girl. I remember her personality being really bubbly, anything for a laugh, I think she liked her social life. She had a real kind of East Enders, London accent. If you understand what I mean. 'Cor Blimey,' one of those. I remember walking with her on patrol and when she got a joke into her mind or something funny happened she just used to cry with laughter. She was very positive, very happy, a really nice girl to be with. When I heard the news it just shocked me to the core. It's always the good ones that get taken.

Laura Ruth Williams
Died 19 February 2009 aged 41

Laura collapsed and fell unconscious while on duty at Greenwich Park police station. She was taken to hospital but died in the early hours of the following day, having suffered a brain haemorrhage.

Police Roll of Honour Trust

Adele Cashman
Died 5 November 2012 aged 30

After responding with other Crime Squad Officers to assist uniform patrols chasing suspected thieves in Belsize Park, North London, and whilst pursuing a suspect on foot she collapsed and died soon afterwards.

Police Roll of Honour Trust

'Adele was a much-loved and wholly dedicated officer. It is always devastating when a colleague loses their life, especially when it is someone so young who

devotes their life to keeping others safe. Adele was such an officer and was held in very high regard by all who met her – she continues to be sorely missed by everyone at Camden who had the privilege of working alongside her.'

Richard Tucker, Acting Borough
Commander for Camden

21

WHO SAID WE COULDN'T DO IT?

The hundred-year pursuit of equality for women police has been a long hard struggle. Even now I can't say we've achieved parity with the men because there are still a lot more of them than there are of us. What I can say is we have come a long way, thanks to the female pioneers and the generations of women who have followed them. Who knows what will be achieved in the future.

It seems fitting to end this century's trials and tribulations by celebrating the fact that we now have, for the first time in our history, a female Commissioner of the Metropolitan Police: Cressida Dick.

The Commissioner is not alone in breaking down those barriers and shares her success with all female officers, past and present, who have made possible the achievements of today.

Jenny

Linda (Recruitment Div) 1980s

I recruited the current Metropolitan Police Commissioner, Cressida Dick. She turned up at the 'Job Shop' at Scotland Yard in Victoria Street. It was our recruiting centre, and she just came in one day. She was a graduate and we had our graduate entry recruiting scheme. She seemed such a nice girl and it was clear she was going to go places; I just didn't realise how high she would go.

She had the same haircut as she has now, but her hair was jet-black in those days; sorry Cressida, you've gone a bit grey. She was memorable even then – and how could you forget her name? You didn't get to meet too many Cressidas.

I missed out her whole career, but I know people who worked with her when she was going through the ranks, and no one had a bad word to say about her. She remembers everybody's name, that's one of the things that's so amazing about this girl. I didn't actually speak to her again until she was a Commander. I'd been to a meeting and afterwards was in this pub when I noticed her. I said to the boys, 'I've got to go and speak to that lady because I recruited her. I haven't seen her for a long time; see if she remembers me!' And I said, 'Hello Cressida, you probably don't remember me but I was in recruiting when you joined.' 'Of course I do,' she said, 'Don't be silly.' And we just had a general chit-chat and I said how lovely it was to see she had done so well, and then I went back to the boys.

Mary (Inspector) 1980s–2000s

I got promoted twice ... but each time had a fight on my hands. Both times I passed the exams with one of the top-scoring passes, yet the men were all recommended and I wasn't. Nor was the other female, even though we were both Acting

Sergeants at the time and the men who got promoted were not.

I had been on the Operational Command Unit for thirteen years, but my personnel manager said he did not know me so couldn't comment. When I qualified for the rank of Inspector I did not get recommended for three years. Only men had been recommended in that period. The next year, with a change of management at the OCU, only female candidates got promoted because there were no eligible men left!

As a result of my experience I joined the Federation and sat on the Promotions Sub-Committee. Although retired, I still hear of similar stories now. Promotion for women was – and still is – difficult; I could write a thesis! In a nutshell, the majority of us prefer the qualities that we admire or possess. This means that white, straight men tend to favour white, straight men . . . whether they mean to or not. I saw it happen on Murder Investigation Teams where Detective Superintendents would select officers they liked onto their team.

Sue (B Div) 1990s

I sat the sergeants' exam and came in the top hundred. As a result I was automatically eligible to apply for the accelerated (Special) Promotion course. I applied and had an in-force interview. I then went to Preston for a couple of days and sat the extended interviews. During one of these I was asked, 'We shouldn't ask this, but we notice that you are getting married soon. Are you a career officer or do you intend to have children?' Lovely! I said I was a career woman and left it at that. It was an exhausting selection process to go through and the odds were steep so I just forgot about it afterwards. But on my wedding day I got a phone call while we were holding the reception. They said I'd passed. I burst into tears and all the guests thought something awful had happened!

Many of my contemporaries on the Special course achieved senior ranks, including several Chief Constables. However, I didn't feel that the Met was very good at supporting Special course people; other forces took it more seriously. But I didn't want to move out of the Met. I also believe that having two children definitely slowed my career. There were opportunities and roles that I just couldn't take and remain sane and married. An example was hostage negotiating. I'd love to have done it but essentially it would have meant even more time on-call, getting out of bed to negotiate for no extra money, and leaving my husband to manage the family.

If you succeeded then people sometimes thought it was because you were a woman, not because you were any good. I'm not sure it was harder. In some ways it was an advantage because you stood out from the crowd. However that also put you under the microscope. I think a lot of it was about doubting oneself and over-thinking things sometimes. I retired as a Detective Superintendent.

Dee (T Div) 2000–2010s

In 2004 I saw an advert asking for inexperienced detectives like me to work in specialist crime for six months. The idea was that we would learn more elite skills to take back with us to the CID. Not only was I accepted, but I was given the top posting: a covert Intelligence cell investigating high-value robbery hijacks at Heathrow airport. This was an exciting new world for me: my first experience of surveillance and other 'sneaky-beaky' methods. I absolutely loved it. I felt like I belonged although I was the only female in a unit of fifteen to twenty people.

Shortly afterwards I became pregnant. I cried when I told my husband. I had just landed my dream job, and was terrified I was going to lose it. I was, of course, happy to be having a child; I just felt the injustice of being a woman who wants a career. I needn't have worried. My new colleagues saw me as an asset and fought to keep me in the unit until I went on maternity leave. We did of course have to make adjustments to my work, but not as many as I had thought.

A few weeks before my pregnancy became headline news in the office, I was needed to identify a particular suspect as I was the only one who could point him out . . . I was now six months' pregnant.

After lots of paperwork I went out. I was sat up in a light turquoise car (not exactly considered a police car) with lots of women's magazines, pretending to eat lunch. When I saw the suspect, I radioed to others who then followed him. Because I was surrounded by undercover officers, all aware of my vulnerability, I couldn't see what all the fuss was about: I was sat in a locked car, eating lunch and reading. Needless to say, my sergeant gave a huge sigh of relief when it was over. I am not sure we would get away with doing that now, but at the time it worked. Who would suspect a big fat pregnant lady in a turquoise car?

In 2006 I returned from maternity leave. With a young baby at home I worked part time. From over 300 applicants I became one of twelve who joined a Surveillance support team in Special Branch. I was the guinea pig. They had never employed a part-time female before. I take it as a compliment that I was given the opportunity to be that person. My Detective Inspector only had really young officers or those approaching retirement, and recognised the need for women in their 30s. He said that women were much better surveillance officers. We are!

We can change our look quickly and are less likely to be suspected by those we are watching.

On my return to work after having my second child I studied for the Inspectors' exam and, after a rigorous selection process, became the only uniformed female inspector and the only female in the management team. Sometimes I still feel isolated, especially when talk of golf or other activities are said in front of me, and without including me, but otherwise I feel that being a woman in the Metropolitan Police has been without disadvantage. I do talk about my children, I do promote flexible working, and I especially encourage women to go into specialist roles.

With the Met's ever-increasing number of women officers, embracing diversity, and now with our first female Commissioner, I can only look forward to an even more positive future for women in the Met.

Louise (Firearms Command Unit CO5) 2000s–2010s

In 2009 the Tactical Firearms Command Unit was set up to professionalise Tactical Firearms Commanders after the de Menezes shooting incident. I was one of two women who were recruited into the newly formed role. The other one only lasted a couple of months, so I became the only woman doing this as a full-time role in the UK. It was like going back to the Ark. When I represented the Met in Firearms Command in Coventry I was the only woman in a room of sixty firearm command trainers, operational firearms cadres and advisers from all over the UK.

When I was deployed on armed operations I had a lot of armed officers around me but I never needed to carry a firearm. The rationale being that, as Tactical Firearm Commander, I should be thinking about command decisions such as whether to give the order to shoot or not shoot someone. All intelligence for an operation is fed to me and I make my decision based on that intelligence. I might have visuals on the situation depending on the operation, but that's unlikely.

In terms of running a terrorist situation, for example, we would either be in the control room, a specially designed room, making command decisions and running the firearms troops remotely; or we'd be with the firearms teams in a separate vehicle at the rear of whatever formation they were in and we'd be making the decisions at the kerbside.

When Barack Obama first came to the UK I was in charge of his wife's safety. I was at the back of the motorcade following her round London, being fed information from everyone and dealing with the services wrapped around her. Interestingly, on her visit to an Oxford girls' school to talk, amongst other things, about female empowerment, I was the woman governor looking after her and in charge of her security.

I ran Command on some high-profile visits and events. In preparation for the Olympics I had to have some awareness of protection work because that was not my normal remit. I therefore acted as a stooge, role-playing being different VIPs in training exercises to see how they worked, so when they came on to my venues at the Olympics I would know how they were going to operate.

I was 'The Queen' for a day, working with her Personal Protection Officers in one of her vehicles for a mock protection exercise on the M20 going from London to Kent. There are various exercises we have to do along the route. At one, there was a terror attack so we ended up driving fast with the Special Escort Group as our outriders, giving us protection and escorting us through the traffic in order for it to be as life-like as humanly possible.

We got to a barracks and had a mock terrorist exercise where I'm meant to be Liz and they run and drag me fast back to the car to protect me. The Protection Officer was a young fit whippet who was clearly some triathlete, and I slipped on some wet moss, skidded, went front down like a sack of shit, ripped my jeans, had cuts all over my hands and knees and grazed my elbows. I was bashed up like you'd never know . . . and I was meant to be The Queen.

Another time I was a 'Principal' at an airbase in a scenario where they have to jump on top of you. So you lie on your back, and this very good-looking Protection Officer jumps on top of me, with my legs akimbo. Had we not been fully clothed on a training exercise we could have been accused of all sorts of things. Again I was supposed to be Her Majesty The Queen and that guy was actually one of her Protection Officers, a young ex-military, yeah a very 'compromising situation' you'd call it. My face got grazed as he jumped on me. Every time I acted as a Principal, either as a Royal Highness or another VIP, I ended up with both a war wound and a story to tell. That was my initiation to the protection world: I got bashed up. I'd love to know what they'd have done if it was 'Liz'.

I'm now in charge of ARVs (Armed Response Vehicles) operational support. All the operational support functions that keep the ARVs on the road, it's quite a big portfolio, pan-London [across London].

When Westminster and London Bridge hit I had to manage the uplift in requirement and the deployment of staff. When London Bridge hit I was at home when I got the phone call, and again we had to look at mobilising everyone and get the staff in that support me delivering that function.

In 2009 it was very male-dominated, even at command level, but now it's becoming much more represented by women officers. It is still very under-represented, but we're getting there.

Lorraine (Specials) 2007–2012

I was the first woman to be promoted to Chief Officer for the Specials in the Met, but even then I went out as a Chief Officer and did traffic duty on the North Circular when I was out visiting Boroughs. I used to go out on Friday nights and visit the Specials on the areas; I didn't just stay in the office because it was important for Specials to see their senior management.

During the royal wedding I went out to the regulars' feeding station. It was about 5 a.m. The Specials were on the serials with the regulars and I looked at all the SCs on the shoulders and I had to say, 'Any Specials here, thanks for coming out, I'm really grateful.' And then I went out and round by Buckingham Palace talking to the Specials there. One of our Inspectors was driving me round and one of the regular officers said, 'There are no senior officers here thanking us for coming out this morning.'

I said, 'Well, it's important. Specials don't get paid, we're all volunteers.' And in my service very few times did people thank us for what we did.

Ellie (B Div) 2010s

I am proud to say I have been a career detective. I became a Temporary Detective Constable in 1991 and rose through the ranks to Detective Chief Superintendent, never giving up my detective status even when I became Borough Commander. Anything at that level is stressful nowadays, particularly so because you end up dealing with people with lots of money and lots of power and lots of influence. People very high up across government who think that they know how to do business, and that you're to be told what to do. I treated everyone the same, whether they lived in a high-rise block or an £80 million mansion.

My role as Borough Commander was to interact with people at every level right across all organisations. One minute you're sitting with Lady X beside you at the Mayor's table for lunch, and then you're down the road at the Chelsea Hospital dealing with the Lord Lieutenant for London. You know you're sitting right behind the royal family. It's surreal. But the community got a real kick out of having a female Borough Commander; they'd never had a female Commander for Kensington and Chelsea. I think as a woman you can deal with things differently. You have a different opportunity.

There are so many more career options now than there were forty years ago. Literally every avenue in policing is available; it's not there yet, but it's becoming more reflective.

I have a great belief that in my last few years, God was having a laugh because he tested me at every level: spiritually, emotionally and professionally. The last two years of my service were particularly hard as I was mentally and physically ill. I collapsed during the minute's silence on Remembrance Sunday. I wasn't sleeping, I wasn't eating. It turns out I'd had an infection for over a month that went undetected and I physically collapsed and ended up in hospital in November 2015. When I went back to work I had to fight to get my own job back.

And then in March 2017 we copped Westminster all the way through to Grenfell in June. During the terrorist attack at Westminster my teams obviously have to commit to it being a neighbouring Borough. The threat is there because of all the tourism; London Bridge is the same. My teams were helping out, my teams were some of the first responders to that and again because I have the high footfall of tourists it's a very, very difficult patch.

Grenfell is on my Borough; I was there within a few hours of the fire starting. My deputy was on night duty because he was covering for me because I hate doing night duty but it's my community, it's my staff. I realised that from day one but in that first moment I saw it for real. There is no book that teaches you how to do it so I threw away what was in my head and listened to my heart. And when someone said, 'I need a hug,' I gave them a hug. And that's why I gave these guys a hug, no handshakes any more even with the fire fighter, the ambulance crew. I remember at the first public meeting I helped a young woman out who was distressed, her father was still in the building and even the Family Liaison Officer was crying; we were all crying, and the para-medic wouldn't let me back in the room because I was crying. He said, 'Normally I would offer you pastoral care, but sod it,' and he gave me a hug. You go beyond the point of worrying what people think and the number of tears you've cried every day. I cried for months.

It was the emotional intelligence that got me through. I had one mission. I decided on night one when I wasn't sleeping, forget the book, forget the forms, focus on the people. I always figured if I tried to do something and I got it wrong, people would forgive me if I was doing it from my heart. And I wanted to make sure before I left I was leaving them in a firmer place emotionally.

Cressida Dick QPM CBE Commissioner of Police

Being the Commissioner, I have to pinch myself . . . often . . . because every day is genuinely a joy. I'm one of those people who never expect anything, definitely not planned, much. I know it sounds ridiculous, but I've never been ambitious in a promotion sense. I've been supported and encouraged, pushed and pulled and I've tried to do my best, but I've tried to do my best in the job I'm in rather than thinking about where's the next job. I left policing, I'd retired. I didn't expect to come back to policing at all.

One of the reasons I took the job was because a female friend, not in fact in policing but very successful in her world, took me to one side and said, 'I know, Cress, you're thinking of taking this job and I know you haven't made up your mind whether to apply or not.' And I thought, 'That's quite right.' She said, 'I think you should have a go and if you did it, you could do it your way. You might be surprised by how much your way might be different from how other people have attempted to do that role but one thing's for sure, I know you, and you will be *you*. I think that's a job you can do your way.' And I've always tried to have no inconsistencies between the personal me and the professional me.

Obviously we all put on a uniform and we perform a role. I do a lot of ceremonials, state visits, commendation ceremonies, passing out parades. I meet a lot of angry, bereaved families. I meet a lot of excited officers or sad officers. I'm there in a lot of emotional occasions for people and I have to be the leader in many situations so I must be the Commissioner but I am 'Cress' through and through, and if you saw me here and saw me at home, you wouldn't see a difference.

In the job I'm in at the moment I have a commitment of getting out every fortnight at least. I've just, before you arrived, been walking out in the West End. I spend two weeks a year, operationally, working shifts: Earlies ... Lates ... Nights ... with different teams, just seeing what their world is like. I think that is useful for me doing my job not just because it's fun but also because it gives me credibility; I can see to some extent through their eyes, because I've done some of that myself.

I'm not trained in the way they're trained now, and they wouldn't want me next to them in certain types of situations because I'm not a TSG officer; but the TSG are very happy to have me seeing them at work. I think I have the same basic kind of recognition of what can be demanding personally, professionally, financially, all the strains that the Job can put on people depending on what's happening at home. I have been the person who has stood at Notting Hill year, after year, after year, after year, after year. I've been the person who, four-teen years in a row, was on New Year's Eve, thinking I might get to that party and never got to it. I know the world is different now and policing is different now, but I think that helps me a lot in my job and my decision-making.

I've made the choice. There's lots of challenging and inter-esting and fun aspects of the work that isn't racing round the streets or dealing with 'the case'. I was a hostage negotiator for years. I loved that. I was Public Order Commander on all sorts of levels for years. I loved that. And then obviously as Chief Officer I spent an enormous amount of time in the heart of the biggest and most difficult investigations, from major incidents to phone hacking and Stephen Lawrence, you know, surrounded by top, top, top Detective Constables who really know their business.

I've been to more mass-casualty mortuaries than I care to remember and I've dealt with more bereaved people than probably the average person has in one way and another. I think it is quite important as a senior person. I don't meet all the parents of all the teenagers who have been killed in the last two years in London – but I have met a lot of them. Sometimes

I've been visiting an area and they'll hear I'm around and they'll come and say, 'Can I come and speak to you?' And I always do. Hopefully I can help them a tiny bit. I can definitely learn from them, and it reminds me of what my officers have to deal with all the time. How difficult it can be. Throughout my service – and I'm sure all officers will say the same – there are things you're glad other members of your family don't see, don't deal with, don't have to think about.

There are still not enough women in the Met. For women, it is something like 38 per cent at the point of entry, which converts for the whole of the Met at about 28 per cent of women police officers. The best Police Force is 37 per cent or something. I think we should be the best. Child care remains a challenge, and I want to make it less of a challenge than it currently is. We have gone through phases where we've lost a lot of women, but I don't think we are at the moment. We should have some greater flexibilities built in for men and women to make the early days of child care easier than it now is. It's a balance.

I would say that when I joined it seemed like you could do anything, but it soon became apparent there were jobs which were not explicitly barred to you but that there were quotas. Quotas in the CID office, where you weren't going to have this number or that number of women, all that. There were jobs where you weren't explicitly barred but they made it very hard – you had to be able to pick up the enormous motorbike, or put the dog over the wall, all these.

That all applied in the 1980s. I would say, in the Met, for the past twenty years, everything has genuinely been open to both men and women; that's what it's been like for me. However, people's circumstances are different and if you're a young mum with your third child it gets blooming hard to do operational police work because our society is structured in the way it is. That's how it often works. There are units of mine, for example, some of the CID teams, the homicide teams, that are more than half women. Women have been flooding into the CID over the last ten years, flooding in. That's great. There have always been female CID officers, almost from time immemorial, but they've been coming in in large numbers. Not so in firearms – and we can argue about why that is – but I know some women still feel they might not, even though it is technically put to them, be that welcome; it might not be as easy as it should be.

Police officers have a fantastic sense of humour. Whatever anyone says – and you hear people say, 'Oh it's not like the old days, we used to have far more laughs' – I don't agree at all. It's different things people laugh about now. I left policing for several years and went to the Foreign Office, and what I found was that there people enjoyed themselves, but it's not the same. There's not so much sheer laughter and there's not so much down-to-earth, straightforward honesty. That's what I love about policing: people say it how it is, they say it how they see it, they deal with facts mainly, with evidence rather than high-faluting hypothesis or strategies and then they laugh their way through the day. You can find yourself in hilarious situations quite often. You can't laugh at the time, but afterwards you can.

If you said to me today, 'It's April Fool. You're not the Commissioner – you're going to be on the response team at Lambeth,' I'd say, 'Wow'; or, 'You're going to be the custody person out at Leyton,' I'd say, 'Thank you, that'll be great'; because I still get a buzz from dealing with the public, being involved in police work. Every aspect of it gives me a buzz, an excitement, an interest.

I know it won't last forever, and it's probably my last job in policing. They won't take me on as an Area car driver, I don't think. I'm making sure I enjoy every minute because it could be over tomorrow, couldn't it? I'm having a good time, but I do pinch myself literally when I walk in the building. It's amazing and I've felt that almost continuously ever since I joined. Every job I've been in, I've thought this is just . . . it suits me, it's great. I can't believe I get paid.

ACKNOWLEDGEMENTS

Our sincere thanks to our wonderful contributors. Without their generous contributions, this book would not have been possible. Many are listed below. However, there are others who wished to remain anonymous but have nevertheless contributed to this book. Our thanks go to them also. They know who they are.

Contributors

Amanda Davidson, Angela Toal, Ann Fox, Annette O'Reilly, Annie Gooch (MBE), Audrey Roche, Carol Squires, Cheryl Cummings, Cressida Dick, Daisy Wood, Debbie Gibbs, Dee O'Brien, Deryl Rennie, Diana Adams, Diane Ralph, Eileen Eastlake, Elaine Bennett, Ellie O'Connor, Eugenie Brooks, Eve Hluszczak, Francine Twitchett, Gina Negus, Helen Baxter, Jacqui Douglas, Jan Cheal, Jane Day, Jane Scotchbrook, Janet Douglas, Janis Anderson, Jean Gordon, Jo Nagy, John Murray, Julie Ferguson, June Courtney, Karen Rhodes, Kate Chamberlain, Kathy Pinfold, Kim Bartlett, Kim Stanley,

Linda Bailey, Liz Kenworthy (MBE), Lorraine Woolley (MBE), Louise Venables, Lyn Lindsay, Lyn Niland, Margaret Bleet, Margaret Giles, Margaret Rickard, Margaret Wilson, Marion Young, Mary Riley, Mary Williams, Mary Wood, Maureen Ridout, Megan Knight, Monica Tett, Pamela Northing, Pat House, Patricia Dyer, Pauline Borwick, Pauline Mills, Richard Keil, Sally Mills, Sally Maybanks, Petura Paulwell, Sam Cailes, Sandra Tucker, Shirley Malyon, Steve Church, Sue Knight, Susan Beckley, Terri Rayner, Wendy Davenport, Wendy Rowe.

Metropolitan Women Police Association
Sioban Clarke and Beverley Edwards.

Metropolitan Police Archives
Dr Clare Smith.

Police Roll of Honour Trust
Dr Peter Kennison and Sidney MacKay.

Our acknowledgements would not be complete without thanking our agent Caroline Montgomery, of Rupert Crew Ltd., for her guidance; Duncan Proudfoot, Publishing Director of Robinson, for his invaluable support; Amanda Keats and Rebecca Sheppard for their help; and Sue Viccars for her editing skills. Finally, our thanks to our families for their support and encouragement throughout.

INDEX